A History of the Republic of Biafra

The Republic of Biafra lasted for less than three years, but the war over its secession would contort Nigeria for decades to come. Samuel Fury Childs Daly examines the history of the Nigerian Civil War and its aftermath from an uncommon vantage point – the courtroom. Wartime Biafra was glutted with firearms, wracked by famine, and administered by a government that buckled under the weight of the conflict. In these dangerous conditions, many people survived by engaging in fraud, extortion, and armed violence. When the fighting ended in 1970, these survival tactics endured, even though Biafra itself disappeared from the map. Based on research using an original archive of legal records and oral histories, Daly catalogues how people navigated conditions of extreme hardship on the war front and shows how the conditions of the Nigerian Civil War paved the way for the long experience of crime that followed.

SAMUEL FURY CHILDS DALY is Assistant Professor of African and African American Studies, History, and International Comparative Studies at Duke University. A historian of twentieth-century Africa, he is the author of articles in journals including *Journal of Imperial and Commonwealth History*, *African Studies Review*, and *African Affairs*.

A History of the Republic of Biafra

Law, Crime, and the Nigerian Civil War

SAMUEL FURY CHILDS DALY
Duke University

CAMBRIDGE
UNIVERSITY PRESS

CAMBRIDGE
UNIVERSITY PRESS

University Printing House, Cambridge CB2 8BS, United Kingdom

One Liberty Plaza, 20th Floor, New York, NY 10006, USA

477 Williamstown Road, Port Melbourne, VIC 3207, Australia

314–321, 3rd Floor, Plot 3, Splendor Forum, Jasola District Centre, New Delhi – 110025, India

79 Anson Road, #06–04/06, Singapore 079906

Cambridge University Press is part of the University of Cambridge.

It furthers the University's mission by disseminating knowledge in the pursuit of education, learning, and research at the highest international levels of excellence.

www.cambridge.org
Information on this title: www.cambridge.org/9781108840767
DOI: 10.1017/9781108887748

© Samuel Fury Childs Daly 2020

First published 2020

A catalogue record for this publication is available from the British Library.

Library of Congress Cataloging-in-Publication Data
Names: Daly, Samuel Fury Childs, 1986– author.
Title: A history of the Republic of Bafra : law, crime, and the Nigerian Civil War / Samuel Fury Childs Daly, Duke University, North Carolina.
Description: New York : Cambridge University Press, 2020. | Includes index.
Identifiers: LCCN 2020013563 (print) | LCCN 2020013564 (ebook) | ISBN 9781108840767 (hardback) | ISBN 9781108887748 (ebook)
Subjects: LCSH: Nigeria, Eastern – History. | Civil war – Nigeria, Eastern. | Nigeria – History – Civil War, 1967–1970.
Classification: LCC DT515.5 .D35 2020 (print) | LCC DT515.5 (ebook) | DDC 966.905/2–dc23
LC record available at https://lccn.loc.gov/2020013563
LC ebook record available at https://lccn.loc.gov/2020013564

ISBN 978-1-108-84076-7 Hardback

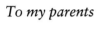

To my parents

Contents

Figures

Maps

Acknowledgments

This incomplete list cannot fully express how grateful I am for the time and energy other people have given this book. Historians are only as good as their sources, and this account would not exist without the work of the librarians, archivists, and registrars who preserve them (sometimes in difficult circumstances). I thank the stewards of collections in Enugu, Umuahia, Lagos, Calabar, Onitsha, Owerri, Kaduna, Ibadan, Nsukka, London, Oxford, Dublin, Nantes, Pretoria, and others listed at the end of this book. I am especially grateful to Florence Chukwu and the staff of the Enugu State High Court library and registry. Valentine N. Alakwe, Georginia Anogbatu, Francisca Morchi, and others at the Nigerian National Archives in Enugu allowed me to work there, as did Salamu Olatunji in Kaduna. Justin Nwaneri of the National War Museum in Umuahia not only permitted me to rummage through the cupboards but included me in the museum's intellectual and social life. Uwem Eteng and Kemi Olowu made the Nigerian Institute of Advanced Legal Studies at the University of Lagos a rewarding place to work. Victor Osasah welcomed me at the Federal Court of Appeal in Enugu, and David Chukwu introduced me to the first tranche of people to interview. I thank the many lawyers who gave me so much of their valuable time – and never billed me for it.

This book started as a doctoral dissertation at Columbia University. Gregory Mann was a perfect advisor, and he has been a model of how to be a scholar and a person at several different stages of my life. Mamadou Diouf was unfailingly supportive and always full of ideas. Abosede George and Brian Larkin grounded me in Nigeria but also encouraged the agile and creative thinking that they exhibit in their own work. Frederick Cooper provided ideas to work with, along, and against and read with great depth and generosity. Collectively, they were an extraordinary committee. Luise White's books made me want to be a historian, and her friendship has proven to be just as rich as her writing. Comments by Egodi Uchendu and Steven Pierce pushed this research in new directions at critical junctures, and a question from John Parker was the spark that set everything off. Njideka Akunyili Crosby led me to the National War Museum in Umuahia, which ended up being an astounding source of material. Lisa Lindsay read the entire manuscript in its final stages, as did Vivian Chenxue Lu.

I am fortunate to have an institutional home at Duke University in the Department of African and African American Studies as well as appointments in the Department of History and the International Comparative Studies Program. My colleagues at Duke have made it a wonderful place to work and live. They include Anne Allison, Ed Balleisen, Lee Baker, Nima Bassiri, Dirk Bonker, James Chappel, Leo Ching, Jasmine Cobb, Michaeline Crichlow, Sandy Darity, Laurent Dubois, Janet Ewald, Greg Field, John French, Thavolia Glymph, Ben Grunwald, Michael Hardt, Deonte Harris, Kerry Haynie, Jayne Ifekwunigwe, Tsitsi Jaji, Mbaye Lo, Adriane Lentz-Smith, Wahneema Lubiano, Anne-Maria Makhulu, Jehangir Malegam, Kathryn Mathers, Lorand Matory, Adam Mestyan, Eli Meyerhoff, Jarvis McInnis, Louise Meintjes, Jessica Namakkal, Mark Anthony Neal, Minna Ng, Jocelyn Olcott, Tolulope Oyesanya, Charles Piot, Cate Reilly, Sumathi Ramaswamy, Gabriel Rosenberg, Charmaine Royal, Karin Shapiro, Stephen Smith, Harris Solomon, Philip Stern, Amanda Wetsel, and Joseph Winters. I am grateful to Trinity College of Arts and Sciences for a generous publication subvention grant and to the Franklin Humanities Institute for funding a book manuscript workshop at Duke. I thank its director Ranjana Khanna and all of the participants, especially outside readers Moses Ochonu, Daniel Jordan Smith, and Saheed Aderinto. I also thank Tyra Dixon, Caroline Diepveen, Drew Kenner, Camille Jackson, and Heather Martin.

A postdoctoral fellowship at Rutgers University – New Brunswick provided valuable time and space to write and a rollicking intellectual community. I am grateful to Ousseina Alidou, Carolyn Brown, Barbara Cooper, Seth Koven, Johan Mathew, Judith Surkis, and all of the participants in the Mellon Sawyer Seminar on Ethical Subjects. I owe a special debt to Judith Surkis for first bringing me to the study of law. Courses and conversations with Akintunde Akinyemi, James Brennan, Zoe Crossland, Barbara Fields, Mahmood Mamdani, Abdul Nanji, Richard Reid, and Joseph Slaughter brought me into the world of African studies as an undergraduate student.

Many people have read parts of this work, shaped my thinking, or pointed me in the direction of sources. They include Fati Abubakar, Yusuf Abukar, Funke Adeboye, Jumoke Adegbonmire, Ademide Adelusi-Adeluyi, George Aumoithe, Amiel Bize, Elizabeth Blackmar, Jane Burbank, Emily Burrill, Emily Callaci, KumHee Cho, Rohit De, Reema Fadda, Bunmi Fatoye-Matory, Mary Tibbets Freeman, Devon Golaszewski, Charles Halvorson, Anna Henke, Irvin Hunt, Lauren Jarvis, Martha Jones, Chima Korieh, Daniel Lee, Tim Livsey, Ebele Martins, Dan Magaziner, Wendell Hassan Marsh, Kristin Mann, Bridget Messer, Lang Messer, Naomi Mezey, Andrew Miller, Hlonipha Mokoena, Dirk Moses, Mena Odu, Oghenetoja Okoh, Tejumola Olaniyan, Jimoh Oriyomi Oluwasegun, Remi Onabanjo, Golda Kosi Onyeneho, Emmanuel Osayande, Nana Osei-Opare, Susan Pedersen, Allison Useche Powers, Peter Redfield, Danielle Roper, Kemi Rotimi, Sarah Runcie, Teemu Ruskola, Emmanuelle Saada, Alex Samaras, Tehila Sasson, Chelsea Schields, Mitra Sharafi, Samuel Shearer, Caroline Sherell, Natasha Shivji, Max Siollun, Julie Skurski, Nicholas Rush Smith, Halimat Titilola Somotan, Jonny Steinberg, John Straussberger, Evan Spritzer, Rhiannon Stephens, Scott Straus, Matt Swagler, Geoff Traugh, Elizabeth Thornberry, Megan Vaughan, Charlotte Walker-Said, Ruth Watson, Gary Wilder, Allen Xiao, Lauren Young, and Adrien Zakar.

Portions of this work were presented at the School of Oriental and African Studies, the University of Lagos, the University of Florida, the University of Nigeria – Nsukka, the University of Wisconsin – Madison, the Max Planck Institute for European Legal History, Stanford, Johns Hopkins, the CUNY Graduate Center, the University of North Carolina – Chapel Hill, Duke, the University of Virginia, Columbia, Rutgers, the University of the Witwatersrand, and the Law and Humanities Workshop at the University of Pennsylvania. Among many conferences, audiences at the Lagos Studies Association and the Igbo Studies Association shaped this work in especially significant ways. Sections of Chapters 2 and 3 were published in a different form in "'Hell was let loose on the country': The Social History of Military Technology in the Republic of Biafra," *African Studies Review* vol. 61, no. 3 (2018): pp. 99–118 and "The Survival Con: Fraud and Forgery in the Republic of Biafra, 1967–1970," *Journal of African History* vol. 58, no. 1 (2017): pp. 129–144, which are reproduced here with the permission of Cambridge University

Press. I thank Maria Marsh, Daniel Brown, and Atifa Jiwa of Cambridge University Press, as well as the three anonymous reviewers who provided extremely rich, constructive comments. I thank Linsey Hague for carefully copyediting the book.

"The criminal must choose his comrades in crime carefully," warns a guide for aspirant 419ers. I choose LaToya Adkins, Neil Agarwal, Miriam Sant Arkin, Patrick Barrett, Nishant Batsha, Mark Drury, Elisabeth Fink, James Clinton Francis, Heron Haas, Trina Hogg, Vivian Chenxue Lu, Abigail Marcus, Elizabeth Marcus, Meredith Martin, Dustin Patenaude, Reynolds Richter, Nicholas Smith, and Inga Manuela Thiessen. Jonathan Daly, Gale Fury Childs, and Emily Fury Daly have given endless love and an appreciation of artifice that only a family of actors could provide. Finally, I thank Daniel McCracken. Financial support for this research was provided by the Harry Frank Guggenheim Foundation, the Mellon Foundation, the Council on Library and Information Resources, the Institute for Historical Research (London), the American Historical Association, and Duke University.

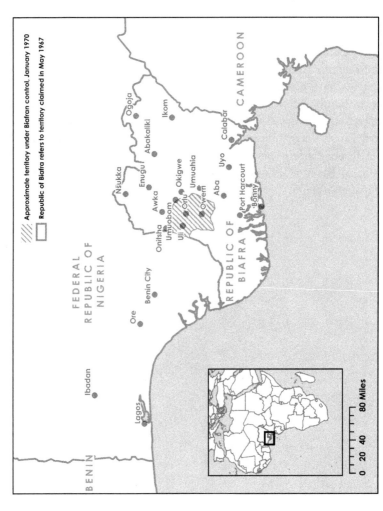

Map 0.1 Map of the Republic of Biafra

Introduction

> That lone rifle-shot anonymous
> in the dark striding chest-high
> through a nervous suburb at the break
> of our season of thunders will yet
> steep its flight and lodge
> more firmly than the greater noises
> ahead in the forehead of memory.
>
> Chinua Achebe, "The First Shot"[1]

On May 30, 1967, Sir Louis Mbanefo brought a new country into the world. Mbanefo was a widely respected judge, known to the Nigerian public as the chief justice of the Eastern Region. To his peers in the judiciary, he was a formidable moralist – a "black Englishman" who "did not mix well at parties" as one would recall.[2] A Cambridge education, a successful law practice, a knighthood, and a term on the International Court of Justice were all behind him.[3] Ahead of him was an uncertain future. A photo taken that day shows Mbanefo, weighed down under his robes and wig, taking an oath from a man thirty years his junior, clad in military fatigues and an unruly beard. The country established that day, through a series of decrees and rituals was the Republic of Biafra, and the soldier being sworn in to lead it was Lieutenant Colonel Chukwuemeka Odumegwu Ojukwu.

The Republic of Biafra broke away from Nigeria in the name of making law and order. It promised to be a new model for Africa, and its leaders pledged to "fulfill the decolonising mission which the 'stillborn' Nigeria failed to do," as they announced in the state newspaper's

---

[1] Chinua Achebe, *Beware, Soul Brother: Poems* (London: Heinemann, 1972): p.11.

[2] Interview with Anthony Mogboh, SAN, Enugu, October 2, 2014.

[3] Ekong Sampson, *Evergreen Memories of Sir Louis Mbanefo* (Lagos: Lomanc Books, 2002).

first issue.[4] Biafra's government would be moderate and modern, guided by humanism and the gospel of prosperity. Yet, in the war of secession that followed, it came to look very different from the country its founders envisioned. As chief justice of the Biafran Court of Appeal, Mbanefo had a prime position to watch things fall apart. Presiding over cases in the dwindling territory that the Biafran Army controlled, he heard accounts of violence that surpassed what he thought people were capable of. Mbanefo came to believe that everyone was lying to him, even his fellow judges. He presided over the expansion of martial law, which went against all his moral instincts, and he came to fear privately that the new country he had thrown in his lot with was actually a "bandit state."[5]

Matters that had seemed black and white before the Nigerian Civil War – the difference between state and private forms of violence, certainties about who engaged in crime and why, even the larger question of what constituted truth in the legal context – all became gray. A constant state of siege, compounded by the desperation of hunger, made violence and deception boom along the front. The survival tactics that people employed to endure the war's hardships were often illegal, which compelled courts to reevaluate the ethics of crime. This reckoning took place as the battle raged just outside the courtroom door. To tell the story of how warfare sowed the seeds of crime, this book mines a new source: a scattered, endangered collection of legal records from the Republic of Biafra and postwar Nigeria. Oral histories, memoirs, and other archives fill in where the legal record trails off. In aggregate, these sources reveal how Biafrans and their government adapted to the war and the humanitarian emergency that accompanied it. Court cases describe the actions that people took to survive in arresting detail, and they reveal how the boundary between crime and the "legitimate" violence of war eroded. Actions that were usually permitted became illegal – ordinary forms of commerce became war profiteering, for example; and actions that were unambiguously prohibited – like acts of killing – became abstruse in wartime. The categories of crime that thrived in Biafra included armed robbery, forgery, and fraud. Not coincidentally, these would become Nigeria's most persistent

---

[4] *Biafra Spotlight*, June 1, 1967, p. 2.
[5] Godwin Alaoma Onyegbula, *The Memoirs of the Nigerian-Biafran Bureaucrat: An Account of Life in Biafra and Within Nigeria* (Ibadan: Spectrum, 2005): p.147.

criminological problems in the late twentieth century. Violence and deception were connected in Biafra, and they became even more tightly interwoven after the war ended.[6]

The lasting image of the Nigerian Civil War is famously a starving child, not a judge presiding over a well-ordered courtroom. It may come as a surprise that tattered, starving Biafra had a legal system at all. A memoirist admitted how uncanny it seemed to find a divorce hearing in session on the front, or to see "a convict being led away while the enemy plane whine[d] overhead."[7] Biafra's courts, however, were in session through even the most brutal periods of the fighting, and its legal system was at the center of its political culture. Administrative tasks usually associated with other organs of state – like providing social services, divvying up humanitarian aid, and articulating a national ethos – became the responsibility of courts. In this setting, law became more than a mechanism for resolving disputes or dispensing justice in the abstract. It was what made Biafra work.

Biafra worked – far more than it seemed to the outside world – but this is not to say that it worked smoothly. The fighting constantly interrupted legal proceedings, and what "justice" meant in the bedlam of wartime life was not a settled matter. Air raids chipped away at the law's physical infrastructure, and the lack of personnel gummed up the appeals process. When the Ministry of Justice tried to conduct an audit of the law reports that had been saved from destruction in 1968, the State Counsel in Awka wrote to the solicitor general to say that "there is no single Law Book in this office."[8] Judges and lawyers cited

---

[6] What to call the war is contentious. I use the name Biafra without the quotation marks or lowercase letters sometimes used to mark its status as an unrecognized state. This is neither an endorsement that the Republic of Biafra *was* a "real" state nor a suggestion that it somehow was not. Similarly, I use the terms Nigerian Civil War, Biafra War, and Nigeria-Biafra War interchangeably. Those who see Biafra as a rebel movement – one that never actually broke Nigeria apart – tend to use the first term, while those who see Biafra as a state that once existed tend to use one of the latter. The conflict described herein was a civil war in that it transpired within the boundaries of an established state – Nigeria – but it is worth noting from the outset that describing something as a "civil war" does not explain much about it. On the application of the term, see David Armitage, *Civil Wars: A History in Ideas* (New York: Alfred A. Knopf, 2017): pp. 232–239.

[7] Ekong Sampson, *The Path of Justice Chike Idigbe* (Lagos: Distinct Universal Limited, 1999): p. 71.

[8] Nigerian National Archives, Enugu [hereafter NNAE] MINJUST 25/1/1, "List of Law Books at Awka," January 26, 1968.

precedent from memory, and they often got the details wrong. Trials were held in the bombed-out shells of schools and government buildings or outdoors under the shade of trees. Proceedings were recorded by hand, and summonses went out on official stationery with "Nigeria" crossed out and hastily replaced with "Biafra." When the blockade exhausted these reserves, scrap paper was used. It is jarring to read testimony of wartime violence and despair written on the back of a prewar love letter, as was one criminal case. The materiality of an archive can sometimes say as much as the words recorded in it.[9]

Crime became so engrained in Nigeria's reputation that it can be difficult to remember that it was not always there. For decades, accounts of planes being held up at gunpoint as they taxied into Murtala Muhammed Airport vied with elaborate kidnappings and embezzlement schemes measured in billions of dollars for what would be the most outrageous crime to come out of Africa's largest country.[10] Although crime – defined here narrowly as the violation of established laws and normative orders – can be found in all periods of Nigerian history (and in the polities that made up Nigeria *avant la lettre*), I argue that the period when crime defined whole areas of Nigerian life began during the war. It ended even more recently; crime today is no longer the crisis it once was, even though it might not seem like it from tabloid reportage and Nollywood films. The forms of criminal violence, deception, and corruption associated with Nigeria

[9] One of postcolonial historiography's most important methodological innovations has been to show how processes of decay and ruination make meaning – both affective and empirical. Nancy Rose Hunt, "History as Form, With Simmel in Tow," *History and Theory* no. 56 (2018): pp. 126–144; Ann Laura Stoler, ed., *Imperial Debris: On Ruins and Ruination* (Durham, NC: Duke University Press, 2013); Luise White, "Hodgepodge Historiography: Documents, Itineraries, and the Absence of Archives," *History in Africa* vol. 42 (2015): pp. 309–318. Archives and their deterioration have captured the artistic imagination as well, such as in the work of the painters George Afedzi Hughes and Njideka Akunyili Crosby.

[10] Until 2001, one could find a reminder of how the outside world saw Nigeria at any international airport in the United States. Signs were posted warning that the Federal Aviation Administration did not advise travel to Lagos because the safety of the airport could not be guaranteed – a warning that was not even made for war zones. On the airport robberies, see "Criminal Acts Against Civil Aviation," Report by the U.S. Department of Transportation, Federal Aviation Administration, Office of Civil Aviation Security, 1992. Teju Cole paints a stark picture of the Lagos airport in *Every Day is for the Thief* (Lagos: Cassava Republic, 2007): pp. 14–16.

in the late twentieth century became embedded in public life during and after the civil war – temporally speaking, in the middle distance between colonialism and the democratic present. Crime did not begin in 1967, and the elements of Nigeria's peculiar criminological condition were already in place during colonial administration (and perhaps before).[11] Yet it took a major crisis to catalyze a reaction between those elements. The Nigerian Civil War would be the spark that started a long blaze.

Nigeria's reputation for crime was destructive and exaggerated, but it was not spun out of thin air. Crime was a stubborn social and political problem, and the questions of what caused it, how it operated, and how it might be suppressed animated Nigerian public life for many years.[12] The Nigerian Civil War and the forms of misconduct that it

[11] On the relationship between colonial rule and the African present generally, see Frederick Cooper, *Colonialism in Question: Theory, Knowledge, History* (Berkeley: University of California Press, 2005); Bonny Ibhawoh, *Human Rights in Africa* (Cambridge: Cambridge University Press, 2018); Richard Reid, "Past and Presentism: The 'Precolonial' and the Foreshortening of African History," *Journal of African History* vol. 52, no. 2 (2011): pp. 135–155.

[12] The large historical and ethnographic literature on Nigerian crime, often oriented by the idea of "corruption," includes Andrew Apter, *The Pan-African Nation: Oil and the Spectacle of Culture in Nigeria* (Chicago: University of Chicago Press, 2005); Moses Ochonu, *Colonial Meltdown: Northern Nigeria in the Great Depression* (Athens: Ohio University Press, 2009); Daniel Jordan Smith, *A Culture of Corruption: Everyday Deception and Popular Discontent in Nigeria* (Princeton: Princeton University Press, 2008); Wale Adebanwi, *Authority Stealing: Anti-Corruption War and Democratic Politics in Post-Military Nigeria* (Durham, NC: Carolina Academic Press, 2012); Steven Pierce, *Moral Economies of Corruption: State Formation and Political Culture in Nigeria* (Durham, NC: Duke University Press, 2016); Stephen Ellis, *This Present Darkness: A History of Nigerian Organised Crime* (Oxford: Oxford University Press, 2016); Charles Edet, *The Dangers of Political Thuggery and Rumour* (self-published, 1992); and many of the contributions in Wale Adebanwi and Ebenezer Obadare, eds., *Encountering the Nigerian State* (Basingstoke: Palgrave, 2010). As is often the case, crime in Nigeria is most vividly described in fiction. See, for example, Seffi Atta, *Swallow* (Northampton: Interlink Books, 2010); Patrick Oguejiofor, *Fast Track* (Ibadan: Constellation Books, 2015); Leye Adenle, *Easy Motion Tourist* (Lagos: Cassava Republic, 2017); Adoabi Nwaubani, *I Do Not Come to You By Chance* (New York: Hyperion, 2009); E. C. Osondu, *This House is Not For Sale* (New York: HarperCollins, 2015). On crime, deceit, and "corruption" in the colonial period, see Stephanie Newell, *The Forger's Tale: The Search for Odeziaku* (Athens: Ohio University Press, 2006); M. G. Smith, *Government in Zazzau, 1800–1950* (London: Oxford University Press, 1960); Simon Ottenberg, "Local Government and the Law in Southern Nigeria," *Journal of Asian and African Studies* vol. 2, no. 1 (1967): pp.

spawned are a critical part of this story. The war routinized actions that violated the law – theft and fraud most prominent among them. They became embedded in daily life, and the ethics surrounding crime changed as this happened. In the long period of military rule that followed Biafra's defeat, the crimes that had become common there thrived. Theft from the state became unofficially tolerated as judges and policemen threw up their hands or in some cases joined in. Battle had blurred legal and ethical lines, and they could not easily be redrawn when the fighting ended. Legal records show how the problem of crime in postwar Nigeria was a continuation of wartime circumstances – not a wave that surged out of nowhere.

Biafra's history is short, and, like Nigeria's reputation for crime, its origins lie in the relatively recent past. Most accounts interpret secession in May 1967 as a response to the events immediately preceding it – a series of pogroms against members of the Igbo ethnic group the year before and the string of coups and assassinations that brought down Nigeria's First Republic.[13] Biafra's population was predominantly Igbo, but it was not a straightforwardly ethnic project. It did not emerge out of grievances stretching back for generations, nor was it the reflection of an old identity, however much its propagandists tried to present it as such. There was no clear historical precedent for an Igbo state. There was even less of one for a country that governed the many communities of eastern Nigeria under one flag, as Biafra tried to.[14] To be sure, there were deeper structural reasons for the war's outbreak, despite the foreshortened way that most people understood it. The danger that permeated Biafran life was deeply felt, but it was historically shallow. This gives credence to Achille Mbembe's claim that "for many people caught in the vortex of colonialism and what comes after, the main indexes of time are the contingent, the ephemeral, the fugitive, and the fortuitous – radical uncertainty and social volatility."[15] Biafra

26–43. For a synthesis touching on many forms of government malpractice, see Max Siollun, *Oil, Politics, and Violence: Nigeria's Military Coup Culture 1966–1976* (New York: Algora Publishing, 2009), and *Soldiers of Fortune: A History of Nigeria (1983–1993)* (Lagos: Cassava Republic, 2014).

[13] Nigeria attained independence from the United Kingdom in 1960 and became a republic in 1963.

[14] Except, of course, for the Federal Republic of Nigeria itself.

[15] Achille Mbembe, "Africa in Theory," in Brian Goldstone and Juan Obarrio, eds., *African Futures: Essays on Crisis, Emergence, and Possibility* (Chicago: University of Chicago Press, 2016): p. 222.

provides a social-historical picture of how people lived in this "vortex," and how it shaped their decisions.

The way Biafra worked was improvisational, unpredictable, and ideologically agnostic. Like the Rhodesia of Luise White's description, Biafra "made up its governmentality as it went along."[16] Its leadership was famously indifferent when it came to Cold War allegiances. As Ojukwu reputedly said at a trying moment of the war, "I would take help from anybody. I would take help from the devil himself in order to survive."[17] The Biafran state, including its judiciary, was a fly-by-night operation, and the fact that Biafran courts remained open did not mean that they dispensed "justice" as most people defined it. In the later stages of the war, the core of the state's purpose was whittled down to maintaining order, which it evermore failed to do. Biafra was a disorderly example of a "law and order" state, but it is an instructive one for the era of military rule in Africa, when order and discipline became political watchwords across the continent.[18] Biafra would shape Nigeria's politics long after 1970, both for what it taught the country's leaders and for how the public remembered it.

Historians have said very little about Biafra's inner life. This is partially a problem of sources, but it is also because a consensus emerged that Biafra had never quite been a real place. "You either believe that Biafra existed or you don't," Ojukwu later stated matter-of-factly. "In my vision, Biafra did exist, it was a state."[19] Few people were so confident. As one prominent lawyer recalled, Biafra's state institutions "never had a moment of peace in which they could fashion a separate identity," and even those who were deeply committed to the

---

[16] Luise White, *Unpopular Sovereignty: Rhodesian Independence and African Decolonization* (Chicago: University of Chicago Press, 2015): p. 17.

[17] School of Oriental and African Studies [hereafter SOAS] Nigerian Civil War Collections MS 321463 Box 14, "Report of the visit to Biafra and San Tome by T. McNally," November 7–16, 1968.

[18] I use the terms "order" and "disorder" here as they were used in Nigeria and Biafra itself; they are native categories to the history of Nigeria in this period. In the writings of judges, journalists, and others, "order" invokes the idea of a society organized and bound by legal institutions and their various agencies of enforcement. "Disorder," conversely, was associated with a high incidence of violent crime, chaos in the political system, and corruption. Neither term had much coherence, but both were rhetorically powerful.

[19] "Chief Chukwuemeka Odumegwu-Ojukwu," in H. B. Momoh, ed., *The Nigerian Civil War, 1967–1970: History and Reminiscences* (Ibadan: Sam Bookman, 2000): p. 763.

Biafran cause often felt like their government was a façade or a mimicry of what a state should look like.[20] Biafra's adversaries constantly reminded the outside world that it was not a "real" country. Biafra never received the diplomatic recognition that would make it sovereign in the eyes of other states, and Nigerian propaganda consistently (and poetically) referred to it as "Ojukwu's Dream Empire." They were right that there was something dreamlike about Biafra. Even in its own records Biafra comes across as fleeting; sometimes the state could interpellate its citizens and provide structure to daily life, but at other moments it wholly failed to do so. The Biafran experiment lasted less than three years, but the fact that Biafra's state institutions (including its courts) were ephemeral did not mean that they had no force of compulsion.[21] The postcolonial state is not only, as Jean-François Bayart called it, a "shadow theatre" of ethnic politics masquerading as governance. Nor is it always a "relatively empty shell," outside of which real politics takes place, per Patrick Chabal and Jean-Pascal Daloz.[22] Even a postcolony as skeletal as Biafra had internal factions, an administrative philosophy, and a political culture, all of which are visible in the remains of its legal record. If this chaotic place

---

[20] Interview with Jerome H. C. Okolo, SAN, Enugu, September 17, 2014.

[21] Whether Biafra can be considered to have been sovereign is a related question. It fails some tests, including that of broad international recognition by other sovereign states, but passes others, like the acceptance of its currency, stamps, official documents, and other trappings of state. See Douglas Howland and Luise White, "Introduction: Sovereignty and the Study of States," *The State of Sovereignty: Territories, Laws, Populations* (Bloomington: Indiana University Press, 2008); Charles Piot, *Nostalgia for the Future: West Africa After the Cold War* (Chicago: University of Chicago Press, 2010); Nathaniel Berman, "Sovereignty in Abeyance: Self-Determination and International Law," *Wisconsin International Law Journal* vol. 7 (1988); Martti Koskenniemi, *The Gentle Civilizer of Nations: The Rise and Fall of International Law, 1870–1960* (Cambridge: Cambridge University Press, 2002); Brenda Chalfin, *Neoliberal Frontiers: An Ethnography of Sovereignty in West Africa* (Chicago: University of Chicago Press, 2010).

[22] Jean-François Bayart, *The State in Africa: The Politics of the Belly* (Cambridge: Cambridge University Press, 2009): p. 41; Patrick Chabal and Jean-Pascal Daloz, *Africa Works: Disorder as Political Instrument* (Oxford: Oxford University Press, 1999): p. 95. On theorizations of postcolonial states in general, see also Jean Comaroff and John Comaroff, eds., *Law and Disorder in the Postcolony* (Chicago: University of Chicago Press, 2006); Achille Mbembe, "The Banality of Power and the Aesthetics of Vulgarity in the Postcolony," *Public Culture* vol. 4, no. 2 (1992): pp.1–30. See also Didier Fassin, ed., *At the Heart of the State: The Moral World of Institutions* (London: Pluto Press, 2015).

can have a meaningful, distinct form of governmentality, it stands to reason that other African nation-states – including ones much more tangible and lasting – would as well.[23] Biafra was a passing and unusual example of the nation-state form, but the forces that emerged there were not unique to it. Broader conclusions about the relationship between crime, warfare, and governance can be drawn from its brief, bloody history.

The Argument

Certain behaviors that are permitted – even encouraged – during wartime become crime once the war is over. Along the Biafran war front, people regularly used forgery, robbery, and extortion as tools to survive in impossible circumstances. After the war, as one prominent lawyer told me, those who had lived through it "did not forget how to forge a document, or how to use a gun."[24] In the heat of battle, a soldier might legitimately requisition property from civilians, but if he "appropriates" a car or a bag of grain after the fighting has ended, most courts would consider that action to be theft. Similarly, the cloak-and-dagger intrigue that takes place in any conflict – spying, espionage – looks more like fraud once the fog of war has lifted. The difference between survivalism and crime becomes murky. "Only the vision of the jurist," wrote Jean-François Bayart of Zaire, where people lived "mysteriously" through similarly hard times, "imposes a difference between these categories, labelling one criminal and another not."[25] Biafra's history offers a larger lesson for the study of war and society: when a war ends but the *habits* of the war do not, the situation that results is often something like a crime wave. The persistence of a "martial spirit" in times of peace has serious implications not only for

---

[23] The idea that the African nation-state has no ideology reaches its apogee in works on Nigeria, many of which posit that categories like "left" and "right" mean little in national politics. A valiant counterargument is made in Adam Mayer, *Naija Marxisms: Revolutionary Thought in Nigeria* (London: Pluto Press, 2016).

[24] Interview with Kola Babalola, SAN, Port Harcourt, March 5, 2015.

[25] Jean-François Bayart, "The 'Social Capital' of the Felonious State, or the Ruses of Political Intelligence," in Jean-François Bayart, Stephen Ellis, and Béatrice Hibou, eds., *The Criminalization of the State in Africa* (Oxford: James Currey, 1999): pp. 38–39.

politics, as many historians have understood, but for the everyday problem of crime.[26]

In 1986, Chinua Achebe wrote that "indiscipline pervades our life so completely today that one may be justified in calling it the condition *par excellence* of contemporary Nigerian society."[27] The notion that Nigerian life was defined by unruliness, deceit, and wariness, while not universally shared, became common enough to be cliché in the decades after the war. Ojukwu would write in 1989 that Nigerian society "is imbued with every quality of the unreal, of fantasy and of a grotesque spectacle."[28] Their depictions were perhaps overdrawn – lamenting Nigeria's unruliness is something of a national pastime – but there was a kernel of truth in them. The country Achebe and Ojukwu described was not only a postcolonial society but a post*war* society – and one where the conditions of conflict were still very present.[29] Violence, vulgarity, indiscipline, and grotesqueness are all common features of war, and Nigeria was contorted by them long after Biafra was wiped off the map. Crime was perhaps the war's most durable legacy, even though few people made that connection at the time.

It was not just any crime that emerged from the crucible of the war – two overlapping types of lawbreaking were connected to it. The first was armed robbery and the second was the expansive category of misconduct known as "four-one-nine." Today, 419 is known as an opportunistic form of advance-fee fraud usually conducted over the Internet, and its poetics will be familiar to anyone who has had an email account in the last thirty years. "Dear friend," begins a typical example

[26] I borrow the term "martial spirit" from John Hope Franklin's study of the militaristic culture of the antebellum American south, which informs this study in many ways. John Hope Franklin, *The Militant South, 1800–1861* (Cambridge, MA: Harvard University Press, 1956). On the lasting effects of military cultures forged in war, see also Isabel V. Hull, *Absolute Destruction: Military Culture and the Practices of War in Imperial Germany* (Ithaca, NY: Cornell University Press, 2005); Mary Dudziak, *War Time: An Idea, Its History, Its Consequences* (Oxford: Oxford University Press, 2013).
[27] Chinua Achebe, *The Trouble with Nigeria* (Oxford: Heinemann, 1984): p. 27.
[28] Emeka Odumegwu-Ojukwu, *Because I Am Involved* (Ibadan: Spectrum, 2011 [1989]): p. xii. This language prefigures Achille Mbembe's description of the outlandish "aesthetics of vulgarity" at the center of the postcolonial African state. Mbembe, "The Banality of Power and the Aesthetics of Vulgarity in the Postcolony."
[29] In this respect, it bears similarity to the Kenya of Daniel Branch's description. *Defeating Mau, Creating Kenya: Counterinsurgency, Civil War, and Decolonization* (Cambridge: Cambridge University Press, 2009): p. xvii.

from my inbox, "I am Mrs. Mariam Abacha, widow of the former Nigerian Head of State Sani Abacha. I am presently in great distress and I solicit your kind assistance with a matter that may interest you." The writer goes on to describe frozen bank accounts and hidden stashes of money and ends with a proposition: "Please, I beg your assistance with removing this money from the country, if you assist me I am prepared to offer you twenty percent (20%) of the sum total." Millions of such emails are sent each year, and enough of them succeed that 419 is a major industry – one that is larger, if statistics can be trusted, than the gross domestic product of several of the countries that border Nigeria.[30] It became famous in Europe and North America, where the "Nigerian scammer" became a menace, then a joke, and eventually a kind of folk archetype. Yet 419 has a complicated place in Nigerian society and politics, and the question of where it came from is an important one. I argue that fraud was a survival tactic during and after the civil war, and a by-product of its obliterating violence.

The war's connection to armed robbery is intuitive – it is not hard to imagine how people habituated to war might turn martial skills against one another in hard times. Its connection to fraud is less obvious. It is difficult to pin down exactly what "419" is. Technically, its meaning is clear: 419 is named after the section of the Nigerian criminal code that prohibits obtaining money or goods through false pretenses.[31]

[30] They probably cannot be trusted – confidently measuring 419's scale is impossible. Nonetheless, see Jerome P. Bjelopera and Kristin M. Finklea, "Organized Crime: An Evolving Challenge for U.S. Law Enforcement," United States Congressional Research Service Report 7–5700, 2010: pp. 17–18; "419 Advance Fee Fraud Statistics 2013," Ultrascan Advanced Global Investigations Report, 2014: p. 2.

[31] Section 419 states that "any person who by any false pretence, and with intent to defraud, obtains from any other person anything capable of being stolen, or induces any other person to deliver to any person anything capable of being stolen, is guilty of a felony, and is liable to imprisonment for three years." Since Biafra continued to use the criminal code it inherited from Nigeria, "419" had the same applied meaning there. Armed robbery, also a topic of this book, is the subject of chapter 37 of the code. For a general history of the code, see A. G. Karibi-Whyte, *History and Sources of Nigerian Criminal Law* (Ibadan: Spectrum, 1993). See also Emmanuel Fakayode, *The Nigerian Criminal Code Companion* (Benin City: Ethiope Publishing, 1977): pp. 35–48; C. O. Okonkwo, *Okonkwo and Naish on Criminal Law in Nigeria* (London: Sweet and Maxwell, 1980): pp. 309–317; A. G. Karibi-Whyte, *Groundwork of Nigerian Criminal Law* (Lagos: Nigerian Law Publications, 1986); Kharisu Sufiyan Chukkol, *The Law of Crimes in Nigeria* (Zaria: Ahmadu Bello University, 1988).

However, what is popularly called "419" encompasses a much broader range of activities than what the actual section 419 prohibits. It has come to be shorthand for deceit, cheating, and the illegitimate acquisition of wealth in many different forms. It includes practices as varied as bank fraud, currency counterfeiting, the forging of contracts and oil prospecting licenses, and the charlatanry of false prophets, bogus ritualists, and fortune tellers.[32] It is often invoked to describe state corruption as well. "In our country," wrote a pamphleteer in the early 2000s, "advance fee fraud has been elevated to an art. Nowadays an infant can easily tell his or her playmate in the school not to cheat in the game by mentioning the number '419.'"[33]

The 419 scam is a hydra of deceptive practices – a "serpent without a head," as Daniel Jordan Smith calls it – which regenerates when it is dismembered and adapts quickly to new policing strategies.[34] It has transitioned seamlessly from the post, to the fax machine, to email, and today to social networks.[35] It has gone by many other names, most recently "The Fast Lane," or "wayo," after the Hausa word for cleverness. In the 1980s, it was known as "OBT" ("Obtain-By-Tricks"), "money doubling," or the "gather-gather" business, all alluding to the acquisitiveness supposedly at is core. A tract from the early 1990s described the many forms 419 could take:

Some are highly organised. Others poorly organised. Some lethal, others not so lethal. While some are found in the offices, others are discoverable in the markets, still some others are at the roadsides and others are simply peripatetics. As places where they are found vary, so do their activities and modes of operation. In all, however, behind their diversity a uniform principle of action is discoverable.[36]

---

[32] See Sajo Dahiru Bobbo, *The 419 Syndrome in Nigeria: Common Practices* (Abuja: Dikko Printing, [2000]). On fraud, see the remarkable guide to identifying false prophets by Adesina Adedipe, *Nigeria Set Aside by God for Greatness* (Lagos: Paramount Communications, 2004).

[33] Henley O. Agbonkhina, *419 Syndrome and Its Effects in Nigeria* (self-published, 2002): p. vi.

[34] Smith, *A Culture of Corruption*, p. 33.

[35] Harvey Glickman, "The Nigerian '419' Advance Fee Scams: Prank or Peril?" *Canadian Journal of African Studies/Revue Canadienne des Études Africaines* vol. 39, no. 3 (2005): pp. 460–489, 473.

[36] Chuu Anoliefo, *419 & the Rest of Us: Our Quest for Survival* (Lagos: Delence Publishing Company, 1992): p. 20.

The author of the pamphlet proposed that greed was behind it all. Perhaps, but the legacy of the civil war was there as well, albeit silently. There is not a straight line between the war and 419 as it is known today. A full account of Nigerian 419 would require a wider time frame – one that includes both colonialism, which made the place called "Nigeria," and the more recent history of technology that made 419 an international phenomenon.[37] That said, this book argues that it is impossible to understand Nigeria's long experience of crime without the context of the Nigerian Civil War – specifically, the survival tactics that Biafrans and Nigerians developed to cope with wartime dangers and postwar hardships.[38]

Everyday life in the Republic of Biafra was shot through with hunger and danger, and these conditions drove people to acts of self-preservation that were illegal. The forms of lawbreaking that emerged during the war forced judges, military administrators, and the public to revise their ideas about what types of people were predisposed toward crime. Many of the defendants in these cases did not see themselves as "criminals" – crime was a necessity of survival rather than a conscious decision to break the law. Judges sometimes agreed with them. In prewar Nigeria, like in the Europe of Clive Emsley's description, there had been a "logical simplicity and a comforting morality" in the idea that criminals were always others.[39] In the public imagination,

---

[37] The fullest and most original description of 419's connection to colonialism is Pierce, *Moral Economies of Corruption*. The authoritative history of the Internet in Africa is yet to be written, but, on the relationship between crime and technology in Nigeria, see Dara N. Byrne, "419 Digilantes and the Frontier of Radical Justice Online," *Radical History Review* vol. 117 (2013): pp. 70–82.

[38] Many aspects of Nigerian life have become marked by this ethos of endurance and survival, including everyday speech. "How are you coping?" is a common greeting in Nigeria today, "coping" having become shorthand for the daily struggle to prosper in a world full of enemies and pitfalls. This language is not unique to Nigeria, but it is worth considering what conditions evoke it there versus, for example, in the Democratic Republic of the Congo, where the phrase "je me débrouille" – "I get by" – became a slogan during the waning years of Mobutu Sese Seko's rule. Guillaume Iyenda, *Households' Livelihoods and Survival Strategies Among Congolese Urban Poor: Alternatives to Western Approaches to Development* (Lewiston, ME: Edwin Mellen, 2007): p. 184. See also Jane MacGaffey and Vwakyanakazi Mukohya, *The Real Economy of Zaire: The Contribution of Smuggling and Other Unofficial Activities to National Wealth* (Philadelphia: University of Pennsylvania Press, 1991).

[39] Clive Emsley, *Crime, Police, and Penal Policy: European Experiences 1750–1940* (Oxford: Oxford University Press, 2007): p. 269.

crime was a problem of the "residuum," to use a term from Victorian England that remained in use in late twentieth-century Nigeria – members of a corrupt lower class, the psychologically deviant, and outsiders. The war troubled this notion that crime came from lowly places. As the circle of people engaged in crime widened to include every class and walk of life, judges and the public could no longer mark criminal offenders as villains and be done with them. The *context* of crime increasingly had to be taken into consideration. When crime continued after Biafra's defeat, the problem thickened.

What was most striking about misconduct during and after the war was the way it ignored ethnicity, class, and gender. Armed robbery and 419 were not the domain of any one segment of Nigerian society – least of all Igbos – and ethnicity was not a useful tool in understanding who engaged in crime and why. Defendants in criminal cases from Biafra were not only Igbo but Ibibio, Ijaw, Itsekiri, and indeed Yoruba and Hausa – groups associated with Nigeria, whose presence in Biafra has been quietly forgotten in a historiography that takes Biafra's Igbo identity at face value. Similarly, no Nigerian region or ethnic group was untouched by crime in the years following the war. Soldiers and civilians of all backgrounds – from both sides of the conflict – partook in crime in the reintegrated east and later in the Nigerian federation as a whole. Crime was a worryingly broad problem, and it was committed by people judges did not see as "naturally" disposed toward lawbreaking.[40] For example, armed robberies conducted by women, while uncommon, went against the idea that violent property crime was a vocation for impulsive young men.

Asking why people across the social spectrum break the law is a better way to approach crime than shoehorning it into a typology, but it is also a more confounding task. Criminology does not capture gray areas very well, and even in its more progressive precincts it posits a world organized into victims and perpetrators. I challenge this way of seeing things, but in the interest of understanding how crime was seen in context I also reproduce some of its language. Terms like "indiscipline," "lawlessness," and even "crime" have unspoken connotations, often discriminatory ones. Historians often resist treating crime as a

---

[40] Both the crimes and the types of people engaged in it baffled and alarmed criminologists of the time. See, for example, Tekena Tamuno, "Trends in Policy: The Police and Prisons," in Tekena Tamuno, ed., *Nigeria Since Independence: The First Twenty-Five Years*, Vol. 4 (Ibadan: Heinemann, 1989).

real phenomenon, for fear that doing so might give credence to the things that are done in the name of combating it. Indeed, crime is a powerful political tool – governments use it to warrant discrimination and to induce the kind of fear that gives them a blank check for repression. Yet crime also has a social history; it is something that people do and experience, and the fact that it can be a political instrument does not preclude it from also being an important feature of daily life. The danger arises when crime is treated as something that explains, rather than something to *be* explained as a historically situated phenomenon, and when the patterns that seem to appear in it – which are almost invariably those of race, class, and gender – are made the basis of how people are governed.

It is easy to imagine that crime might have been a fantasy of Nigeria's paranoid military rulers or a specter propped up to justify their authoritarianism. One of many examples of this was Muhammadu Buhari's 1984 coup against the short-lived civilian government of Shehu Shagari. Corruption and indiscipline, he argued, were the "twin evils in our body politic," and he justified his coup as a revolution against "forgery, fraud, embezzlement, misuse and abuse of office, illegal dealing in foreign exchange and smuggling."[41] Many military leaders used the fear of crime to buttress their legitimacy. The war served a similar purpose. As an anxious judge noted in the ruling of a 1971 counterfeiting case, "the continued prevalence of the atmosphere of the last Civil War" could be used as the pretext to violate individual rights, from unlawful arrests to outright disappearances.[42] The war and its memory would provide the justification for thirty years of nearly uninterrupted military rule in Nigeria, most of it under brutal regimes of emergency.[43]

Crime, however, was not just an alibi for repression, and Biafrans and Nigerians experienced it as something more than an epiphenomenon of military rule. It was a real and obdurate social problem – as

---

[41] Hoover Institution Archive [hereafter HIA], Nigerian Subject Collection XX787, Box 6, "Facts About the Military Takeover," February 1984.

[42] Enugu State High Court [hereafter ESHC] uncatalogued collection, High Court of the East Central State, *Commissioner of Police v. James Usong*, September 8, 1971.

[43] Military rule lasted from 1966 until Olusegun Obasanjo's election as president in 1999, with two brief interruptions. The first was the civilian government of Shehu Shagari from 1979 to 1983, the second the annulled 1993 election that gave way to the administration of General Sani Abacha.

thousands of court cases, frenzied editorials, and the memories of those who lived through it attest. Crime really existed, but that did not mean that a despotic form of military rule was the only way to stop it. Harsh policing and stringent sentencing were not reflections of a broad social consensus about the need for security but tools of repression, as many Nigerians came to understand them during the period of military rule. That said, criminal law was not inherently tyrannical, and whether it was "just" was a matter of perspective. Police and criminals could be both villains and heroes, often simultaneously. Seeing them as one or the other occludes the dialectical relationship between law and crime – a relationship that exists everywhere but is especially salient in contemporary Africa.[44]

None of this figures prominently in how the rest of the world remembers the Nigerian Civil War. For the generation of people who watched it unfold on television, Biafra brings to mind a different kind of horror – starvation. The war was a spectacle for the international press, and the images of emaciated children that flowed out of Biafra drowned out its politics. The Nigerian Civil War has long been understood through those images, and a large literature posits that it was not just an episode in Nigeria's history but a global one.[45] The war shaped

[44] On this dialectic, see Jean Comaroff and John Comaroff, "An Introduction," *Law and Disorder in the Postcolony* (Chicago: University of Chicago Press, 2006); Achille Mbembe, "Necropolitics," *Public Culture* vol. 15, no. 1 (2003): pp. 11–40; Achille Mbembe, *On the Postcolony* (Berkeley: University of California Press, 2001); Paul Nugent, *Africa Since Independence: A Comparative History* (Basingstoke: Palgrave Macmillan, 2004).

[45] The history of the war has most often been told from foreign diplomatic records, the international press, and Biafra's voluminous propaganda, much of which was produced in the United States and Europe. See John Stremlau, *The International Politics of the Nigerian Civil War* (Princeton: Princeton University Press, 1977); Suzanne Cronje, *The World and Nigeria: The Diplomatic History of the Biafran War, 1967–1970* (London: Sidgwick and Jackson, 1972); Bola A. Akinterinwa, *Nigeria and France, 1960–1995: The Dilemma of Thirty-Five Years of Relationship* (Ibadan: Vantage Publishers, 1999). Recent studies of the war have paid greater attention to international dimensions that are not captured by a strictly diplomatic approach, including its relationship to changes in humanitarian practice, human rights, and the question of genocide. See, for example, Daniel Sargent, *A Superpower Transformed: The Remaking of American Foreign Relations in the 1970s* (Oxford: Oxford University Press, 2015); Dirk Moses and Lasse Heerten, eds., *Postcolonial Conflict and the Question of Genocide: The Nigeria-Biafra War, 1967–1970* (London: Routledge, 2017); Roy Doron, "'We are doing everything we can, which is very little': The Johnson Administration and the Nigerian Civil War, 1967–1969," in

many larger matters, including the practice of humanitarianism, the consensus over what political responses genocide compelled, and the politics of the Cold War (though not always in the ways one might expect). Biafra also changed the way the West fundamentally understood warfare – it was among the first televised wars, exposing people to the atrocities of a distant conflict more intimately than perhaps ever before. A connection between Africa, violence, and humanitarian crisis crystallized in the global public imagination.[46] This was a consequence – not entirely unintended – of partisan reportage and activism, which pulled no punches in describing the crisis in Biafra.[47] The famines in the Sahel in the 1970s and in Ethiopia in the 1980s would have similar effects, but it was in Biafra where violence, hunger, and disorder first converged as postcolonial Africa's lot.

The diplomatic history of the war is also well known. Biafra's allies included France, Portugal, and South Africa, all of which had designs on carving an ally out of Nigeria (a regional power that each found threatening for various reasons). Only a few states recognized Biafra formally, most importantly Haiti, Tanzania, Ivory Coast, and Gabon. Nigeria's allies included a much wider group, and one that cut across the major geopolitical divides of the time – the United Kingdom, the United States, and the Soviet Union all supported Nigeria, though in a somewhat ambivalent manner. Most African states were against Biafra's independence, recognizing that they, too, were diverse countries where secession movements might manifest like they had in Nigeria.[48] The Organisation of African Unity took an especially firm stance against Biafran independence.

Yet Biafra is not just a case study in humanitarian intervention or the complexities of Cold War diplomacy. Understanding the international and humanitarian dimensions of the war is necessary but not sufficient

---

Toyin Falola, Roy Doron, and Okpeh O. Okpeh, eds., *Warfare, Ethnicity and National Identity in Nigeria* (Trenton: Africa World Press, 2013): pp. 126–133.

[46] The role of the international press has been addressed by several scholars. See, for example, Roy Doron, "Marketing Genocide: Biafran Propaganda Strategies During the Nigerian Civil War, 1967–1970," *Journal of Genocide Research* vol. 16, no. 2–3 (2014): pp. 227–246; Brian McNeil, "'And starvation is the grim reaper': The American Committee to Keep Biafra Alive and the Genocide Question During the Nigerian Civil War, 1968–70," *Journal of Genocide Research* vol. 16, no. 2–3 (2014): pp. 317–336.

[47] An account of this process can be found in Lasse Heerten, *The Biafran War and Postcolonial Humanitarianism: Spectacles of Suffering* (Cambridge: Cambridge University Press, 2017).

[48] See, for example, *Uganda Argus* [Kampala], May 18, 1967, p. 1.

for understanding what happened in Nigeria between 1967 and 1970. Historians of international institutions increasingly write of human rights, humanitarianism, and nongovernmental organizations as if their histories are synonymous with the history of Africa. I do not deny that international agencies were important in Biafra, including for its internal history; the humanitarian aid Biafra received saved many lives while also prolonging the war – a fact that makes any kind of argument about its morality complicated.[49] In broader terms, Biafra also precipitated a new, more partisan form of humanitarianism; famously, Doctors Without Borders was inspired by events there.[50] However, in Biafra, like in many places where international organizations dirtied their hands, much is obscured by paying attention to the global at the expense of the national and local.[51] To be sure, those organizations have a prominent place at the table in many African states, and it can be difficult to see where the boundary lies between African politics and foreign charities.[52] However, dressing up the history of humanitarianism as the history of the people whom it serves confuses events that happen *in* Africa with the history *of* Africa.[53] The

[49] Alex de Waal, *Famine Crimes: Politics and the Disaster Relief Industry in Africa* (Oxford: James Currey, 1997): p.77.

[50] See Eleanor Davey, *Idealism Beyond Borders: The French Revolutionary Left and the Rise of Humanitarianism, 1954–1988* (Cambridge: Cambridge University Press, 2015): pp. 29–44. On the International Committee of the Red Cross, see Marie-Luce Desgrandchamps, "'Organising the Unpredictable': The Nigeria-Biafra War and its Impact on the ICRC," *International Review of the Red Cross* vol. 94, no. 888 (2012): pp. 1409–1432; Arua Oko Omaka, *The Biafran Humanitarian Crisis, 1967–1970: International Human Rights and Joint Church Aid* (Madison, NJ: Fairleigh Dickinson University Press, 2016). See also Tehila Sasson, "Milking the Third World? Humanitarianism, Capitalism, and the Moral Economy of the Nestlé Boycott," *American Historical Review* vol. 121, no. 4 (2016): pp. 1196–1224.

[51] On this tension in the study of Africa, see Steven Feierman, "African Histories and the Dissolution of World History," in R. H. Bates, V. Y. Mudimbe, and J. O'Barr, eds., *Africa and the Disciplines: The Contributions of Research in Africa to the Social Sciences and Humanities* (Chicago: University of Chicago Press, 1993); Andrew Zimmerman, "Africa in Imperial and Transnational History: Multi-Sited Historiography and the Necessity of Theory," *Journal of African History* vol. 54, no. 3 (2013): pp. 331–340.

[52] See Gregory Mann, *From Empires to NGOs in the West African Sahel: The Road to Nongovernmentality* (Cambridge: Cambridge University Press, 2015).

[53] This is true even of accounts that emphasize the agency of African actors in international organizations or enumerate the failures of humanitarian and rights-based interventions in Africa. Some works move back and forth across this boundary. See, for example, Matthew Hilton, "Charity, Decolonization and

global historiography of the war says little about events in Biafra itself, rendering it the object of its own history rather than the subject. In the end, the Nigerian Civil War meant the most to Nigerians, not to the humanitarians, reporters, and diplomats who fed on it.

What happened in Biafra was not just a blur of tragedy. I take the humanitarian crisis as a starting point, but here that crisis is important for the problems it made locally, not in the corridors of international institutions.[54] Nigeria's vastness, with its huge population and its global diaspora, means that this is not a small question. Looking at Biafra as an episode in Nigerian history rather than international history does not diminish its stakes – if anything it raises them. The Nigerian blockade created a famine affecting millions of people, killing a very large number of Biafrans and inflicting permanent damage on many who survived. Hunger was recorded on bodies and in names; a woman who gave birth in the final months of the war named her child Nwaohia ("child of the wilderness"), and another christened a malnourished daughter Aguru ("hunger").[55] Photographs of starving Biafran children became emblems of human suffering; but these images, which entreated the viewer to see Biafra as an incomprehensible disaster, have done it a disservice.[56] Starvation is not the only story there is to tell about Biafra, and it should not conceal the full sweep of its brief, eventful history. This was neither an apolitical tragedy nor a place of unmitigated death.[57]

Development: The Case of the Starehe Boys School, Nairobi," *Past and Present* vol. 233, no. 1 (2016): pp. 227–267; Florian Hannig, "The Biafra Crisis and the Establishment of Humanitarian Aid in West Germany as a New Philanthropic Field," in Gregory R. Witkowski and Arnd Bauerkamper, eds., *German Philanthropy in Transatlantic Perspective* (Cham: Springer, 2015).

[54] Of course, the line between the local and the global consequences of the war should not be drawn too firmly. Small-scale events there informed the larger international dynamics that historians of the war have made familiar. In the realm of law, crime shaped how Biafra articulated its identity as a sovereign state, which in turn affected how the international community responded to it.

[55] Interview with Flora Udechukwu, Port Harcourt, February 15, 2015; IWM 6687, Papers of Rosina Umelo, "Biafra, A World of Our Own," p. 145.

[56] On the social dynamics that famine can generate, see Megan Vaughan, *The Story of an African Famine: Gender and Famine in Twentieth-Century Malawi* (Cambridge: Cambridge University Press, 1987).

[57] This statement vis-à-vis the international literature should not be mistaken for a generalized argument about agency. That Biafrans acted in their own interests and made decisions about their lives, even in the constraints of warfare, should not be surprising. The argument that Africans are agentive, both in the context

Sources: Legal Records, Oral History, Memoirs

The methodological challenges for this project are immense, as they are
for postcolonial African history in general. Many African state archives
from the period after independence are inaccessible to researchers,
pertaining as they often do to governments that are still in power or
to historical periods still within living memory. The archives of independent Nigeria can seem more inscrutable than those of the colonial
state it supplanted, with the British Empire's strong documentary
impulse and the United Kingdom's open records (even if, as recent
discoveries have made clear, more was concealed than the British
admitted as they departed their former colonies).[58] The most intract-
able problem is not transparency, however, but the fact that the
Nigerian National Archives have not accessioned records systematically since the early 1960s.[59] The problems of decay and neglect that
afflict nearly all archives were exacerbated by intentional acts of era-
sure. In Biafra, many people feared how government records might be
used against them. In the final days of the war, a clerk in the Research
and Production Directorate witnessed buses being packed with documents, likely to be taken away and destroyed.[60] Civil servant Godwin
Onyegbula recalled how after Biafra's surrender, he and his colleague:

occupied ourselves going through the documents in our possession, to ensure
that anything incriminating, which could be used against our people, was

of colonialism and beyond, has the danger of suggesting that there might be
some otherwise; asserting the agency of one group or another implicitly suggests
that other people do *not* act in the social and political world. Unless one is
speaking of people who are in conditions of bare life, these arguments about
agency often have the opposite effect from what they intend. The harder thing to
grapple with is that the agency Biafrans exercised was not always something
positive or redemptive. "Agency" is ugly and unvarnished in the legal record,
where acts of violence and cruelty are recorded more often than acts of care.

[58] Caroline Elkins, "Looking Beyond Mau Mau: Archiving Violence in the Era of
Decolonization," *The American Historical Review* vol. 120, no. 3 (2015): pp.
852–868.

[59] Saheed Aderinto and Paul Osifodunrin, eds., *The Third Wave of Historical
Scholarship on Nigeria: Essays in Honor of Ayodeji Olukoju* (Newcastle upon
Tyne: Cambridge Scholars Publishing, 2012): pp. 6–7.

[60] Chikwendu Christian Ukaegbu, "War and the Making of an Organic Scientific
and Technological Intelligentsia: The Case of Biafran Scientists in the Nigeria-
Biafra War," in Apollos O. Nwauwa and Chima J. Korieh, eds., *Against All
Odds: The Igbo Experience in Postcolonial Nigeria* (Glassboro, NJ: Goldline
and Jacobs Publishing, 2011): pp. 73–94, 91.

destroyed. Indeed, it was a painful task, reliving the experience of Biafra, and dumping into the toilet-bin, documents which stirred emotion. This we had to do, for in spite of Yusufu's [Gowon's] warm-heartedness, we could not predict what the Nigerian authorities would do with us.[61]

Personal archives fared no better. At the war's end, a British school-teacher named Rosina Umelo walked the thirty miles to Enugu from her Biafran husband's village, where she had taken refuge. She remembered that, along the way, "[I] noticed quite often scores of pages from someone's carefully preserved files, abandoned at the last torn out and thrown away along the roadside in the dust."[62] Countless personal documents were lost in the upheaval of the war and its aftermath. In 1972, the East Central State government issued a public appeal for people to send records relating to the war to an administrator in Onitsha where they would be "kept in the archives." The administrator guaranteed that "people with such documents should not entertain any fears in sending them to his office."[63] Shortly thereafter, the Nigerian Federal Government decided that posterity had no place in the reconciliation process, and what could be found of Biafra's state records was intentionally destroyed.[64] Of course, burning documents did not obliterate the war's memory.

The near-total absence of state recordkeeping since 1960 is most obviously a problem of scarcity, exacerbated by the impulse to conceal that all states exhibit to some degree. Yet perhaps there is something other than austerity and secrecy at work here. Freedom had many meanings in postcolonial Africa, and the freedom to be unknown to the state was one of them. The upside of shoddy recordkeeping is that it is hard to build a police state without paperwork – even Nigeria's most tyrannical regimes had a limited capacity to monitor their enemies or suppress dissent from within. It is not unreasonable to think that some

---

[61] Onyegbula, *The Memoirs of the Nigerian-Biafran Bureaucrat*, p. 193.
[62] IWM 6687, Papers of Rosina Umelo, "Biafra, A World of Our Own," p. 240. Umelo's memoir is one of the more detailed accounts of daily life in Biafra, told from the perspective of a British woman who stayed in Biafra for the duration of the war. Her manuscript, held in the archive of the Imperial War Museum in London, remained as obscure as most Biafran records until 2018, when it was published with extensive commentary. See S. Elizabeth Bird and Rosina Umelo, *Surviving Biafra: A Nigerwife's Story* (London: Hurst, 2018).
[63] *Nigerian Tide* [Port Harcourt], November 7, 1973, p. 4.
[64] Sampson, *The Path of Justice Chike Idigbe*, p. 71.

civilian bureaucrats intentionally kept poor records because they feared how military regimes or subsequent administrations might use them.

Historians' reliance on (and affection for) state archives leads us to argue that documentation is critical to the work of governing, but this is not necessarily how administrators think about the preservation of paper. For most civil servants, the archive is an unseen and unknown place – one which resembles a waste disposal service more than anything else. It is only a highly articulated state, and one that has a keen sense of its own past, that will devote scarce resources to documenting its activities for posterity. Biafra was not such a state, and arguably nor is Nigeria.[65] To speak generally, independent African states oriented their politics toward the future, and if they were interested in history it was for how it might serve that future – the "usable past" being the one most worth reconstructing.[66] One Biafran bureaucrat admitted in his memoirs that during the war he

hardly kept records; nor did I consider that there was much in my life deserving of such attention [...] I was initially persuaded to commence this work, after a discussion with General Ojukwu, in those heady days. He asked

[65] There is a vibrant literature on the meanings of archives – real and figurative – in postcolonial Africa. Selectively, see Stephen Ellis, "Writing Histories of Contemporary Africa," *Journal of African History* vol. 43, no. 1 (2002); Gabrielle Hecht, *Being Nuclear: Africans and the Global Uranium Trade* (Cambridge, MA: MIT Press, 2012); Samuel Aniegye Ntewusu, "Serendipity: Conducting Research on Social History in Ghana's Archives," *History in Africa* vol. 4, no. 1 (2014), pp. 417–423; Luise White, "Introduction – Suitcases, Roads, and Archives: Writing the History of Africa after 1960," *History in Africa* vol. 42 (2015), pp. 265–267; Achille Mbembe, "The Power of the Archive and Its Limits," in Carolyn Hamilton et. al., eds., *Refiguring the Archive* (Dordrecht: Springer, 2002), pp. 19–28; Antoinette Burton ed., *Archive Stories: Facts, Fictions, and the Writing of History* (Durham, NC: Duke University Press, 2005); Ann Laura Stoler, *Along the Archival Grain: Epistemic Anxieties and Colonial Common Sense* (Princeton: Princeton University Press, 2009); Todd Shepard, "'Of Sovereignty': Disputed Archives, 'Wholly Modern' Archives, and the Post-Decolonization French and Algerian Republics, 1962–2012," *The American Historical Review* vol. 120 no. 3 (2015): pp. 869–883. Innovative approaches to postcolonial history from the literary archive include Ato Quayson, *Oxford Street, Accra: City Life and the Itineraries of Transnationalism* (Durham, NC: Duke University Press, 2014); Emily Callaci, *Street Archives and City Life: Popular Intellectuals in Postcolonial Tanzania* (Durham, NC: Duke University Press, 2017).

[66] Bogumil Jewsiewicki, "African Historical Studies Academic Knowledge as 'Usable Past' and Radical Scholarship," *African Studies Review* vol. 32, no. 3 (1989): pp.1–76.

if I was keeping some records, and I answered in the negative: he was also not keeping any. What a pity, we thought, that both of us, students of history, were so a-historical.[67]

For this reason, those who write Biafra's history have generally sought out their sources from far away, in aid organizations, foreign governments, and the international press. Historians of the recent African past often bypass national and local archives, relying instead on the "shadow archives" and "hidden corridors" of international history, as Jean Allman calls them.[68] These are records that tend to underscore Africa's extraversion – its imbrication in international politics, and not its inner life.[69] As a result, the study of Africa after independence has taken a more "global" tack than the study of colonialism did (even when it worked in an imperial frame). I make use of these outside sources, keeping fully in mind that the diplomats, journalists, and "observers" of various types who visited the war zone came with their own agendas and could only see what they were shown.[70] Foreign records can only say so much about what happened in Biafran households, villages, and courtrooms. The originality of this work lies in its use of sources that were *internal* to Biafra.

These Biafran sources were cobbled together from many places, most of which do not lend themselves easily to historical research. What remains of the Biafran archive is fragments of its legal record, preserved haphazardly in the storerooms and cupboards of courthouses across the former republic.[71] None, to my knowledge, have ever been used by

[67] Ojukwu had studied history as an undergraduate at Oxford University. Onyegbula, *The Memoirs of the Nigerian-Biafran Bureaucrat*, p. ix.

[68] Jean Allman, "Phantoms of the Archive: Kwame Nkrumah, a Nazi Pilot Named Hanna, and the Contingencies of Postcolonial History-Writing," *The American Historical Review* vol. 118, no. 1 (2013): pp. 104–129.

[69] It is worth noting that most of these materials are held in Europe and North America, where ever-tighter travel restrictions have made them inaccessible to scholars from African institutions.

[70] The British and French state archives figure most prominently here, but the archives of other foreign governments, especially Ireland and South Africa, also proved unexpectedly rich as sources on Nigeria in this era. Most foreign observers viewed the war from arm's length. Notable exceptions included aid workers, priests, and the spouses of Nigerians and Biafrans, who stayed longer and were more embedded in the conflict. See, for example, the American Peace Corps volunteer John Sherman, *War Stories: A Memoir of Nigeria and Biafra* (Indianapolis: Mesa Verde Press, 2002).

[71] In addition to these, a small number of Biafran cases from early in the war are preserved in the Biafra Court of Appeal series of the National Archives of

historians, and without intervention many of them will literally turn to dust in the near future. Biafra's far-flung records are dispersed and decaying, but these conditions reveal something about the state and its afterlife. Biafra's legacy is submerged, and it is not surprising that its paper trail is halting and difficult to follow. These records will probably never be digitized, for reasons both practical and political. Maybe this is just as well, since some of their meaning is contained in where they are kept, what condition they are in, and how they are accessed.[72] Some documents gave me feelings rather than facts: a stiff piece of blood-stained cloth that tumbled out of an evidence folder, a restricted file surreptitiously passed to me in a bathroom stall, or a Biafran veteran's army papers that he kept hidden at the bottom of a box of pornography – both of which he seemed ashamed of but eager to show me. Documents like these have an aura, independent of what they actually say.

Why legal records were preserved is not always clear. Some seem to have been maintained because it was not worth going to the trouble of disposing of them. Others, especially civil records, were probably kept because a registrar thought that someone might one day request a record of, say, their divorce proceedings – even if their Biafran stamps rendered them useless for most legal purposes in postwar Nigeria. In the Enugu State High Court, which constitutes the largest single repository for this project, digests of Biafran cases were preserved by the judges who decided them, possibly "for reasons of vanity," as a current librarian hypothesized.[73] They are irregularly organized, incomplete, and deteriorating. Perhaps because they are so thoroughly forgotten, or

Nigeria in Enugu, along with a smattering of administrative files from the Biafran Ministry of Justice and an incomplete run of the *Biafra Sun* newspaper. Odd issues of other Biafran periodicals can be found in the Special Collections of the Nnamdi Azikiwe Library at the University of Nigeria – Nsukka. In the branch of the national archives in Ibadan, there is a collection of Biafran propaganda that is duplicated in a number of repositories abroad, most completely at Michigan State University. In the zonal office of the national archives in Calabar there are some irregular files from Biafra. A unique collection of materials from Biafran civil defense organizations can be found in the storeroom of the National War Museum in Umuahia.

[72] I am skeptical of the "digital turn" in historical research, from which African archives have been largely excluded. See Samuel Fury Childs Daly, "Archival Research in Africa," *African Affairs* vol. 116, no. 463 (2017): pp. 311–320.

[73] With the exception of village-level customary courts, courts and tribunals in the east operated largely in English. In cases where speakers of Igbo or other languages testified, translation was made into English or occasionally Pidgin. In the interest of maintaining consistency, I have left errors and idiomatic

because they are of no practical value to the legal practitioners who use the institutions where they are held, in most cases I was given free rein to view them.[74] This was labor-intensive work, conducted in cobwebby sheds and the back rooms of working courts, all while wearing the formal attire expected of court visitors. I tried to leave these archives in better condition than I found them, but much work would have to be done to ensure that they survive.

Most of these records are of criminal trials. Many legal histories of Africa take civil dispute as their point of entry,[75] but a different picture emerges when one starts from *criminal* law, as this book does. Criminal law is important not only for the teleological reason that crime became important in Nigeria, but because it was at the center of both Biafra's and Nigeria's sovereign identities. Criminal law was critical to the maintenance of "order," "discipline," and "security," all of which were maxims of military rule.[76] Discipline animated Nigerian politics

expressions intact, without the use of *sic.* Occasional clarifying notes appear in brackets. As had been the case in the colonial period, the recording and translation of proceedings shaped legal process in important ways. See Derek R. Peterson, *Creative Writing: Translation, Bookkeeping, and the Work of Imagination in Colonial Kenya* (Portsmouth: Heinemann, 2004); Benjamin N. Lawrance, Emily Lynn Osborn, and Richard L. Roberts, eds., *Intermediaries, Interpreters, and Clerks: African Employees in the Making of Colonial Africa* (Madison: University of Wisconsin Press, 2006).

[74] In the interest of protecting privacy, I have changed the names of criminal defendants in unreported cases cited here. Location descriptions and file numbers for these cases have not been altered.

[75] This stands to reason, given that the sharpest points of dispute in many African societies in the colonial period (and after) were civil matters like land ownership and divorce. The question of how people use the legal system to make claims is of secondary importance here, since most of the cases from Biafra's courts are criminal rather than civil. They therefore involve the state pursuing people rather than people pursuing outcomes from the state; but, even in the criminal court, legal persons are made and law itself is shaped (at least in the tradition of the English common law, of which both Biafra and Nigeria are a part). See Richard Roberts, *Litigants and Households: African Disputes and Colonial Courts in the French Soudan, 1895–1912* (Portsmouth: Heinemann, 2005); Sara Berry, *No Condition is Permanent: The Social Dynamics of Agrarian Change in Sub-Saharan Africa* (Madison: University of Wisconsin Press, 1993); Emily Burrill, *States of Marriage: Gender, Justice, and Rights in Colonial Mali* (Athens: Ohio University Press, 2015).

[76] In many ways, this followed on from colonialism. Criminal law had been at the center of British administration, both as a mechanism of repression and as the place where the privileges of rulers and the obligations of the ruled were sorted out. Echoing a larger current in imperial history, Martin Wiener writes that "law lay at the heart of the British imperial enterprise. And criminal justice was at the

across the late twentieth century – it was a goal for both military regimes and their detractors, and criminal law was its bludgeon. In Biafra, the state also used criminal law as a semaphore to express its ideology to its citizens and to the wider world. For these reasons, criminal records reveal much more than the history of crime.

My other main source material consists of oral interviews, mostly with people who worked as lawyers, magistrates, or legal administrators in Biafra and postwar eastern Nigeria. The majority of my informants were men, which reflects the composition of the bar and the bench at the time. I also interviewed several men who were soldiers during the war and became lawyers after its end, forging their professional and civic careers as veterans of the "rebel" army. A smaller number of interviewees appeared before Biafran and Nigerian courts as defendants, though it proved difficult to trace them into the present. Most identify as Igbo, although like many people of high social position, they are more likely to describe themselves in terms of their class, profession, or religion than their ethnicity. Even those who had no desire to be part of Biafra and feel no nostalgia for it, like members of ethnic minorities in Port Harcourt or Calabar, rarely expressed their reflections on the war in ethnic terms. To them, the war had many dimensions and ethnicity was only one of them.

Most conversations took place in their busy chambers, often in down-at-heel office buildings that did little to outwardly suggest their success – which in some cases was substantial. More than once I was taken home from interviews in a chauffeured Mercedes-Benz. Other interviews took place in people's homes, in court canteens, or after church. Some introduced me to friends and colleagues whom I then interviewed, invariably accompanying their recommendations about who to talk to with warnings that I should not trust everything I hear.[77] As lawyers, their livelihoods depend on telling convincing stories, and the risk of being taken in by smooth talk was not lost on me. The hospitality I enjoyed was almost always gracious, and I was received as

---

core of law." Martin J. Wiener, *An Empire on Trial: Race, Murder, and Justice under British Rule, 1870–1935* (Cambridge: Cambridge University Press, 2009): p. 5. For an analysis of how crime could dovetail with colonial politics, see Richard Rathbone, *Murder and Politics in Colonial Ghana* (New Haven, CT: Yale University Press, 1993).

[77] Some spoke to me under the condition that they remain anonymous, which I have respected.

a hapless foreigner in need of protection and tutelage. I left interviews with gifts of books or photocopied cases and, once, a brand-new tin of polish when my scuffed shoes were found lacking. My gender, age, race, nationality, and professional standing (or, as a non-lawyer, lack thereof) inflected this research in many ways. My position no doubt influenced what I was told and how it was told to me, but it is worth noting that the power differential cut in a different direction to what foreign anthropologists and historians who work in Africa often describe; in most cases, I was less educated, worldly, and affluent than the people with whom I spoke.[78] Although this book is a social history, it is not exactly written "from below."

Perhaps because of their success, most of the lawyers I interviewed exhibited little bitterness toward Nigeria. Some may privately mourn the lost cause of Biafra, but no person I spoke to openly expressed desire for the east to secede again. Nearly all lived in the east throughout the war and its aftermath, and they have had to forge their professional and personal lives in the shadow of Biafra's defeat. Over the last half century, most have concluded that the best way to live is "to let go of the past."[79] Many of their children feel differently, as do the Biafrans who remained in exile after the war. Those who made their lives abroad were never forced to make a personal peace with Nigeria, and they could speak freely about their experiences in a way that those who stayed behind could not.[80] They recall the war with undiminished bitterness and anger. For Igbos who were born after 1970, Biafra remains an unfulfilled, idealized dream. Unconstrained by actual memories, young people can speculate about what Biafra might have been. On the Internet, photoshopped images of "Biafran embassies" in foreign capitals and planes in the livery of "Biafra Airlines" circulate widely, and rapturous prophecies of Biafra as an oil-rich "African Dubai" describe a place that never was, and likely never will be.[81]

Like in Nigerian history broadly, memoirs are an important body of knowledge about the civil war. There are hundreds of personal accounts

---

[78] See Charles Piot, *Remotely Global: Village Modernity in West Africa* (Chicago: University of Chicago Press, 1999): pp. 59–62.
[79] Interview with Jerome H. C. Okolo, SAN, September 17, 2014.
[80] See Bibi Bakare-Yusuf, "Scattered Limbs, Scattered Stories: The Silence of Biafra," *African Identities* vol. 10, no. 3 (2012): pp. 243–248.
[81] See Vivian Chenxue Lu, "Agitating the State: Biafran Money, Memes and Mobility," *The Republic*, November 2017.

of Biafra, many of them self-published. They are subject to the same exaggerations and distortions of autobiographies anywhere, and they have fed back into public memory and academic scholarship in complicated ways.[82] As one Biafran administrator candidly warned in his own memoirs, "biography becomes boring when entirely true."[83] Their embellishments and half-truths are historical data in and of themselves. This biographical tradition has created a historiography that is tightly focused on individuals. Chukwuemeka Odumegwu Ojukwu, Olusegun Obasanjo, Yakubu Gowon, and other prominent figures of the war have been the subjects of many biographies, sometimes written by their political rivals to set the record straight, and even lesser-known figures like Victor Banjo and Isaac Boro have received the same treatment.[84] They depict the war as a battle of wills between forceful personalities; they explain Biafra's secession through psychology or personal ambition and the war itself through the strategic genius (or cowardice) of commanders.[85] This venerable military historical tradition of describing war as a falling-out between "a handful of men" is not always inaccurate, but it represents a narrow view of how war happens.[86] I turn to their

---

[82] Comparatively, see Luise White, *Fighting and Writing: The Rhodesian Army at War and Post-War*, forthcoming.

[83] Onyegbula, *The Memoirs of the Nigerian-Biafran Bureaucrat*, p. 193.

[84] Among many examples, see Val Obienyem, *Ojukwu: The Last Patriot* (Ibadan: Wisdom Publishers, 2005); Chukwuemeka Odumegwu Ojukwu, *Because I Am Involved* (Ibadan: Spectrum Books, 1989); Olusegun Obasanjo, *Nzeogwu: An Intimate Portrait of Major Chukwuma Kaduna Nzeogwu* (Ibadan: Spectrum Books, 1987); J. Isawa Elaigwu, *Gowon: The Biography of a Soldier-Statesman* (London: Adonis and Abbey, 2009). See also F. Adetowun Ogunsheye, *A Break in the Silence: A Historical Note on Lt. Colonel Victor Adebukunola Banjo* (Ibadan: Spectrum Books, 2001); Isaac Boro, *The Twelve-Day Revolution* (Benin City: Ibodo Umeh Publishers, 1982).

[85] See, for example, Victor Olu Taiwo's hypothesis that Ojukwu brought about Biafra's secession in order to impress his father. Victor Olu Taiwo, *Nigeria on Gunpowder: The Climax of Misrule* (Ibadan: Omo-Ade Publications, 2000): p. 193.

[86] Philip Roessler and Harry Verhoeven, *Why Comrades Go To War: Liberation Politics and the Outbreak of Africa's Deadliest Conflict* (Oxford: Oxford University Press, 2016): p. 12. Two important military sociologies that give the grounding of this idea are Samuel Decalo, *Coups and Army Rule in Africa: Studies in Military Style* (New Haven, CT: Yale University Press, 1976); Claude E. Welch, Jr., ed., *Soldier and State in Africa: A Comparative Analysis of Military Intervention and Political Change* (Evanston, IL: Northwestern University Press, 1970).

memoirs not for stories of valor or intrigue but for what they say in passing about what was going on in the background.

Biafra gives lie to the cliché that history is written by the victors. The most widely read accounts of the war – those by Chinua Achebe, Chimamanda Ngozi Adichie, John De St. Jorre, Frederick Forsyth, Chukwuemeka Ike, Buchi Emecheta, and others – are by people who either fought on the Biafran side or were sympathetic to it. There are many general histories of the war, most of which emphasize its military dimensions.[87] A small but important body of social-historical work has fleshed out how Biafran civilians experienced the war, often through oral historical research.[88] *A History of the Republic of Biafra* brings these bodies of sources to bear on one another to provide a picture of how people survived this cataclysm and how they lived in its aftermath.

The Nigerian Civil War is important not only for what it reveals about Nigeria, but for the comparative history of warfare. Accounts of warfare in Africa take many forms, bridging methodologies from history, anthropology, and political economy.[89] Some narrate war as a consequence of scarcity, interpreting local forms of violence in light of

---

[87] Among many, which often bridge the genres of history and memoir, see Alexander Madiebo, *The Nigerian Revolution and the Biafran War* (Enugu: Fourth Dimension, 1980); Olusegun Obasanjo, *My Command: An Account of the Nigerian Civil War, 1967–1970* (Ibadan: Heinemann, 1980); Godwin Alabi-Isama, *The Tragedy of Victory: On-the-Spot Account of the Nigeria-Biafra War in the Atlantic Theatre* (Ibadan: Spectrum, 2013); Philip Efiong, *The Caged Bird Sang No More: My Biafra Odyssey, 1966–1970* (Pinetown: 30 Degrees South Publishers, 2016); Luke Nnaemeka Aneke, *The Untold Story of the Nigeria-Biafra War* (Lagos: Triumph, 2008); Michael Gould, *The Struggle for Modern Nigeria: The Biafran War, 1967–1970* (London: I.B. Tauris, 2012); John De St. Jorre, *The Brothers' War: Biafra and Nigeria* (Boston: Houghton Mifflin, 1972); Ralph Uwechue, *Reflections on the Nigerian Civil War: Facing the Future* (Victoria: Trafford, 2004); Fredrick Forsyth, *The Biafra Story* (Baltimore: Penguin, 1969). See also Zdenek Cervenka, *A History of the Nigerian War, 1967–1970* (Ibadan: Onibonoje Press, 1972).

[88] See, for example, Axel Harneit-Sievers, *A Social History of the Nigerian Civil War: Perspectives From Below* (Enugu: Jemezie Publishers, 1997) and many of the contributions in Siyan Oyeweso, ed., *Perspectives on the Nigerian Civil War* (Lagos: OAP Humanities Series, 1993). See also the extensive oral historical materials of the University of South Florida's Memorial Project, available at http://asabamemorial.org/, and the website compiled by journalist Chika Oduah available at https://biafranwarmemories.com/ (both available at the time of publication).

[89] For an overview of the questions that have structured the study of warfare in Africa, especially in the period before colonial rule, see John Lamphear, ed., "Introduction," *African Military History* (Aldershot: Ashgate, 2007).

larger economic forces. Others privilege the international dimensions of warfare, fitting complex conflicts into categories like proxy war or religious fundamentalism, rendering them legible to outsiders but leaving their internal dynamics opaque. A further body of literature brings the social, spiritual, and gendered dimensions of African civil wars to the fore.[90] Some combine explanatory frameworks, arguing against monocausal determinism.[91] One important study inverts the question of why African states go to war, asking instead why Guinea "chose" peace at a time when its neighbors were embroiled in armed conflict.[92] In a different vein, several recent works have revisited colonial ideas about "martial races" to understand the ethnic politics of African militaries.[93] Some use nationalist historiography as their foil, narrating the histories of civil wars against older attempts at nation-building, which papered over deep divisions.[94] Nearly all share a common enemy in the "new barbarism" thesis – a sensationalist approach to African warfare that treated it as inscrutable, primordial, apolitical, and

---

[90] Michelle R. Moyd, *Violent Intermediaries: African Soldiers, Conquest, and Everyday Colonialism in German East Africa* (Athens: Ohio University Press, 2014); Alicia C. Decker, *In Idi Amin's Shadow: Women, Gender, and Militarism in Uganda* (Athens: Ohio University Press, 2014); Heike Behrend, *Alice Lakwena and the Holy Spirits: War in Northern Uganda, 1985–1997* (Oxford: James Currey, 1999); Joseph Hellweg, *Hunting the Ethical State: The Benkadi Movement of Côte d'Ivoire* (Chicago: University of Chicago Press, 2011); Stephen Ellis, *The Mask of Anarchy: The Destruction of Liberia and the Religious Dimension of an African Civil War* (New York: New York University Press, 2007); Danny Hoffman, *War Machines: Young Men and Violence in Sierra Leone and Liberia* (Durham, NC: Duke University Press, 2011).

[91] See, for example, Gérard Prunier, *Africa's World War: Congo, the Rwandan Genocide, and the Making of a Continental Catastrophe* (Oxford: Oxford University Press, 2009); William Reno, *Warlord Politics and African States* (Boulder, CO: Lynne Rienner, 1998); Richard J. Reid, *Warfare in African History* (Cambridge: Cambridge University Press, 2012); Christopher Clapham, ed., *African Guerrillas* (Bloomington: Indiana University Press, 1998).

[92] The author's answer has to do with Guinea's successful, if heavy-handed, process of nation-building under socialism. Mike McGovern, *A Socialist Peace?: Explaining the Absence of War in an African Country* (Chicago: University of Chicago Press, 2017).

[93] Moses Ochonu, *Colonialism by Proxy: Hausa Imperial Agents and Middle Belt Consciousness in Nigeria* (Bloomington: Indiana University Press, 2014); Myles Osborne, *Ethnicity and Empire in Kenya: Loyalty and Martial Race among the Kamba, c. 1800 to the Present* (Cambridge: Cambridge University Press, 2014).

[94] See, for example, Justin Pearce, *Political Identity and Conflict in Central Angola, 1975–2002* (Cambridge: Cambridge University Press, 2015); Branch, *Defeating Mau Mau, Creating Kenya*.

uniquely violent.[95] I combine these heterodox approaches to the study
of armed conflict and add to them an analysis of how law functions
during and after war.

***

"Sitting on the Bench," recalled Dulcie Oguntoye of her career as a
magistrate, "one does see much of the worst of human nature."[96] War
stories and court records have something in common in that both speak
more often of cruelty than kindness.[97] Biafra was a vast theater of
tragedy, and this book catalogues many acts of self-preservation,
often staged at the expense of others. Yet this should not be taken as
a cynical argument that the country was built of crooked timber.
Biafrans also acted selflessly, sacrificing their own lives for friends,
relatives, or strangers. The legal record seldom captures these acts but
other sources do.[98] One poignant figure of altruism is the medical
orderly Peter Ozekweo. He attended to seventy-two patients, alone,
in a looted hospital at Awomama for several months in 1969, with no
drugs and no clean water, only to succumb to disease himself in the
final days of the war.[99] Or there is the story of Innocent Chijindu, the
nine-year-old son of a university lecturer who hid in the forest after his
parents were killed. Hunger drove him to a village in mid-1969, where
someone pieced together who he was by some scraps of paper that he

[95] Derived from the work of the American journalist Robert Kaplan, it explained
African wars in Somalia, Liberia, Sierra Leone, and Rwanda as conflicts over
resources and greed compounded by environmental factors, in which fighters
were "loose molecules" with no particular allegiances or ideologies. Paul
Richards aptly described it as "Malthus with guns." Paul Richards, *Fighting for
the Rain Forest: War, Youth, and Resources in Sierra Leone* (Oxford: James
Currey, 1996): pp. xiv–xxv.

[96] Dulcie Adunola Oguntoye, *Your Estranged Faces* (self-published, 2008): p.154.

[97] As Axel Harneit-Sievers succinctly put it, "there are few wartime tales about
togetherness and solidarity, but many about conflict and social or moral decay."
Axel Harneit-Sievers, *Constructions of Belonging: Igbo Communities and the
Nigerian State in the Twentieth Century* (Rochester, NY: University of
Rochester Press, 2006): p. 127.

[98] See, for example, a description of an Ikwerre man who sheltered a group of Igbo
children during the Nigerian recapture of Port Harcourt. Diliorah Chukwurah,
Last Train to Biafra: The Memoirs of a Biafran Child (Ibadan: Constellation
Publishers, 2015): p. 66.

[99] Interview with Mary Okehe, Lagos, July 17, 2013. Unusually, his story found its
way into the archival record as well. National Archives of the United Kingdom,
Kew [hereafter NAUK] PREM 13/3378, "Report of Incoming Save the Children
Fund Team at Orlu, Hospitals Located as at 1st January 1970," n.d.

carried with him – he had been rendered mute by months of wandering alone. Chijindu and a dozen other children were adopted by the head-master of the Holy Rosary School in Umuobom, who somehow found a way to provide for them despite the crippling shortage of food.[100] Acts of heroism, compassion, and self-sacrifice took place during the war, even though they are less perceptible than its violence.

War, as historians of many places have long argued, makes worlds. The world that the Nigerian Civil War made was shaped by what took place inside Biafra. In turn, the history of Biafra is largely about law. Finding a functional legal system operating in the depths of a civil war challenges the idea that the postcolonial state in Africa is inherently despotic, dysfunctional, or despoiled. If a legal order can be found in Biafra, surely one can be found anywhere. I admit that there are limits to this argument; although Biafra was founded in the name of law and order, the war made it impossible to meaningfully implement the ethos of discipline that it promised. Biafran law was more honored in the breach than in the observance, which makes it a tricky kind of legal system to study. Both the *rule* of law (the constraint of power by a judiciary) and the *force* of law (its ability to maintain order) would ultimately be casualties of the war; and, of course, the fact that there *was* a legal system does not mean that it was fair or just to those caught up in it. Even so, the story of Biafra's birth, life, and death is critical for Nigeria's history – and for the larger question of what warfare does to normative orders.

Historians of Africa long enjoined their readers to treat African societies on their own terms – to eschew models of change made in Europe, to take local knowledge seriously, and to develop new ways of marking time that better served African societies. These are worthy admonitions, and they should still be heeded. However, arguing for Africa's distinctiveness risks parochializing African history, preventing us from seeing that ecumenical arguments might emerge *from* the African past. The Nigerian Civil War is important because it reveals something about war in general – more, in some ways, than it says about

---

[100] National War Museum, Umuahia [hereafter NWM] uncatalogued collection, "An abandoned boy picked up," July 28, 1969. The most famous cases of Biafran children orphaned by the war are the children who were airlifted to other African countries and adopted there, especially Gabon – where unsubstantiated rumors would later hold that President Omar Bongo's son Ali, who became president himself, was one such child.

Africa in the 1960s.[101] Biafra is an important episode in the history of Africa after independence, but its lesson is portable beyond that context: Biafra shows how the "legitimate" violence of warfare can bleed into crime. "Ours is not a unique experience as the history of other nations illustrates," wrote Nnamdi Azikiwe toward the war's end. "Our country is passing through a crucible. From its experiences we can set aright the course of our human history."[102] Azikiwe was right, even if he overestimated how much the rest of the world would learn. Biafra does not reveal much about the African condition, if such a thing exists, but it says quite a lot about the human condition in times of conflict.

Finally, I offer a disclaimer. The story of Nigeria's civil war is not mine to tell, although who among the partisans ought to tell it is not a settled question.[103] This is *a* history of Biafra, not *the*, and it is far from being the only one that could be told. As far as possible, it is partial to neither the Biafran side nor the Nigerian one. Historical characters are

[101] The war does not follow the script of its time and place; it was neither an anticolonial war nor a Cold War proxy, and it had nothing to do with communism. The war that was closest to Biafra (in both character and timing) was Katanga's secession from the Democratic Republic of Congo in 1960–1963, where the politics of ethnicity, natural resources, and international statesmanship converged, albeit in a different arrangement, to create a new African nation-state that was never internationally recognized. See Erik Kennes and Miles Larmer, *The Katangese Gendarmes and War in Central Africa: Fighting Their Way Home* (Bloomington: Indiana University Press, 2016). Despite these similarities, Katanga's secession and reintegration did not give rise to crime in the way that Biafra's did. Over the border in Cameroon, the violence that attended the decolonization process muddled state and personal acts of violence in ways consistent with what I describe here. See Meredith Terretta, *Nation of Outlaws, State of Violence: Nationalism, Grassfields Tradition, and State Building in Cameroon* (Athens: Ohio University Press, 2014).

[102] Azikiwe had been Nigeria's first president. He briefly sided with Biafra when it seceded but would return to the Nigerian fold midway through the war. Lagos State Research and Archives Board, Lagos [hereafter LASRAB] CSG 1.4, Nnamdi Azikiwe to Lagos State Military Governor Mobolaji Johnson, October 15, 1969.

[103] Consider, for example, the fictionalized debate over the historical monograph at the center of Chimamanda Ngozi Adichie's *Half of a Yellow Sun*, as well as the very real controversy about Adichie's representation of the war. See, among others, Meredith Coffey, "Ethnic Minorities and the Biafran National Imaginary in Chukwuemeka Ike's *Sunset at Dawn* and Chimamanda Ngozi Adichie's *Half of a Yellow Sun*," in Toyin Falola and Ogechukwu Ezekwem, eds., *Writing the Nigeria-Biafra War* (Woodbridge: James Currey, 2016): pp. 265–283.

not always heroes and not always victims, and I make no attempt to efface acts of violence committed by either of the belligerents. I take as positivist an approach to the "plot" of the war as possible. That plot as I tell it is riddled with holes, twists, and double-backs, and it is full of details that trouble the stories stalwarts from both sides would prefer to tell. For this reason, this book will likely please no one.

Organization of the Book

A History of the Republic of Biafra covers the period from the 1966 pogroms that sparked Biafra's secession to its defeat in January 1970, and through its trailing effects in the 1970s and 1980s. The events of the narrative are clustered in the period from May 1968, when Biafra was fully blockaded and the humanitarian crisis became acute, to the coup that overthrew Yakubu Gowon in 1975. Chapter 1 gives a short general history of the war, after which it describes the Biafran state in the early stages of the fighting, paying particular attention to the important place that law and order occupied in Biafra's national imagination. Chapter 2 moves into the later period of the war, when Biafra was cut off from the outside world and its carefully constructed legal system began to unravel. In particular, the chapter focuses on the emergence of vigilantism, the blurring of lines between the battlefield and civilian life in Biafra, and the Biafran state's loss of its monopoly on violence. Chapter 3 analyzes how forged documents and fraudulent identities emerged in Biafra, considering how they overlapped with legitimate state practices that the war had thrown into flux. These records show how the logics, tools, and skills of the battlefield inflected confrontations in Biafra, leading some people to survive in ways that the norms of war permitted but the law classed as "crime." Chapter 4 analyzes the political, legal, and social problems of reintegration, starting with the minority areas that fell to Nigeria early in the war and moving into the central Igbo provinces that held out until 1970. Chapter 5 uses legal records to describe the shape of crime in the postwar East Central State – the core of the former Biafra and the last region to fall to Nigeria – where poverty, unemployment, and a variety of social and political ills caused by the war conspired to make everyday life in the 1970s very violent and precarious. Chapter 6 considers the long tail of wartime 419, using a variety of sources to understand why wartime practices of deception and subterfuge continued long after the war was over.

1 | *Law, Order, and the Biafran National Imagination*

On the first day of June 1967, the day after the Republic of Biafra seceded from Nigeria, a state-run newspaper described a picture of perfect order in the new country:

Biafrans in the capital city of Enugu went to work yesterday morning carrying small portraits of their head of state, Lt. Col. Odumegwu Ojukwu, pinned conspicuously on their breast pockets. On their way, they hailed one another with "Best wishes for a prosperous Biafra Republic," gave out military salutes typical of Col. Ojukwu or shook hands expressing satisfaction that ties with the Northern vandals have been cut.[1]

Three years later, after a devastating war between Biafra and Nigeria had elapsed, the fallen city would be a far cry from the orderly society that Ojukwu had hoped to create. A quarter of the population had been killed. Enugu was a ghost town, occupied only by Nigerian soldiers and a handful of nervous loyalists. The violence of the war did not abate, and crime became rampant in the defeated Biafran territories. A hardened lawyer who defended armed robbers after the war welled up with tears as he looked through some of his casefiles from the early 1970s. "They were ruthless, and the case was so macabre," he recalled, describing the trial of a jobless veteran of the Biafran Army, who fatally shot his victim point-blank after she had already handed over her possessions. Like many members of his generation, his faith in the goodness of people was shaken by what happened during the Nigerian Civil War.[2] Biafra's brief story follows an arc from the optimism and order of Enugu at independence in 1967 to the violence and disarray that the barrister described there following the war's end.

To "piece together the memory of a country that exists only on paper" is, as Fiston Mwanza Mujila argues, an easier task for a novelist than

[1] *Biafra Sun*, June 1, 1967, p. 8.
[2] Interview with anonymous informant, Onitsha, March 2015.

a historian.[3] Historians often treat the study of places like Biafra as a fool's errand. Short-lived governments, unrecognized states, and the losing sides of civil wars – all of which describe Biafra – are poorly served by the tools we have to understand a world made up of nation-states. If they are described at all, they are usually reduced to a single political idea, at the expense of the full picture of how they worked. Their internal orders are difficult to see, or they appear to be poor copies of the states they break away from. They do not quite fit the model of the nation-state – a form that Biafra aspired to but did not perfectly imitate – but nor are they well-served by transnational approaches that disembed them from the particularities of their "national" contexts. This is a problem of studying places ranging from the American Confederacy to unrecognized states like Somaliland and the Sahrawi Arab Democratic Republic, the internal orders of which are overshadowed by their fraught relationships with the rest of the world. This chapter describes the Republic of Biafra from within. What made this embattled place work – to the extent that it did at all? To answer this question, it begins with an overview of the war's history, providing an account of its immediate causes and narrating its major events. It then examines how the Biafran state operated within its own borders, paying particular attention to law.

A Brief History of the Nigerian Civil War

Modern war makes for an unusual kind of time. The dense eventfulness of wartime speeds up the "natural" course of things – a city built over centuries can be destroyed in a day and a generation of men wiped out in a matter of months. Yet the same thickness of wartime that seems to accelerate the pace of change in historical hindsight *slows down* time for those living through it. Survivors of wars often remember them as longer periods than they actually were, and Biafra is no exception. Many people bore lasting psychological damage and, to some of them, the war ended time altogether. An extreme act of violence could become a naked singularity – a moment so traumatic that it collapsed the horizon of the future. After the war, judges expressed sympathy for people who seemed perpetually trapped in shock.[4] The Nigerian Civil

---

[3] Fiston Mwanza Mujila, *Tram 83* (Dallas: Deep Vellum Publishing, 2015): p. 45.
[4] Their minds had been "scattered," as judges called what psychiatrists were
    beginning to call posttraumatic stress disorder. Comparatively, see
    Stefanos Geroulanos and Todd Meyers, *The Human Body in the Age of*

War lasted for only two and a half years, but it cast a long shadow. Biafra made every subsequent Nigerian government obsessed with law and order, and it profoundly shaped how Nigerians thought about themselves as a national community.

The Republic of Biafra was born of cataclysm. On January 15, 1966, five years after Nigeria had gained independence from Britain, a group of five majors in the Nigerian military staged a coup, overthrowing the civilian government of Prime Minister Abubakar Tafawa Balewa in the name of ending the venality that had infected the Nigerian First Republic. The coup faltered, and the plotters were unable to seize control of the government. After a brief period of grappling, Major General John Aguiyi-Ironsi came to power as the highest-ranking surviving officer in the military. He had not participated in the coup, but he shared some of the plotters' goals. Like many military takeovers that pledge to clean up corruption, the January putsch was initially popular among Nigerians who had lost faith in civilian politics. In Kano, the All Nigeria Cinemagoers Union wrote to the military governor to celebrate the end of the First Republic, with its "dishonest politicians and plutocrats surrounded by hogs and sycophants."[5] However, enthusiasm for the coup dissipated quickly, especially in the north.

Ironsi's first action was to consolidate power, upsetting the delicate federal arrangement that administered Nigeria along regional lines. The shift of power from the states to the federal government threatened the interests of the northern political elite, which feared being margin-alized if the distant federal government in Lagos became stronger. The fact that Ironsi and most of his advisors were Igbo, and that most of the federal officials and politicians killed in the coup had been northerners and westerners, led many in the north to believe (incorrectly) that the coup had been an Igbo conspiracy to take over the government all along.[6] Northerners registered their protest by lashing out, not at

---

Catastrophe: Brittleness, Integration, Science, and the Great War (Chicago: University of Chicago Press, 2018).

[5] Arewa House, Ahmadu Bello University, Kaduna [hereafter ABUAH] PR1/59/ 429, President, Nigeria All Cinemagoers Union to Military Governor, Northern Provinces, February 1966.

[6] This is a subject of controversy but the multiethnic composition of the coup's leadership and their rhetoric – which described an ambition to create a center-left, ethnically plural Nigerian state – suggest that ethnic politics were not at the heart of their actions. See Adewale Ademoyega, *Why We Struck: The Story of the First Nigerian Coup* (Ibadan: Evans Brothers, 2012): pp. 124–130. For an

Ironsi but at the Igbos who lived among them as their neighbors. Acts of ethnic violence against Igbos residing in the north – most of whom worked there as merchants, technicians, professionals, and government employees – began to take place in the first months of 1966, with the first mass killings in May. Igbos had lived in the *sabon gari* ("strangers' quarters") of northern towns throughout the twentieth century where, as one memoirist recalled, they "thoroughly [enjoyed] the process of making money and often [made] plenty of it as traders or contractors, in property, hotels and transport."[7] Affluence bred resentment, and tension between Igbos and their neighbors manifested as disputes over resources, politics, and religious observance. This was not the first time that this entrepreneurial minority had been targeted, but Igbos' presence in the north had usually been peaceable until this point.

Six months after the first coup, on July 29, 1966, a group of northern officers staged a countercoup and installed a young major general, Yakubu Gowon, as head of state. This did not bring the violence in the north to an end, and the killings of Igbos accelerated at the end of 1966. Over the space of three months, tens of thousands of Igbos were killed in northern towns and cities. Isolated instances of anti-Igbo violence also happened outside of the north, including in Lagos. Some, like the killing of civilians by a gang of soldiers outside a barracks in Apapa, were investigated in the moment but most were not.[8] The violence did not take place evenly and the degree to which it was directed by state and military officials varied from place to place. In some towns, it was directed by members of the police or the military. In others, there were individual acts of violence by private citizens but "no consistent pattern of revolt against command" by soldiers, as a sociologist observed at the time.[9] In Jos, the ethnically diverse city in the middle belt region, Chief Rwang Pam placed Igbos under his personal protection. Jos became a temporary refuge until a series of killings overwhelmed Pam's forces.[10]

alternative viewpoint, see Usman Faruk, *The Victors and the Vanquished of the Nigerian Civil War, 1967–1970: Triumph of Truth and Valour over Greed and Ambition* (Zaria: Ahmadu Bello University Press, 2011).

[7] IWM 6687, Papers of Rosina Umelo, "Biafra, A World of Our Own," p. 17.

[8] ABUAH G1/36/1293, "Deaths of Odinle and Duru," September 19, 1966.

[9] Robin Luckham, *The Nigerian Military: A Sociological Analysis of Authority and Revolt 1960–1967* (Cambridge: Cambridge University Press, 1971): p. 305.

[10] Diliorah Chukwurah, *Last Train to Biafra: The Memoirs of a Biafran Child* (Ibadan: Constellation Publishers, 2015): pp. 12–13.

Why anti-Igbo pogroms broke out with such vehemence at this point is difficult to understand.[11] In some circles of the Northern Region government, Igbos were thought to have brought the situation on themselves. "Rightly or wrongly," an administrator wrote, "our present generation has been indoctrinated to think racially, and perhaps southern tribes are the worst offenders in this respect."[12] Some understood it as retribution for the killing of Ahmadu Bello, the north's spiritual and political leader, by Major Chukwuma "Kaduna" Nzeogwu, an Igbo officer who had spent most of his life in the north, during the coup of January 1966. A false report of attacks against northerners in Onitsha sparked a mutiny of thirty-one soldiers on October 1 – the sixth anniversary of Nigeria's independence. Before it was put down the following day, the mutineers murdered a group of Igbos boarding a flight at Kano airport in full view of many witnesses.[13] This would become the most infamous moment of a violent year.

Others argued that religious affronts had set off the bloodshed. Most Igbos were Christians, and the northern towns where they lived were largely Muslim. Stories circulated about acts of disrespect against Islam – that an Igbo grocer had labeled his goods with a slogan demeaning the prophet Muhammad or that Igbo merchants had laced the food and drink they sold to Muslims

[11] I use the term "pogrom" to describe these acts of organized violence against Igbos. Other historians, notably Douglas Anthony, have chosen instead to use the terms "disturbance" and "riot" on the grounds that "pogrom" suggests too unambiguous a degree of *state* organization in these events. It is true that there is ambiguity here; local governments (especially Native Authority Police Forces) were often enthusiastic participants in the violence, while the federal Nigeria Police Force often went to great lengths to protect Igbos. In some towns, it was the other way around. Does a local police force or a federal agency have a greater claim on being representative of "the state"? It is not my aim to answer this question. I use "pogrom" because, in its historical usage, the term captures the combination of popular organization and an ambivalent state response. For a full account of the war's prelude, see Douglas A. Anthony, *Poison and Medicine: Ethnicity, Power, and Violence in a Nigerian City, 1966–1986* (Portsmouth: Heinemann, 2002). On the deeper history of federal and local police jurisdictions, which has long been contentious in Nigeria, see Kemi Rotimi, *The Police in a Federal State: The Nigerian Experience* (Ibadan: College Press, 2001).

[12] NNAK MOI/272, "Memorandum by the Permanent Secretary, Ministry of Establishments and Training," January 28, 1966.

[13] Anthony, *Poison and Medicine*, p. 98. The act is also immortalized in *Half of a Yellow Sun*, among other accounts.

with alcohol or pig fat.[14] The governor of the North-Western State
later claimed that Igbos brought the violence on themselves by
"circulating insulting and highly provocative pictures of the late
Sardauna in a Drum Magazine owned by their people." In fact,
Drum was a South African publication, but this kind of detail
mattered little in the heat of the moment. He continued, with little
remorse, "that was what fueled and ignited the northern riots or
'*Araba*,' which for all intents and purposes, underlined the true
inherent Igbo callousness and their lack of inherent diplomatic
approach to issues of high sensitivity."[15]

   Whether or not these stories were true, and I find no evidence that they
were, the larger reasons for the violence were structural. By 1966, claims
that there was an Igbo conspiracy to control the government had become
a familiar trope of Nigerian politics. Many northerners saw Igbos as an
exploitative class and suspected that they had larger political designs. As
early as 1957, an eastern politician had decried "that mean and ruthless
weapon the 'Ibo Domination Stunt', so well known in Nigerian
politics."[16] It had only become more common since independence in
1960. Anti-Igbo sentiment had been building in the north for some time,
and petitions from northerners in the lead-up to 1966 reveal mounting
animosity.[17] A Hausa engineer who had recently lost a job to an Igbo
rival wrote to the military governor to register his disapproval of
"unwanted Dictators, Black Imperialists, and Foreigners" – local chiefs,
Igbos, and the British, respectively – who did not employ northerners in
their enterprises. "Leave Nigeria now or dance to the tune of one
Nigerianism," he warned.[18] The Northern Region government seldom
responded to these complaints, but taken together they reveal a growing
enmity by the northern public. Ethnic resentment was built out of small

---

[14] The fact that Igbos were the proprietors of most of the north's bars and hotels
      contributed to their association with alcohol and other un-Islamic vices.
      Interview with anonymous informant, Kaduna, April 2014.
[15] Faruk, *Victors and the Vanquished*, p. 96.
[16] Rhodes House Library, GB 0162 Micr. Afr. 608, Papers of Adegoke Adelabu,
      "A memorandum presented at the Nigeria Constitutional Conference by the
      Dr. the Hon. S. Moke, Minister of Finance, Eastern Region on behalf of the
      people of Ogoja Province, Reference the issue of Calabar Ogoja Rivers State
      Movement" [1957].
[17] The active petitionary culture that had developed during colonialism carried
      over into independence.
[18] ABUAH G1/35/1287, "A Call for Review of Establishment and Administration
      and Enterprises in Kano Area," January 29, 1966.

economic and personal complaints, which amassed into popular conspiracies about what Igbos "really" aspired to.

The presence of Igbos and other easterners in the north's civil service was a common grievance. The civil service had real power, and northern "indigenes" resented Igbos for occupying government positions that might otherwise have gone to local people. Others were suspicious of what they perceived as Igbos' close relationship to state authority. Their ability to corner the state bureaucracy is best explained not by conspiracy, nor by a "natural" aptitude for administration, as the British had construed it, but by historical circumstances. The boom of missionary activity in the east in the early twentieth century led to more and better schools and higher rates of English literacy. This set Igbos up well for jobs in the colonial administration.[19] They found positions throughout Nigeria and, by the time of independence, Igbos occupied some of Nigeria's highest bureaucratic ranks. Under the First Republic, this pattern continued. In the early 1960s, there were so many prospective applicants to the Eastern Region civil service that the region began requiring a university degree.[20] Easterners who did not have this qualification began to go elsewhere. They often found positions in the north, where pressure to "indigenize" the regional administration – still staffed by Europeans, now in the employ of independent Nigeria – was building. In this context, the highest-qualified African applicants were often from the east. As a result, the face of state authority in the north was increasingly neither British nor local, but Igbo.

The killings continued until the end of 1966, giving Igbos the impression that they were being planned – or at least tacitly permitted – by the new military regime. They decided, nearly to a person, that the only part of Nigeria where they would be safe was the east. Several million people fled to their ancestral homes in the Eastern Region, completely overwhelming the country's transportation infrastructure. Some carried the bodies of their loved ones back with them. The handful of Igbos who chose to stay in other parts of Nigeria found themselves taken into protective custody by local police or the military.[21] Many feared that

[19] Ogbu U. Kalu, *The Embattled Gods: The Christianization of Igboland, 1841–1991* (Lagos: Minaj Publishers, 1996).
[20] NNAK MOI/46, J. Reynolds to Permanent Secretary, Ministry of Internal Affairs [March 1960].
[21] NAUK FCO 38/287, "Ibo civil prisoners," July 25, 1968. A Lagos magistrate who visited Igbo detainees at Kirikiri Prison recalled that they "had no

this was no protection at all but a trap.[22] In January 1967, the military administrators of the Nigerian regions met in the town of Aburi in Ghana to hash out an agreement to restructure Nigeria as a confederation, guaranteeing the security of Igbos while preserving Nigeria's unity. Gowon's government did not implement the agreement when he returned to Lagos, confirming to many easterners that they had no future in Nigeria.

In this context, the military governor of the Eastern Region declared its independence from the Federal Republic of Nigeria on May 30, 1967. He did so on the grounds that Nigeria had failed to protect the lives and interests of easterners, and especially Igbos, resident elsewhere in the Nigerian federation. The new country called itself the Republic of Biafra – a seldom-used historical name for the curve of the Atlantic that its coastal provinces faced. It had a population of about 14 million people, of whom roughly two-thirds were Igbo.[23] Its leader was Lieutenant Colonel Chukwuemeka Odumegwu Ojukwu, an Oxford-educated military officer who, up to that point, had been a model Nigerian soldier. Like Gowon, he was young and charismatic, and he cultivated a brash and unpredictable affect. A student of history, Ojukwu had a deeply held, sometimes delusional sense of Biafra's destiny. Ojukwu's philosophy held that "never in history have a people lost a war of independence," which he repeated constantly, as one of Biafra's top bureaucrats recalled, like "a magical axiom, of which the Biafran situation was a natural and automatic proof."[24] As Rosina Umelo recalled, "he looked stern but so very young, of medium

complaints ... except for loss of liberty." She further noted that, unlike regular prisoners, they enjoyed "clean white bedsheets." Dulcie Adunola Oguntoye, *Your Estranged Faces* (self-published, 2008): p.146.

[22] This included some figures within the Nigerian government. In the Western Region, Bola Ige compared a proposal to incarcerate Igbos in Ibadan to the creation of concentration camps, convincing the Military Governor there to scrap the plan. Bola Ige, *People, Politics and Politicians of Nigeria (1950–1979)* (Ibadan: Heinemann, 1995): p. 341.

[23] The remainder were eastern minorities. Small communities of Nigerians from the north and west were also present, though most departed immediately. Foreigners in Biafra included a small number of Cameroonian migrants, most of whom left for home, and several hundred Irish Catholic clergy, many of whom decided to stay. Their decision to do so helps to explain why the Irish government took such an interest in Biafra.

[24] Ntieyong U. Akpan, *The Struggle for Secession, 1966–1970: A Personal Account of the Nigerian Civil War* (London: Frank Cass, 1971): p. 133.

Figure 1.1 Ojukwu inspecting troops, June 1968 (Rob Burton/Mirrorpix, via Getty Images)

height, heavily built with broad shoulders. Perhaps he spoke so slowly to add authority to his youth but at the time he was alarming and gave an impression of tightly reined anger."[25] Authority was located in his personality; Ojukwu would ride through the streets of Enugu atop a motorcade, solemnly repeating the mantra "power" to the crowds cheering him on.[26]

Nigeria was not willing to let Biafra go. Gowon initiated a "police action" to reclaim the east, which quickly escalated into a full-fledged war between the Federal Military Government of Nigeria and the Republic of Biafra. On the day of Biafra's secession, Gowon declared that Nigeria would be divided from four states into twelve, acceding to the long-standing demands of ethnic minorities in the east for their own state governments. The Eastern Region was split into the East Central State (comprising the inland, Igbo-majority areas), the South-Eastern State (neighboring Cameroon, with its capital at Calabar), and the Rivers State (home of both the oil economy and the major city of Port

---

[25] IWM 6687, Papers of Rosina Umelo, "Biafra, A World of Our Own," p. 24.
[26] *Sunday News* [Dar es Salaam], November 26, 1967, p. 1.

Harcourt). This was an attempt to head off any support for Biafra's independence that non-Igbo people in the coastal and riverine regions of the east might have given. Since all three states were held by Biafra, the new boundaries existed only on Nigerian maps. The stakes of Biafra's secession were high. Gowon understood that allowing the east to secede would embolden other groups to do so as well, and Nigeria could shatter into pieces. Territorial integrity, however, was not the only thing that Nigeria wanted to preserve. Nearly 70 percent of Nigeria's oil reserves were located in territory that Biafra claimed, so secession represented an economic threat to Nigeria as well as a political one.

The war that transpired was chaotic, brutal, and dense with misinformation. Nearly all of it would be fought on eastern soil. This was a region unaccustomed to war, the last major conflicts having taken place at the time of colonial conquest.[27] Warfare's unfamiliarity made it especially disruptive. Unlike most Europeans, who knew total war intimately by the mid-twentieth century, few people in Nigeria had been in situations that would help them navigate life on the front. Civilians had to invent the tools of survival in the moment. The Nigerian Army was the better organized and provisioned of the belligerents, even though many of its technicians had defected to Biafra. The Biafran Army was conjured from almost nothing in the first months of the war, and it would only become less regular as it went on. Recruitment into the army was initially well-organized, and the hastily constructed training camp for Biafran officers successfully produced a workable class of commanders;[28] but the situation devolved quickly. Ntieyong Akpan, Biafra's chief secretary, described how men, armed with machetes, stones, and shotguns that they had not been trained to use, were dispatched to the Nsukka front in the thousands. "It was this exercise which convinced me of the hopelessness of the situation.

---

[27] Eastern Nigerian men had fought in the European World Wars, of course, but their service had been on the distant fronts of Burma and North Africa. The Women's War of 1929, while occasionally violent, was more a mass protest than an armed conflict. Aside from those old enough to remember the European invasion, eastern Nigerians had no experience of war at home until Biafra.

[28] Nigerian National Archives, Calabar [hereafter NNAC] 609 CAD 396/1/vol. x 3/3/356, "Recruitment Into Biafra Army," July 7, 1967. The early stages of recruitment are also described in Chukwuemeka Ike, *Sunset at Dawn: A Novel About Biafra* (London: Collins and Harvill, 1976): pp. 9–15.

I actually went aside and wept for those innocent men, huddled in the lorries and driven to certain death."[29]

Soldiers who described the war in their memoirs used the language of conventional military conflict to describe its progress – with clearly delineated fronts, towns that "fell" to advancing forces, and tactical maps with areas colored green for Nigeria and red for Biafra. In fact, the conduct of the fighting was more diffuse than this would suggest. Biafra's stance for most of the war was defensive, and the front shifted constantly. Biafran forces briefly controlled the Mid-West State in August and September 1967, but this was their only major incursion into Nigerian territory. The invasion was led by Lieutenant Colonel Victor Banjo, and it culminated in the declaration of a Biafran puppet state called the Republic of Benin.[30] In an act of insubordination, Banjo chose not to march on Lagos and retreated at the town of Ore, for which he was executed when he returned to Biafra.[31] Biafran forces were driven back across the Niger River in late September.

Following their brief occupation of the Mid-West State, Biafran troops retreated eastward, into Biafran territory, blowing up a major bridge behind them. Igbo civilians were left stranded in Asaba, a town across the Niger River from Onitsha, which became the site of one of the war's most extreme episodes of ethnic cleansing. In October 1967, Nigerian troops under the command of Murtala Muhammed killed more than 700 Igbo civilians in an organized, unprovoked massacre.[32] In a petition to the Irish government, a group of survivors described the killings:

---

[29] Akpan, *The Struggle for Secession*, p. 95.

[30] Not to be confused with the present-day Republic of Benin, known at this time as Dahomey.

[31] His reasons for turning back are a subject of dispute, and this act of treason would be the subject of one of Biafra's first major trials. See Samuel Fury Childs Daly, "The Case Against Victor Banjo: Legal Process and the Governance of Biafra," in Lasse Heerten and Dirk Moses, eds., *The Nigeria-Biafra War, 1967–1970: Postcolonial Conflict and the Question of Genocide* (London: Routledge, 2017): pp. 95–112.

[32] See S. Elizabeth Bird and Fraser M. Ottanelli, *The Asaba Massacre: Trauma, Memory, and the Nigerian Civil War* (Cambridge: Cambridge University Press, 2017). One of the most vivid descriptions of the massacre is by a woman who was a teenager at the time: Celestina Isichei-Isamah, *They Died in Vain* (self-published, 2011).

[Nigerian] soldiers after repeatedly extorting money from many homes, led men out on gun point to be machine-gunned in cold blood at an open playground at Ogbeosewa, Asaba on 5th to 8th October, 1967. There are picturesque but somber descriptions of how corpses clad in the Asaba traditional white costumes had also littered the playground at Ogbeosewa. These corpses were those of dancers who had come out to welcome your army. Asaba, then became a ghost town.[33]

Violence took place in many Biafran towns as they fell to Nigeria, but nowhere was it as vehement as in Asaba. Enugu and the university town of Nsukka fell to Nigeria the same week, and the Biafran government withdrew to the town of Umuahia, where it began to draft a largely defensive strategy. Two weeks later, Nigerian troops under Benjamin Adekunle captured Calabar, which had been one of Biafra's main portals to the outside world.

It became a war of attrition. Nigeria tried to strangle the secessionist province by imposing a full blockade. This strategy was accompanied by periodic air raids and a low-level land war, which reached a stalemate by early 1968. Starvation became acute, and Biafrans came to believe that Nigeria's aim was not only to retake the region but to exterminate the Igbo people. The violence took more than one direction, however; acts committed by the Biafran Army against minorities, such as a massacre at Abonnema in March 1968, did little to endear unwilling "Biafrans" outside the Igbo areas to the new government.[34] Nigeria emphasized this and other atrocities to argue that it was Biafra, not Nigeria, which was engaged in war crimes. The Nigerian government was much less adept at publicizing acts of violence against its civilians than Biafra, and the foreign press was generally more inclined to believe reports of atrocities committed by Nigeria. A war of global public opinion began. Many in Europe and North America sympathized with Biafra's cause, but popular support did not translate into the diplomatic recognition that it desperately needed.

Port Harcourt fell to the Nigerian Third Marine Commando in May 1968 – an eventful month in world history and one that played out bloodily in the Niger Delta. Most Igbos fled for the inland territory

---

[33] National Archive of Ireland, Dublin [hereafter NAID] 2000/14/24, Asaba Union of Great Britain and Ireland to Major-General Y. Gowon, June 17, 1968.

[34] Nabo B. Graham-Douglas, *Ojukwu's Rebellion and World Opinion* (Lagos: Nigerian National Press, [1969]): p.15.

that Biafra still controlled, leaving it a quiet and tense city – and a very dangerous one for the small number of Igbos who stayed behind, many of whom were killed. From May 1968 to Biafra's final surrender in January 1970, the country was in a state of unrelenting crisis.[35] The loss of Port Harcourt cut it off from the outside world except for dangerous and irregular airlifts by humanitarian organizations. Famine set in. Horrifying images of children suffering from the protein deficiency called kwashiorkor began to come out of Biafra, which galvanized public opinion against Nigeria among students, Catholics, and others worldwide.[36] Without the humanitarian aid that the international community provided to Biafra, the war would likely have ended at this point.[37]

Biafra lasted longer than even its staunchest supporters thought it would. Nigeria's greater military capacity was undercut by its internal disorganization and balanced out by Biafra's willingness to use guerilla tactics.[38] The blockade and a strategy of sporadic aerial bombardment were not enough to defeat Biafra outright, but they made daily life in the enclave desperate and nervy. Toward the beginning of the war, British intelligence had reported that "the military picture, as it slowly unfolds, looks more and more like turning out to be a stalemate."[39]

---

[35] When exactly conditions became a "crisis" is disputable. As Brian Larkin writes, calling the war a crisis "is an intellectual act that tells us not just about the event but about the system of distinctions that makes the event appear. Did the crisis begin in 1967 with the declaration of secession by Biafra? Did it begin in 1960 with the establishment of an independent Nigerian state? Or did it begin with Hausa riots against Igbo in the 1950s?" Arguments can be made for all of these periodizations, but the rapid deterioration of conditions in Biafra after May 1968 made for a "crisis" of a different order, at least in the eyes of those who lived there. Brian Larkin, "The Form of Crisis and the Affect of Modernization," in Brian Goldstone and Juan Obarrio, eds., *African Futures: Essays on Crisis, Emergence, and Possibility* (Chicago: University of Chicago Press, 2016): p. 42.

[36] Biafra resonated with Europeans and North Americans especially, and the events of the war spoke to their domestic political concerns in various ways. A detailed autopsy of the war's international dimensions can be found in Lasse Heerten, *The Biafran War and Postcolonial Humanitarianism: Spectacles of Suffering* (Cambridge: Cambridge University Press, 2017).

[37] See Marc-Antoine Pérouse de Montclos, "Humanitarian Aid and the Biafra War: Lessons not Learned," *Africa Development* vol. 34, no. 1 (2009): pp. 69–82.

[38] "Chief Chukwuemeka Odumegwu-Ojukwu," in H. B. Momoh, ed., *The Nigerian Civil War, 1967–1970: History and Reminiscences* (Ibadan: Sam Bookman, 2000): p. 756.

[39] NAUK FCO 38/203, E.G. Norris to Minister of State, September 26, 1967.

Hit-and-run tactics became Biafra's primary mode of engagement. "Guerrilla activities by our men are on the increase," Ojukwu told the foreign press in 1968. "The enemy is not wanted in any part of Biafra so that even the villagers are also potential guerrillas. The enemy cannot be said to be in complete control of any part of Biafra because he is being harassed by guerrillas wherever he goes."[40] Peace talks, encouraged by the major international institutions and facilitated by a group of American Quakers, were convened in Kampala in May under the aegis of the Commonwealth and in Addis Ababa in July by the Organisation of African Unity. Both collapsed almost immediately.[41] As 1968 went on, Nigeria came to fear that an incomplete defeat of the Biafran Army would splinter it into a Vietnam-style "people's war," so they held the blockade and hoped that Biafra could be starved into surrender.

The effect of this tactical decision was a slow, strangling defeat, in which the state of crisis was constant but the fighting was not. The unevenness of Nigeria's assault meant that there were always some parts of Biafra under siege and others that were tensely quiet. Biafrans' conviction to fight was stoked by the fear of what would happen should Biafra lose. "I keep looking," said a woman whose house overlooked the hills leading into Enugu, "expecting the Hausas to come over the skyline like the Indians on the warpath in a cowboy film."[42] To Aba Province administrator Ben Gbulie, the stakes of defeat were high:

I could not help conjuring up all kinds of ugly scenes to which an outright military defeat was liable to give rise ... Nuremberg-type trials as well as kangaroo courts, with convictions based on perjured evidence; public executions by firing squads; deportations, especially of pro-Biafra aliens; widespread anti-Igbo measures, including suppression of liberties, calculated to destroy for good the much-envied Igbo psyche.[43]

These fears were given credence by the massacres of civilians in Biafran towns that fell to Nigeria. The memory of what had happened at Asaba

---

[40] NAID 2000/14/22, "Address by Lt. Col. C. Odumegwu Ojukwu to an international press conference," July 18, 1968.

[41] Donald Rothchild, "Unofficial Mediation and the Nigeria-Biafra War," *Nationalism and Ethnic Politics* vol. 3, no. 3 (1997): pp. 37–65.

[42] The unnamed woman was a friend of Rosina Umelo. IWM 6687, Papers of Rosina Umelo, "Biafra, A World of Our Own," p. 49.

[43] Ben Gbulie, *The Fall of Biafra* (Enugu: Benlie Publishers, 1989): p. 207.

loomed particularly large.[44] As a result, Biafra continued the fight even as conditions became untenable – and long after it had ceased to be the orderly and peaceful place that its founders had promised.

The war would ultimately end with a whimper, but Nigeria's reoccupation of Biafran territories before the final surrender of 1970 was more like a bang. The Nigerian government promised that the residents of recaptured Biafran territories could expect decent treatment, humanitarian assistance, and whatever resources they needed to reclaim their property and resume their peacetime occupations.[45] Whether these promises were fulfilled differed from place to place. The treatment of Igbo civilians ranged from welcoming them into the federal fold with open arms in some places to enthusiastic acts of ethnic cleansing in others. The characteristics of the occupation were shaped by factors including the attitude of the local leaders, the personality of the Nigerian commanders, and the degree of visibility to the international press.

The journalist (and Biafra sympathizer) Frederick Forsyth described how Igbo villages were abandoned in advance of the Nigerian troops: "On six occasions I have accompanied Biafran commandos behind the Nigerian lines to places apart from the show villages set up by the Nigerians for the foreign press. The prospect each time was of a landscape of total desolation. Nothing moved except the vultures."[46] The Nigerian military's representatives did little to assuage

---

[44] The Nigerian Armed Forces printed and distributed a code of conduct for soldiers to carry with them at all times, outlining Nigeria's commitment to uphold the Geneva Conventions, admonishing that civilians must not be molested and rights in property must be respected. A personal message from Gowon addressed to the troops stressed that "you must remember that some of the soldiers Lt. Col. Gowon has now forced to oppose you were once your old comrades at arms and would like to remain so. You must therefore treat them with respect and dignity except any one who is hostile to you." NAID 2000/14/23, "Operational Code of Conduct for Nigerian Armed Forces" [1968]. The Irish ambassador noted that despite its assurances, "it is unlikely that a large number of his troops can, in fact, appreciate this document even if they are able to read it. Nonetheless the need for restraint and civilized behaviour is being impressed on the commanding officers." NAID 2000/14/23, Paul Keating, ambassador of Ireland to Nigeria to Department of External Affairs, Dublin, September 5, 1968.

[45] Centre des archives diplomatiques, Nantes [hereafter CADN] 332PO/1 Box 4, "The 'Biafran' Illusion: Fate and future of the non-Ibo peoples in the Eastern States of Nigeria," [May 1968].

[46] Quoted in SOAS Nigerian Civil War Collections MS 321463 vol. 68, Manuscript, "Biafra – As I See It," Carl Gustaf von Rosen, 1969, pp. 94–95.

the perception, established by Forsyth and others, that discipline fell quickly when troops captured towns. A British source described how, after Murtala Muhammed's negotiated capture of Onitsha, "the Divisional Commander held court in a pair of shocking-pink pyjamas and the fruits of victory were widely enjoyed. One emotionally involved Senegalese girl who had been an officer in the Biafran militia was shot dead while trying to escape in a sports car."[47] Onitsha's experience of defeat was unusual among towns in the East Central State, since Muhammed had made a separate peace with the city council – they surrendered to him in exchange for agreeing not to destroy the city.[48] Muhammed kept his promise in Onitsha, but most Biafran towns that were occupied while the war still raged fared worse.

The corridor between Biafra's first capital at Enugu and Nsukka was the region that Nigeria occupied earliest, having captured it five months after secession. There was a "see-saw struggle" to make the occupation stick in the first year of the war, but Nigeria was never at serious risk of losing Enugu.[49] It was, however, constantly harassed by Biafran guerilla units. Biafran snipers hid out in vacant buildings, and periodic raids were made on the city's outlying neighborhoods.[50] There was a draconian regime of curfews and restrictions. These apparently did little to prevent looting, which was "the principle off-duty pursuit of the soldiers."[51] It took nearly a year for Enugu to become, as British intelligence found, "physically secure. However, civilian government officers are still very wary, and have been issued rifles which they keep in vehicles when they travel. (This probably reflects loyalist Ibo nervousness over fears of assassination more than 'Biafran' threat to security of town itself.)"[52] A government doctor stationed there recalled that sentries were posted on every major corner, and anyone

---

[47] I do not know who this woman was. The possibility of there being a foreign, female officer in a Biafran militia is unlikely but not impossible. NAUK FCO 38/287, Maj. G.A. Shepherd, British High Commission, Lagos to Col. P. H. Moir, Ministry of Defence, April 10, 1968.

[48] NAUK FCO 38/285, Sir David Hunt to Commonwealth Office, October 7, 1967.

[49] NAID 2000/14/19, "Civil War in Nigeria: Military Situation at mid-December 1967," December 15 1967.

[50] Linus U. J. T. Ogbuji describes one such raid in his memoirs, *Seeing the World in Black and White* (Trenton: Africa World Press, 2007): pp.70–71.

[51] NAUK FCO 38/287, Maj. G. A. Shepherd, British High Commission, Lagos to Col. P.H. Moir, Ministry of Defence, April 10, 1968.

[52] NAUK FCO 38/286, "Re: Iboland Sitrep," April 3, 1968.

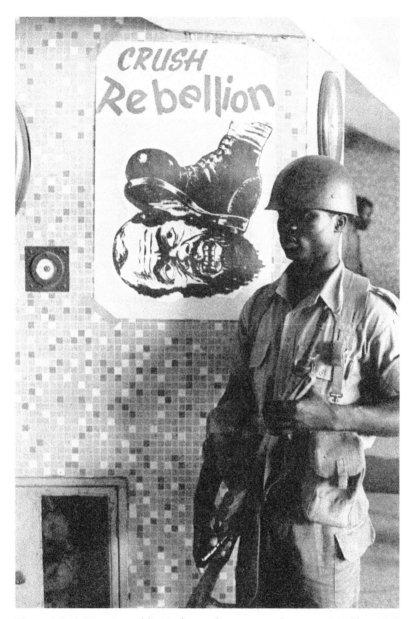

Figure 1.2 A Nigerian soldier in front of a propaganda poster, Nsukka, 1967 (Bruno Barbey/Magnum Photos)

attempting to travel after dusk could only do so by giving a password that changed daily. "If a person did not know it and tried to run away, he could be taken for a rebel infiltrator and shot."[53] Insecurity and repression were not antithetical in occupied Enugu – they went hand in hand.

It was in this region where the largest refugee camps were set up, mostly for Igbo women, children, and elderly people who had not been able to flee ahead of the Nigerian troops. They also contained some combatants who had defected to the Nigerian side. The people who were interred in the camps were glad not to have been killed (contrary to what Biafran propaganda had told them to expect), but they constantly feared that they might be. Some ran away, preferring an uncertain fate in the Biafran forest to waiting out the end of the war in detention. Occupied towns remained empty, but people trickled back into the rural areas throughout 1968.[54] Nigerian control of a region by no means guaranteed an end to the fighting, and Biafran militias continued to operate covertly.[55] Nigeria's occupation was arterial – it was concentrated along main roads, and it lost its grip as the east's sprawling towns gave way to woods and farms. Even around Nsukka, where the Nigerian presence was densest, resistance continued throughout the war.[56] This fragile occupation expanded as the Republic of Biafra shrank to a small, famine-stricken nub.

Relations were tense between Nigerian soldiers and the civilians who lived under their guns. Igbos in the East Central State faced greater hostility from the Nigerian rank-and-file than eastern minorities in Biafra's coastal provinces, who were generally seen as "loyal" Nigerians. At the same time, there was also more oversight in the heart of Biafra, where international observers, humanitarian agencies, and the Nigerian military leadership were all watching the situation more closely than they were in places like Calabar and the Niger Delta. The Mid-West, which had only been part of Biafra briefly, was generally sympathetic to the federal side. Even though it was home to

---

[53]   R. B. Alade, *The Broken Bridge: Reflections and Experiences of a Medical Doctor During the Nigerian Civil War* (Ibadan: The Caxton Press, 1975): p. 54.

[54]   NAUK FCO 38/297, G. D. Anderson, British High Commission, Lagos to Commonwealth Office, February 10, 1968.

[55]   NAUK FCO 65/213, E. G. Donohoe, British High Commission, Lagos to Foreign and Commonwealth Office, November 1, 1969.

[56]   NAUK FCO 38/297, "Report from the Nordic Team (Ruusuvuori)," January 31, 1968.

a large Igbo population, many considered themselves culturally and politically distinct from Igbos who lived east of the Niger, and few embraced the Biafran cause. The Nigerian government often brought foreign journalists to the Mid-West to show them that reintegration was welcomed by Igbos – sidestepping the fact that most who lived there had not supported Biafra in the first place.[57] During the Nigerian occupation, Igbos from west of the Niger distanced themselves from both Biafra and the Igbo identity, instead emphasizing their historical connections to the Edo Kingdom of Benin directly to the west. Other communities that had seen themselves as "Igbo" or close to it, like the Ikwerre to the south, would follow suit in claiming other origins in the war's aftermath.[58] Often, the end goal of this historical revision was to secure separate, ethnically determined states within the Nigerian federation.

In Biafra's coastal provinces, where Igbos were a minority, Nigerian victory was retributive and violent. Calabar and Port Harcourt were taken – "seized" in the Biafran parlance and "liberated" in the Nigerian – by Nigerian troops of the Third Marine Commando under the leadership of Lieutenant Colonel Benjamin Adekunle and Brigadier General Godwin Alabi-Isama. It was in these regions, where few people other than Igbos felt any affection for Biafra, that the Nigerian occupation was bloodiest. South-Eastern State Military Governor Udoakaha Esuene captured public sentiment in an angry speech: "they Ibos want slaves and not allies. We shall not be their slaves."[59] After Calabar fell to Nigeria in October 1967, Igbo civilians there were placed in an extremely dangerous position. Many escaped with the departing Biafran troops, and those who could not leave went into hiding with sympathetic neighbors. Civilians who were found to speak Efik with an Igbo accent were killed on the spot.[60] When he arrived home in Ireland, Calabar's Catholic bishop gave a disturbing account of the city's fall.[61]

---

[57] Some, however, had supported Biafra's brief occupation of the Mid-West. This placed West Niger Igbos in a delicate position, in which both Nigeria and Biafra doubted their loyalties.

[58] A. E. Afigbo, *The Igbo and their Neighbours: Inter-Group Relations in Southeastern Nigeria to 1953* (Ibadan: University Press, 1987): pp. 16–17.

[59] IIIA, Nigerian Subject Collection XX787, Box 6, "Treatise to the Peoples of South-Eastern Nigeria" [1967].

[60] Chinua Achebe, *There Was a Country: A Personal History of Biafra* (New York: Penguin, 2012): p.295, n. 1.

[61] NAID 2000/14/20, Statement of Bishop Moynagh [November 1967].

He described how the federal troops rounded up anyone suspected of being or having been a Biafran soldier, marched them to the riverbank, and shot them into the water: "My tummy was upset because I felt that there were no longer any pockets of armed resistance in town and that the shooting meant the elimination of the Ibo civilians flushed out from hiding," he wrote. "We had felt that there would be fighting – it is what is to be expected in war, but we had not expected wholesale slaughter." Igbos came to the cathedral in Calabar for protection, where the bishop turned them away, since "anyone sheltering men were shot out of hand." An Igbo man and his wife showed up carrying a toy rifle in a vain attempt to defend themselves:

Some of the boys were telling him to get out of the compound and he stopped and looked at him and asked him where was his Christian charity, were we all not living together a few days ago in peace as neighbours, did they not think that [if] they had him killed they would find money inside, or would they be able to eat him. It was dreadful to hear all of these basic questions from a man that had not long to live. He crossed over to the Sacred Heart School and we heard shots after a few minutes and decided that the affair was over ... the mental anguish was beyond bearing.

Within a few weeks of Calabar's surrender, hardly any Igbos remained in the city.

This pattern would be repeated when Nigeria captured Port Harcourt in May 1968. After just under a year as part of Biafra, Ijaw and other non-Igbo "indigenes" welcomed the Nigerian troops. Port Harcourt's prewar population had been approximately half Igbo – and higher in the center of the city, where Igbos owned much of the real estate. Nearly all of them fled into Biafra's central territories ahead of the Nigerian Third Marine Commando, leaving behind houses, valuables, and documents. The process of reclaiming them would be a major point of contention after Biafra's surrender in 1970. Many of those who did not leave in time were killed, both by their neighbors and by Nigerian troops, in violation of their code of conduct, and in some cases against the commands of their superiors.

This points to one of the most contentious questions in the war's historiography, which is its connection to genocide.[62] The Biafran

---

[62] In a large literature, see Apollos Nwauwa and Chima Korieh, eds., *Against All Odds: The Igbo Experience in Postcolonial Nigeria* (Baltimore: Goldline and Jacobs Publishing, 2011); Chima Korieh, *The Nigeria-Biafra War: Genocide*

government made the case to the outside world that Nigeria's conduct was genocidal, which rested on two separate but related lines of argumentation. One was that the pogroms of 1966 in the north constituted genocide because they had been orchestrated by government officials in some towns and cities. The second was that the war itself, especially the blockade policy that created a vast famine, was an attempt to exterminate the Igbo people. The former Western Region Premier Obafemi Awolowo was the public face of the blockade. His fiery rhetoric about starving Biafra out of existence was taken as evidence that the Nigerian government's intent in the war was not only to defeat Biafra but to destroy the Igbo people.[63] There was ample proof of genocide for those who wanted to find it. Adekunle famously told a foreign reporter that if he marched into an Igbo village, "we shoot everything that moves" and that "in the sector of the front which I command – and that is the whole of the south front from Lagos to the Cameroon border – I will not [do not want to] see any Red Cross, any Caritas, any World Council of Churches, Pope, missionary, or U.N. delegation."[64] These statements would later be cited as evidence that the reoccupation of the East Central State was part of a genocidal plan by Nigeria.[65]

---

and the Politics of Memory (Amherst, NY: Cambria Press, 2012); Grace O. Okoye, *Proclivity to Genocide: Northern Nigeria Ethno-Religious Conflict, 1966 to Present* (Lanham, MD: Lexington Books, 2014); Dirk Moses and Lasse Heerten, eds., *Postcolonial Conflict and the Question of Genocide: The Nigeria-Biafra War, 1967–1970* (London: Routledge, 2017).

[63] Awolowo defended starvation as a legitimate tool of war. Later, he would attribute the famine to Biafran mismanagement of aid materials. "You won't hear of a single lawyer, a single doctor, a single architect, who suffered from kwashiorkor," he remarked in 1983, pointing to the uneven effects of the starvation policy. Quoted in Bukola A. Oyeniyi, "Beyond the Blame-Game: Theorizing the War," in Toyin Falola and Ogechukwu Ezekwem, eds., *Writing the Nigeria-Biafra War* (Woodbridge: James Currey, 2016): p. 113.

[64] Some of Nigeria's foreign allies found Adekunle dangerous and mentally unstable and were especially concerned about his "alleged policy of taking no prisoners." Gowon himself was privately concerned about Adekunle's brutality toward civilians – especially Igbos – but publicly stood behind him. NAUK FCO 38/285, Sir David Hunt to Commonwealth Office, January 22, 1968; SOAS Nigerian Civil War Collections MS 321463 vol. 68, Manuscript, "Biafra – As I See It," Carl Gustaf von Rosen, 1969, p. 112.

[65] Adekunle's threats had an important witness in the French doctor Bernard Kouchner, who founded the politically partisan humanitarian organization Doctors Without Borders after being frustrated with the International Committee of the Red Cross's neutral stance toward Nigerian officers like

Yet it was also a matter of perspective. If one was looking at the war from the vantage point of Asaba, or from the pogroms leading up to secession, it seemed obvious that a genocide was taking place. Elsewhere, it was less clear. In Nsukka, the Nigerian reoccupation brought not retribution but food and medical care, followed by attempts to reintegrate Igbos into Nigerian society. As an internal memorandum from the Nigerian Air Force reminded officers, "the aim is to preserve the Federation, not to destroy the Ibos, whom we want to keep in the Federation."[66] In Lagos, the government went to great lengths to assure Igbos that the capital city welcomed them, even though the few who remained there feared for their safety constantly.[67] Former president Nnamdi Azikiwe would make a highly publicized visit to Lagos after defecting to Nigeria midway through the war, which was staged to show Igbos that they had nothing to fear if they went over to the federal side.[68] These promises were not disingenuous, at least in Lagos. In short, the intentions of the Nigerian government looked different from one place to another. As the political scientist Scott Straus writes, the patterns of violence that emerged were "consistent with mass categorical violence, rather than genocide."[69] Classification aside, the loss of life was enormous, and it is measured in the millions. It is not the objective of this work to weigh souls, but many more Biafrans died than Nigerians.[70] Most were civilians, and, because starvation

Adekunle. Alex de Waal, *Famine Crimes: Politics and the Disaster Relief Industry in Africa* (Oxford: James Currey, 1997): p. 77.

[66] NNAK MOI/326, "Priority of Air Force targets and suggestions for prosecuting the war," August 1967, p. 2.

[67] The handful of "loyalist" Igbos from east of the Niger who remained in Nigeria usually concealed their background or lived in hiding. Prominent people lived under the protection of the federal government. Ukpabi Asika, who would later become the administrator of the East Central State, was kept under guard on the campus of the University of Ibadan for the war's duration.

[68] Azikiwe's defection was very demoralizing in Biafra. His reasons for doing so included disillusionment with the Biafran project, personal differences with Ojukwu, and a desire to prevent further loss of life. He would later claim that he had effectively been kidnapped by the Biafran government and that he had supported the cause only with "a Biafran gun at my back." *The People* [Kampala], September 30, 1969, p. 5. Alfred Obiora Uzokwe, *Surviving in Biafra: The Story of the Nigerian Civil War: Over Two Million Died* (self-published, 2003): p. 141.

[69] Scott Straus, *Making and Unmaking Nations: War, Leadership, and Genocide in Modern Africa* (Ithaca, NY: Cornell University Press, 2015): p. 102.

[70] The total number of casualties is a subject of contention, but credible estimates range from one million to three million. A more precise number is probably

was used as a weapon, children and the elderly suffered disproportion-ately high mortality rates.[71]

Finally, there were two factors – commonly evoked though poorly understood – that explain less about the war than one might assume. One was religion and the other was oil. The fact that eastern Nigerians practiced Christianity at rates higher than elsewhere in the federation led some observers (from within and without) to conclude that the Nigerian Civil War was predominantly a religious conflict between Biafran Christians and Nigerian Muslims. In light of Nigeria's more contemporary religious conflicts, some authors have continued to pro-ject this communitarian explanation onto the war.[72] While Biafra did sometimes present itself as a Christian nation, not all Biafrans were Christians, and few saw religion as the force behind the conflict. Moreover, the notion that Nigeria or its military was "Muslim," as propagandists sometimes claimed, ignored the fact that about as many Nigerians were Christians as Muslims. Confessional identities explain little about the war, and their importance in Nigerian politics today should not be superimposed onto the past. The war also cannot be reduced to a conflict over oil. Although the presence of oil in the territory that Biafra claimed raised the stakes of secession, oil was not the only factor in Biafra's decision to secede, nor in Nigeria's to pursue it.[73] Biafra lost control of the oil terminal at Bonny early in the war. Had it truly been a conflict over resources, the war would have ended there. Instead, it accelerated. What Biafra and Nigeria were fighting for was something larger and more abstract than control of the oil spigot. It was a contest over identity, ethics, and the political future.

---

impossible to calculate, but, as Alex de Waal writes, the number "is not the point." The cost of the war in human life was enormous, with political and social consequences to match. De Waal, *Famine Crimes*, p. 75.

[71] Starvation had long-term effects for survivors too. A physician at Biafra's main hospital estimated that only 5 percent of kwashiorkor patients died under his care, but survivors experienced anemia and stunted growth. See Richard Akresh et. al., "War and Stature: Growing Up during the Nigerian Civil War," *The American Economic Review* vol. 102, no. 3 (May 2012): pp. 273–277.

[72] For example, Aliyi Ekineh, *Tears and Weeping of the Niger Delta Struggling for Separation from Islamic Nigeria* (London: Catford Book Centre, 2003).

[73] Oil did, however, play a role in the diplomatic calculations that other countries engaged in over whether or not to recognize Biafra. See Chibuike Uche, "Oil, British Interests, and the Nigerian Civil War," *The Journal of African History* vol. 49, no. 1 (2008): pp. 111–135.

Biafra ceased to be a place on the map in 1970, but it created fault lines that Nigeria still lives with. Biafra's effects lingered long after its defeat, and for this reason this book devotes as much space to the postwar period as it does to the war itself. Perhaps most importantly, the war provided cover for the continuation of military rule. For thirty years after Biafra's defeat, the soldiers who staged coups justified them by invoking the specter of secession or the ongoing problem of crime. The ethnic and regional dimensions of Nigerian politics were not overcome by Biafra's defeat.[74] Peter Ekeh was one of the first intellectuals to grasp how deep the wounds of the war were. His theorization of the "two publics" of African states – one ethnic, one civic – was in many ways a response to postwar politics, even though it located the origins of that divide in colonialism.[75] Nigeria's divisions have become more complex as it has been carved into ever-more states – from three at independence, to four, then twelve at the time of the war, and today thirty-six.[76]

[74] Yakubu Gowon would later argue that the war had not only fractured Nigeria but set back African integration as a whole. After being deposed in 1975, Gowon spent his exile completing a doctorate in political science in the United Kingdom. He eventually produced a thesis arguing, among other things, that other African countries' recognition of Biafra was a betrayal of pan-Africanism. Yakubu Gowon, "The Economic Community of West African States: A Study in Political and Economic Integration" (Doctoral thesis, University of Warwick, 1984). See also the final chapter of Richard Bourne, *Nigeria: A New History of a Turbulent Century* (London: Zed Books, 2015).

[75] In Biafra, these publics substantially overlapped. Many of those who insisted that Biafra was a diverse, ethnically agnostic state also recognized that it existed because of what had happened to Igbos. Biafra's separate identity could not be understood in isolation from that history. Peter P. Ekeh, "Colonialism and the Two Publics in Africa: A Theoretical Statement," *Comparative Studies in Society and History* vol. 17, no. 1 (1975): pp. 91–112. See also Joseph Okpaku, ed., *Nigeria: Dilemma of Nationhood; an African Analysis of the Biafran Conflict* (New York: Third Press, [1972]). Ekeh and his interlocutors spawned some of the most important debates about governance in independent Africa. See Wale Adebanwi, "Africa's 'Two Publics': Colonialism and Governmentality," *Theory, Culture and Society* vol. 34, no. 4 (2017): pp. 65–87; Browne Onuoha, "Publishing Postcolonial Africa: Nigeria and Ekeh's Two Publics a Generation After," *Social Dynamics* vol. 40, no. 2 (2014): pp. 322–337; Eghosa Osaghae, "Colonialism and Civil Society in Africa: The Perspective of Ekeh's Two Publics," *Voluntas* vol. 17, no. 3 (2006): pp. 233–245.

[76] More recently, state and ethnic cleavages have been joined by sharp religious divisions. See Ousmane Kane, *Muslim Modernity in Postcolonial Nigeria: A Study of the Society for the Removal of Innovation and Reinstatement of Tradition* (Leiden: Brill, 2003).

What Was the Biafran State?

Biafra was in flux for all of its short existence. Like its population of refugees, the new country's ideology was constantly in motion.[77] During the first year of the fighting, before it was isolated under a Nigerian blockade, Biafra's administrators tried to make flesh its sovereignty by performing the tasks of a nation-state. They issued stamps and currency and dispatched diplomats to open "embassies" in foreign capitals. In Biafra itself, legalism was the most important tool the government used to assert its legitimacy. Independence demanded a new national identity, and the courts would be where it was hashed out. Biafran judges saw their work as contiguous with the prewar legal system. To them, what mattered was that Biafra retained the English common law tradition, tying it not only to Nigeria but to the "civilization of law" that stretched across the former British Empire.[78] In Biafra, however, like in postcolonial Africa more broadly, the fact that judges and other powerful people saw independence as a point of continuity rather than a break does not mean that it always was one. Even though African states bore a resemblance to the colonial governments they supplanted, self-rule was not business as usual.

Biafra is usually remembered as an Igbo ethno-nation or, less commonly, as an artifact of Nigerian federalism – an arbitrary assemblage of peoples or an "orchestra of minorities," albeit one dominated by Igbos.[79] Yet Biafra had meaning beyond these ethnic definitions. When addressing its citizens, Biafra's leaders defined them not as Igbos but as people who shared a set of commitments; they were law-abiding, loyal, and "orderly" in their comportment, whatever their ethnicity. This language is an important motif of both the legal record and the official writings of Ojukwu and his circle. To be "Biafran" was first and

---

[77] The term "refugee" warrants some explanation. The distinction between refugees (who cross international borders in the course of their displacement) and internally displaced persons (who do not) was not firmly delineated at the time of the war. However, Biafran state officials were aware of the emerging consensus about the connotations of this term, and they insisted that Igbos (and others) who "returned" to Biafra from the north were refugees to underscore that Nigeria was a separate country.

[78] A. A. M. Ekundayo, "The Common Law of Nigeria. A 'Stranger' or an Indigene in Nigeria?" in M. Ayo Ajomo, ed., *Fundamentals of Nigerian Law* (Lagos: Nigerian Institute of Advanced Legal Studies, 1989): p. 228.

[79] I borrow this term from the novelist Chigozie Obioma, *An Orchestra of Minorities* (New York: Little, Brown, 2019).

foremost a statement of ideological commitment and only secondarily an ethnic (or geographic) identity. This goes against the established wisdom about what lay behind the secessionist movement, which continues to equate Biafra with the Igbo. In fact, Biafra was a state with its own ideology and political culture – not all of which was about ethnicity.[80] It tried desperately to construct an identity that had broader purchase, both to appeal to the outside world and to legitimize itself to its own citizens. This was a task Biafra shared with other independent African states, and it was arguably no more or less artificial than the continent's other new countries.

Ethnicity does not explain everything about the war, but the most immediate cause of Biafra's secession had to do with the place of the Igbo people in the Nigerian federation. Biafra was shaped by deeper historical currents. The experience of Igbo societies in the longue durée – or even the whole of the twentieth century – is beyond the remit of this book but that history informed why Biafra seceded and what form it took.[81] Igbos did not share a common origin story or a unified cosmology, and they had not lived in a centralized political unit until the British grouped them together under the pseudo-traditional "warrant chiefs" they empowered to rule on their behalf. This does not mean that Igbo identity was invented by colonialism, however; long-standing patterns of migration and interaction had knit together the people who spoke the various dialects of the Igbo language over centuries.[82] Different legal systems and normative orders operated

---

[80]   See Samuel Fury Childs Daly, "A Nation on Paper: Law and the State in the Republic of Biafra," forthcoming.

[81]   Among many important works, see Nwando Achebe, *Farmers, Traders, Warriors, and Kings: Female Power and Authority in Northern Igboland, 1900–1960* (Portsmouth: Heinemann, 2005); A. E. Afigbo, *The Warrant Chiefs: Indirect Rule in Southeastern Nigeria, 1891–1921* (Ibadan: Humanities Press, 1972); Gloria Chuku, *Igbo Women and Economic Transformation in Southeastern Nigeria, 1900–1960* (London: Routledge, 2005); Kenneth Dike, *Trade and Politics in the Niger Delta, 1830–1885* (Oxford: Clarendon Press, 1956); M. Echeruo and E. N. Obiechina, eds., *Igbo Traditional Life, Culture and Literature* (Owerri: Conch Limited, 1971); Elizabeth Isichei, *A History of the Igbo People* (London: Palgrave, 1976); Toyin Falola, ed., *Igbo History and Society: The Essays of Adiele Afigbo* (Trenton: Africa World Press, 2005).

[82]   On the longer history of the region in the Atlantic context, see Ugo Nwokeji, *The Slave Trade and Culture in the Bight of Biafra: An African Society in the Atlantic World* (New York: Cambridge University Press, 2010); Carolyn Brown and Paul Lovejoy, eds., *Repercussions of the Atlantic Slave Trade: The Interior of the Bight of Biafra and the African Diaspora* (Trenton: Africa World Press, 2011).

in Igbo villages, many of which were horizontally organized and demo-cratic, or "acephalous," to use a contested term from colonial ethnography.[83] The English common law tradition was no older than colonialism in this part of the continent.

Nonetheless, Igbos immersed themselves in law, and the state they created was a highly judicial one (even if, as a military regime, it was also very illiberal). The reasons for this, again, are to be found in the experience of the twentieth century. The same embrace of missionary education that had trained large numbers of Igbo clerks and colonial administrators also produced lawyers and, eventually, judges. This meant that, by the time of independence, many of Nigeria's most eminent legal practitioners were Igbo. For non-lawyers, law was important too. The disputes that arose doing business in far-flung parts of Nigeria had shown Igbo merchants that law could provide protection and furnish remedies, and many came to believe that the English common law protected them better than customary traditions. Some argued that it also reflected their values. They embraced law, both as practitioners and as litigants.[84]

By the mid-twentieth century, "Igbo" had coalesced into an ethnic and linguistic identity. In the federal arrangement established by the 1946 Richards Constitution and its successors, it was one leg of a power balance with Nigeria's two other large ethnic groups – Yorubas in the Western Region and Hausas in the Northern Region.[85] The place of the many minorities who fit none of these categories was a topic of constant negotiation. Igbos had been

---

[83] Many of those legal systems coalesced around oracles, some of which served multiple communities. C. K. Meek, *Law and Authority in a Nigerian Tribe* (London: Oxford University Press, 1937); Simon Ottenberg, "Ibo Oracles and Intergroup Relations," *Southwestern Journal of Anthropology* vol. 14, no. 3 (1958); pp. 295–317; Nonso Okereafoezeke, *Law and Justice in Post-British Nigeria: Conflicts and Interactions Between Native and Foreign Systems of Social Control in Igbo* (Westport, CT: Greenwood, 2002).

[84] A fruitful comparison can be made to the Parsis of Mitra Sharafi's description, for whom identity was deeply imbricated in law and legal process. Mitra Sharafi, *Law and Identity in Colonial South Asia: Parsi Legal Culture, 1772–1947* (New York: Cambridge University Press, 2014).

[85] For a survey of the many currents that feed into the idea of "Igbo" in the twentieth century, see Axel Harneit-Sievers, *Constructions of Belonging: Igbo Communities and the Nigerian State in the Twentieth Century* (Rochester, NY: University of Rochester Press, 2006). On Igbo involvement in the nationalist project through labor organization, see Carolyn Brown, *"We Are All Slaves": African Miners, Culture, and Resistance at the Enugu Government Colliery,*

important in both colonial administration and nationalism. They were proud of their role in building independent Nigeria – a role exemplified by Nnamdi Azikiwe, the northern-born newspaper magnate turned politician who served as president of the First Republic. As Ojukwu stated toward the end of the war in the Ahiara Declaration, "Biafrans were in the fore-front among those who tried to make Nigeria a nation. It is ironic that some ill-informed and mischievous people today will accuse us of breaking up a united African country."[86] A foreign doctor working in Biafra observed that his Igbo colleagues' deep involvement in the nationalist project made the parting with Nigeria all the more painful. "They speak with the bitterness of spurned lovers."[87]

Not all Biafrans were Igbos, however, and not all Igbos were Biafrans. Roughly a third of Biafra's population at the time of secession consisted of non-Igbos, including a small population of northerners and westerners.[88] What relationship the "minority" regions along the coast had to Biafra was especially fraught, populated as they were by people who generally did not share Igbos' galvanizing experience of

Nigeria, 1914–1950 (Portsmouth: Heinemann, 2003); Nnamdi Azikiwe, *A Matter of Conscience* (Nsukka: African Book Company, 1979).

[86] This declaration, written by the literary scholar Ben Obumselu and others, was a statement of socialist ideology drafted late in the war. It was not a charter of how Biafra was actually administered – few of its provisions were brought into force. It is perhaps best understood as a last-ditch attempt to gain the support of the Warsaw Pact countries and China by giving Biafra a socialist cast. Chukwuemeka Odumegwu Ojukwu, *The Ahiara Declaration, 1 June 1969* (Enugu: Heritage, 1993): p. 4.

[87] SOAS Nigerian Civil War Collections MS 321463 Box 14, Report of the visit to Biafra and San Tome by T. McNally," November 7–16, 1968.

[88] Most of these northerners were itinerant cattle-drivers or urban businesspeople. Nearly all left Biafra within the first months of the war, some of them under duress. In keeping with its ideological commitment to legalism, the Biafran government prosecuted some of the perpetrators of violence or theft against northerners, even when the violated parties were no longer there to press charges. These cases usually ended in acquittals, but for judges the trials were important as a performance of the difference between themselves and Nigeria; no such cases were brought by the Northern Region government against those who had participated in the pogroms of 1966. The pogroms had been investigated by the G. C. M. Onyiuke Tribunal of Enquiry between December 1966 and June 1967. Because Biafra seceded during the tribunal's investigation, no action was taken by Nigeria in response to its recommendations. Biafrans saw this as a great miscarriage of justice, and Nigeria's apparent inaction became a point of grievance. The proceedings of the tribunal were published after the war in Ben Obumselu, *Massacre of Ndi-Igbo in 1966* (Enugu: Igbo Youth Movement, n.d.).

ethnic violence in federal Nigeria.[89] A common explanation for Biafra's attachment to the Rivers State and the South-Eastern State was that Igboland itself was too densely populated and resource-poor to be viable as a stand-alone nation-state.[90] The cities of Calabar and Port Harcourt – outside of the Igbo-majority region but linked to it by a long history – were valuable to Biafra, as was the oil in the region; but it was not only oil that led Biafra to claim the Niger Delta. Nearly 2 million Igbo people lived in the delta, and they had been involved in its economy for a century or longer. This made many Biafrans feel that it was "naturally" part of Biafra. Many Ijaw and Efik people in Rivers and the South-Eastern State emphatically disagreed.[91] In these places, Igbos were often seen as interlopers in local politics, agents of colonialism, or "compradors." In the rural areas of the Rivers State, Biafran troops were an unwelcome occupying force. One Biafran infantryman stationed near Brass recalled that he only realized how hostile the local people were to Biafra when he surreptitiously observed a group of civilians "joyously reveling in a ceremony that was heralding the initial but secret entry of Nigerian troops into the community. The continuous chanting of 'One Nigeria, One Nigeria' was loud and clear to us."[92]

The ethnic dimension of the war was important but it was not straightforward. Zooming in from how the war was reported to how it was actually fought, the conflict was fueled by a division not only between Igbos and other Nigerians but between Igbos and eastern

[89] For an expression of their grievances see CADN332PO/1 Box 4, "The Views of the Minority Peoples of the Former Eastern Region of Nigeria by Dr. U.K. Enyenihi, Addis Abeba, Ethiopia," May 10, 1968.

[90] This Malthusian argument about the region's capacity to support its large population had a long genealogy. It had been invoked to explain dynamics ranging from the willingness of local leaders to sell people into the transatlantic slave trade to Igbo labor migration to Fernando Po in the colonial period. See Ige, *People, Politics and Politicians of Nigeria*, p. 332.

[91] The best known denunciation of Biafra's occupation of these regions is Ken Saro-Wiwa, *On a Darkling Plane* (Lagos: Wingspan, 2000). Saro-Wiwa, an Ogoni activist and intellectual, would later become famous as a critic of Shell and its clients in the Nigerian government, but during the war he and many other southeastern minorities threw in their lots with Nigeria against Biafra. Taking a page from Biafra's propagandists, he would later claim Nigeria's actions in Ogoniland were "genocidal." Ken Saro-Wiwa, *Genocide in Nigeria: The Ogoni Tragedy* (Port Harcourt: Saros International Publishers, 1992).

[92] Thomas Enunwe (Omenka), *The Biafran War: The Story of an Orphan* (Ojo: Teg Commercial Enterprises, 2005): p. 117.

ethnic groups *within* Biafra. A third divide in Biafra's domestic politics,
more submerged but no less important, was between different Igbo communities. The division between Nnewi and Onitsha people – which is to
say Igbos who were "indigenes" of those towns – was the most persistent
one in Biafra, but there were many other rifts down to the level of villages
and neighborhoods. The caste system that divides Igbos into people of
slave (*ohu* and *osu*) and freeborn (*diala*) ancestry was also in the background of Biafran politics, although it was rarely mentioned explicitly.
These disputes, made sharper by deprivation and the presence of firearms,
are reflected in the legal record.[93] It was through localized quarrels over
dwindling resources, not only in the grand clashes of the fight with
Nigeria, that many Biafrans understood the stakes of the war. A few
saw class as the central tension of Biafra's politics. Ikenna Nzimiro, an
official in the Biafran Ministry of Information who was responsible for
political education, came to see Biafra as a "bourgeois" regime rather
than a genuinely "revolutionary" one, attributing its defeat to the Biafran
left's failure to reach the proletariat.[94] These and other nuances of the war
are lost in accounts that view it being entirely about the place of Igbos in
the Nigerian federation.

The Ideology of Order

Biafra's propaganda was full of the argot of crime. Nigerians were
"criminals," their military government a "lawless" regime, and
Nigeria was painted as an anarchic, violent place run by a cabal of
"gangsters."[95] In contrast, Biafra presented itself as a regime of law,
one which was disciplined, orderly, and guided by respect for human
dignity.[96] The propagandists who made this argument were elites,

[93] A good example is *Alfred Kalu v. The State*, in which a long-standing dispute
between Aro and Uturu families over the ownership of a cocoa farm bridled into
an armed conflict replete with "units" and "commandos," replicating the
violence of the broader war in miniature. NNAE BCA 1/1/20, in the Biafra
Court of Appeal, Enugu, no. CA/22/67, *Alfred Kalu v. The State*, February 8,
1968.
[94] Ikenna Nzimiro, *The Nigerian Civil War: A Study in Class Conflict* (Enugu:
Frontline, 1982): p. 181.
[95] See, for example, Nigerian National Archives, Ibadan [hereafter NNAI] CWC
1–5, "Nigerian Pogrom 1966," Biafran Directorate of Propaganda [1967].
[96] See Douglas Anthony, "'Resourceful and Progressive Blackmen': Modernity
and Race in Biafra, 1967–1970," *Journal of African History* vol. 51, no. 1
(2010): pp. 41–61.

including literary luminaries like Chinua Achebe and Cyprien Ekwensi, but the Biafran public shared this preoccupation with orderliness. The establishment of the Biafran state was foremost the creation of a legal system. As one petitioner wrote, implementing the rule of law and safeguarding the court system were the most important tasks in "deodorising the region of the diabolical wrongs perpetrated by politicians of the fallen regime."[97] Chief justice of the Biafran Court of Appeal Louis Mbanefo insisted that his government "were not irresponsible rebels who had seized power for the sake of power: on the contrary [we] had maintained law and order and the courts system inherited from the Federation."[98] Indeed, Biafra had an active judiciary and a lively legal culture; as one attorney who practiced there joked, "the one thing that we never had a shortage of was lawyers."[99] "Order" was the barometer by which all things were measured in Biafra, and "discipline" was the constant refrain of judges, government officials, and military officers.[100] In his speech announcing Biafra's independence, Ojukwu said that he saw "the idea of the rule of law [as] one of the driving forces behind the founding of the Republic of Biafra. The future Biafra will be guided by this knowledge."[101]

Of course, this kind of language was hardly unique to Biafra – what modern state does *not* present itself as a guarantor of order or encourage "disciplined" behavior in its citizens? What makes Biafra different is that its legal system was its main – and eventually, only – implement of governance. "Law and order" was more than a rhetorical device. Fundamentally, it was what was being fought over.[102] Precious resources were devoted to the courts' operation, and, aside from the army, the Ministry of Justice was the only part of the Biafran government still operating by the end of the war. The decision to protect the

[97] ABUAH PR1/59/429, Secretary, Zikist Movement of the Far North Provinces to Military Governor, Northern Provinces, May 18, 1966.
[98] NAUK FCO 38/216, Summary of meeting between Lord Shepherd and Sir Louis Mbanefo, June 11, 1968.
[99] Interview with Ejike O. Ume, SAN, Onitsha, March 12, 2015.
[100] This did not end with Biafra's defeat. "Discipline" would become a key word in Nigeria's political culture, culminating with Muhammadu Buhari's "War on Indiscipline" in the early 1980s.
[101] NAUK DO 186/1, "Transcription of Ojukwu's 29th May Biafran Anniversary Address" [May 30, 1967].
[102] Comparatively, see Laura F. Edwards, *A Legal History of the Civil War and Reconstruction: A Nation of Rights* (New York: Cambridge University Press, 2015).

legal system before all else illustrates Biafra's commitment to discipline as a political ideology. Legalism figured prominently in Biafra's performance of its legitimacy, both to its own people and to the outside world. Discipline for the purpose of survival remained its guiding principle even as public order collapsed. The courtroom was the place where that ideology could be put into action. Biafra's obsession with discipline made the criminal court a venue for discussions about politics and ideology – even as criminal procedure became increasingly madcap. Martial obsessions with discipline and regularity found a natural outlet in the criminal justice system, which became one of the military's primary tools for controlling "unruly" or disobedient civilians. It was also the place where Biafrans were most likely to encounter their government. For all of these reasons, criminal law was not a backwater of the legal system but a main channel of state power.[103]

Yet Biafra's legal system fell far short of its ambitions. Lawyers recalled that, although courts remained open, they operated only "at the level of keeping up appearances."[104] They did not feature the "flare, decency, and openness" that eastern Nigeria's eminent judges had demonstrated in peacetime.[105] The standards of dress and comportment at court declined; claimants appeared before judges in work clothes or in "native attire," and the use of the wig and gown fell away as conditions deteriorated, much to the consternation of traditionally minded judges.[106] As famine set in, the problems the Biafran legal system faced would become much greater than the loss of its trappings.

Nigeria also invoked disorder to justify its actions, and the notion that Nigeria's main problem was a deficit of law did not begin with the pogroms of 1966.[107] Along with corruption and "indiscipline," the

---

[103] This central place accorded to law in administration would be one of the war's longest-lasting consequences; under military rule, criminal courts and tribunals were among the most important sites of interaction between civilians and the ruling soldier class.

[104] Interview with Dr. Jacob Ibik, SAN, Enugu, September 26, 2014.

[105] Interview with Jerome H. C. Okolo, SAN, Enugu, September 17, 2014.

[106] The rules of the court remained rigid, though. One lawyer recalled Chief Justice Sir Louis Mbanefo frequently dressing down lawyers who used the conditions of the war to explain poor preparation or informal conduct in court. Interview with Dr. Jacob Ibik, SAN, Enugu, September 26, 2014.

[107] Nor was "disorder" an operative term only in the east. See Ruth Watson, *"Civil Disorder is the Disease of Ibadan": Chieftaincy and Civic Culture in a Yoruba*

claim that Nigeria was ungovernable had been the main justification for the military coup that toppled the First Republic. Six months later, Gowon justified his own coup by claiming that the "lawless" Ironsi regime had failed to prosecute the killers of Northern Region Premier Ahmadu Bello and others assassinated in the first coup. More generally, before Biafra's secession there had been a widespread feeling that Nigeria's national politics were lawless.[108] One eastern political analyst traced the situation back to events five years before, writing that "the beginnings of the breakdown came in 1962 with the crisis in Western Nigeria which necessitated a Declaration of Emergency ... This may be cited as the commencement of the indiscipline and lawlessness which was to lead eventually to civil war."[109] Others pointed to the process of decolonization as the root of political disorder, especially the Willinck Commission's 1957 recommendation to leave Nigeria's large regions intact rather than split them into smaller, ethnically defined states.[110]

In a speech on the eve of Biafra's secession, Gowon argued that the Eastern Region could not be allowed to secede because the rule of law had collapsed there, and the regional government was behaving illegally. It had violated the law by expelling non-easterners, appropriating federally owned railways, and hijacking a plane owned by Nigeria's national airline. In their dueling accusations of lawlessness, both sides drew on the language of legality. Nigeria's first reaction was to stage what it called a "police action" to reclaim Biafra – further evidence that the

City (Oxford: James Currey, 2003). Crime, especially when it was committed by young people, was a major preoccupation of the colonial state. Crime had also been a major site for the articulation of ideas about gender, comportment, and relationships between young and old. See Abosede George, *Making Modern Girls: A History of Girlhood, Labor, and Social Development in Colonial Lagos* (Athens: Ohio University Press, 2014); Laurent Fourchard, "Lagos and the Invention of Juvenile Delinquency in Nigeria, 1920–60," *The Journal of African History* vol. 47, no. 1 (2006): pp. 115–137.

[108] Olushola Fadahunsi, *Nigeria: The Last Days of the First Republic* (Ibadan: AOF Press, 1970).

[109] SOAS Christian Aid Collections, CA/A/6/5, "Information paper written for the Joint International Department of the British Council of Churches and the Conference of British Missionary Societies," November 1967.

[110] See Michael Vickers, *A Nation Betrayed. Nigeria and the Minorities Commission of 1957* (Trenton: Africa World Press, 2010); Oghenetoja Okoh, "Who Controls Warri? How Ethnicity Became Volatile in the Western Niger Delta (1928–1952)," *Journal of African History* vol. 57, no. 2 (2016): pp. 209–230.

war took place under the banner of criminal justice, at least rhetorically. Biafrans and Nigerians alike understood the war as both cause and consequence of "lawlessness," "indiscipline," and "disorder," all of which became embedded in the language of politics. The war's physical terrain was the land between the River Niger and Cameroon, from Ogoja to the Atlantic. Its discursive terrain, however, was law.

Long after the war's end, a reporter asked Ojukwu why a personal friend of his had been executed for treason in Biafra. "You know we were in an emergency situation in the East during the war," Ojukwu replied. "During emergency, anything can happen."[111] Indeed, the English common law was not the only law of the land. Both sides implemented emergency measures immediately, and martial law would last throughout the war and for a long time after. Biafra's history offers a vantage point on the "state of exception" and the social forms it generates. There is a long genealogy of thought that treats the state of emergency or exception as an abstraction – as an "anti-law" that operates so differently from the normal workings of the legal system that it is unrecognizable as law, or nearly so. Emergency, in most analyses, is important for the way it enables and instantiates a form of repressive sovereign power. The state of emergency, in this view, is a force that emanates from the executive, or a vacuum that precludes the possibility of ethical action for those trapped in it.[112] Sovereign power in the state of exception can be found in discrete gestures and rituals, embodied by individual figures of authority who can exceed or supplant law. In literary representations, emergency often appears as a kind of ether – a miasma of repression that is free-floating and immanent.[113] It is arbitrary and ungraspable, evoking the imagery of black holes, the supernatural, and the millenarian. How it actually works is usually left unsaid.

Was Ojukwu correct that "anything can happen" in a state of emergency? Not exactly. Looking at emergency through the lens of

---

[111] Tunde Akingbade, *Ilaro: Memories of "Operation Wet E" and the Civil War Years* (Lagos: Climate International Paperback, 2008): p. 84.

[112] See, for example, Giorgio Agamben, *State of Exception* (Chicago: University of Chicago Press, 2004): p. 51

[113] Of many artistic treatments of the state of emergency that fit this description, see Fela Anikulapo Kuti, "O.D.O.O., Overtake Don Overtake Overtake" (1989); Salman Rushdie, *Midnight's Children* (New York: Avon, 1982).

law shows its limits and logics. The rule of exception worked on people in ways that were not irreconcilable with how they had lived under civilian administration and indeed under colonialism.[114] Emergency was a system that Biafrans navigated like they would any other. It consisted of a tangible body of institutions and a knowable set of rules; tribunals and executive decrees instantiated people as citizens and national subjects, and they shaped public understandings of morality and ethics. They were not always clear or consistent, but they were legible to those who lived with them. Biafrans and Nigerians made the best they could of the state of exception that they inhabited. Some avoided it, others were ensnared in it, and a few found ways to bend it to their advantage. Seeing the state of emergency as a terrain that people moved through, rather than a force that affected them in blunt or mysterious ways, offers a fuller understanding of how Biafra and Nigeria governed. What is true here is true of postcolonial legal systems more broadly, nearly all of which implemented some form of emergency rule in the 1960s and 1970s. Historians have struggled to describe how independent African states ruled through any means other than repression and co-optation. Looking at military rule from the perspective of social history provides part of the answer.[115]

In Biafra, emergency manifested most clearly as a turn to martial law. All of the country's courts were tasked with keeping the new republic intact and functional, but the part of the legal system most explicitly responsible for preserving order was the Special Tribunal of Biafra. The tribunal was established under Biafra's emergency measures, which remained in force for the entire duration of Biafra's existence. The Law and Order (Maintenance) Edict of 1967 was proclaimed in the days after independence, in dense language that nonetheless left little doubt about who would be in charge.[116] The

---

[114] The simultaneous coexistence of an operative legal system law and a system of emergency that suspends law is a feature of many military regimes, including wartime Nigeria as well as Biafra. In Nigeria, the Suppression of Disorder Decree of 1966 had a similar function to the Law and Order (Maintenance) Edict of 1967 in Biafra. These parallel sets of emergency measures established the jumbled practice of martial law that would last until the civilian handover in 1999.

[115] On the colonial genealogy of emergency measures, see Nasser Hussain, *The Jurisprudence of Emergency: Colonialism and the Rule of Law* (Ann Arbor: University of Michigan Press, 2003).

[116] *Biafra Sun*, June 5, 1967, p. 1.

edict gave Ojukwu wide authority to pursue internal enemies – both
real and imagined – and established a bifurcation in the legal system
between the ordinary civilian courts and the Special Tribunal. In the
absence of a constitution, which Biafra never had, the Law and Order
(Maintenance) Edict became the guiding document of public
administration.[117] Civilian and military modes of justice became so
tightly intertwined that they could not be distinguished from one
another. In theory, the emergency measures were checked by civilian
courts, which continued to operate; but the lack of a clear structure of
appeal from the tribunals meant that they were a law unto themselves.
Legal niceties like habeas corpus, the right to legal counsel, and various
rules of evidence were suspended indefinitely. As a Nigerian sociologist
would later describe, in Biafra "the theoretically clear dichotomy of
military-civil law was not maintained in practice."[118] The Special
Tribunal had jurisdiction over acts of sedition, fraud, profiteering,
and sabotage, all broadly glossed as "subversion," which became
a category of crime large enough to accommodate virtually any
activity.[119] Even the robbery of a civilian by a gang of other civilians
would come under the jurisdiction of the Special Tribunal on the
grounds that it was a "disruption of Biafra's economy."[120] Treason
cases, of which there were many, were also usually heard before the
tribunal. Jurisdictional rules came to mean almost nothing in the chaos
of the war; soldiers appeared before civilian courts, and resolutely

---

[117] The Ahiara Declaration would not be proclaimed until the war's final gambit,
      and even then it did not have a constitutional function.

[118] M. Angulu Onwuejeogwu, *A Study in Military Sociology: The Biafran Army,
      1967–1970* (Lagos: UTO Publications, 2000): p. 98.

[119] There were frequent debates in the tribunal over what kinds of crimes could be
      considered "subversion." For example, in a case where the theft of gasoline
      intended for a civilian hospital had been committed, the question arose of
      whether it necessarily constituted subversion. They ruled that it did: "this plant
      generates electricity which is used in the Queen Elizabeth Hospital where the
      inhabitants of this country go for medical and surgical treatment. Without the
      electric plant the welfare of the inhabitants would be adversely affected. The
      surgeons will not see to operate nor can various apparatuses which are
      electrically operated be of any use. Any theft, therefore, of the gas oil used in
      generating the plant is a crime against the inhabitants of the Republic. It is an
      offence of subversion within the context of present emergency." NNAE
      MINJUST 117/1/4, in the Special Tribunal of the Republic of Biafra, no. ST/
      11c/69, *The State v. Gilbert Obazi Ihejiobi*, May 11, 1969.

[120] NNAE MINJUST 116/1/4, in the Special Tribunal of Biafra, *The State v. Simon
      Atulobi and two others*, October 21, 1969.

civilian matters like divorce or probate were brought before tribunals. Any jurisdictional port would do in a storm.

Ojukwu and his circle of advisors were paranoid about spies, saboteurs, and the allegiances of Biafra's own citizens. Paranoia took many forms, from concerns about Nigerian spies to fears of palace coups and sabotage from within. A plot to overthrow Ojukwu by Victor Banjo, a Yoruba officer in the Biafran Army, had made him suspicious of non-Igbos from the very beginning, but even among the Igbo elite trust did not run deep. Ojukwu harbored particular mistrust of people from Onitsha, the home of both Nigeria's first president Nnamdi Azikiwe and his political rival Emmanuel Ifeajuna. Ukpabi Asika, the Igbo loyalist administrator of the East Central State, governing in absentia from Lagos, observed that the Biafran leadership

walks in fear. Afraid of its own shadow. Afraid of the people it is supposed to lead. A leadership that has so corrupted our society with fear and suspicion that today in Orlu, in Umuahia, in Ihiala, in Awo Omama, in Mbaise, in Nnewi, in Okija, in Aro Ndizogu and other places where they still control no man or woman dares open his mouth to his neighbour, his wife, her husband or child.[121]

Demands to be wary were everywhere – car number plates were prefixed with VIG for "vigilance."[122] This suspicion permeated legal processes as well, and the place where it manifested most clearly was in the Special Tribunal of Biafra.

The lawyer Jacob Ibik remembered that the tone of the proceedings in tribunals was combative, treacherous, and improvisational – "we were making it up as we went along."[123] Judges and lawyers who had been trained in the common law tradition were acutely aware of the dangers inherent in this kind of justice. Many legal practitioners privately worried that the expanding remit of martial law threatened to hollow out Biafra's legal culture. The Special Tribunal was shaped by the demands of the war to a greater degree than the civilian side of the Biafran legal system, which exercised judicial independence (at least in theory). The attorney general weighed in on cases frequently. In one, two men stood accused of subverting Biafra's economy for purchasing a large bag of salt above the government control price. The tribunal

[121] NAUK FCO 65/213, "Asika Appeals for a New Era," November 11, 1968.
[122] IWM 6687, Papers of Rosina Umelo, "Biafra, A World of Our Own," p. 38.
[123] Interview with Dr. Jacob Ibik, SAN, Enugu, September 26, 2014.

acquitted the defendants on a technicality – it could not be confirmed that the bag reading "British Salt – 40 lbs." indeed contained salt because the police had not taken a sample of its contents. The acquittal infuriated the attorney general. He wrote,

One recalls the ageless principle of interpretation established in Heyden's Case centuries ago, which is that a law must be interpreted so as to suppress the evil and advance the remedy. The evil here is in the inflation of prices against the welfare of the people of Biafra. The remedy is to stamp it out by means of sanctions provided by law. To avoid those sanctions by means of technicalities is to advance the evil, and this is a thought I do not find refreshing.[124]

To this Biafran administrator, a preoccupation with the rules of evidence should not be allowed to obstruct the need for public order. The protections embedded within the legal system eroded under this pressure.

The business of courts and tribunals continued through the fighting – though not very effectually. Investigations were interrupted by the war, and courts sitting in improvised conditions in schools and village squares were regularly adjourned due to bombings. One case was cut short because the defendant was killed in an air raid during his trial.[125] One of the few descriptions of the atmosphere in a Biafran courtroom was written by the American journalist Renata Adler, who visited the High Court of Biafra in Owerri in 1969:

All the judges and attorneys wore black robes and curled, yellowing wigs. On the table nearest the attorneys was a gray volume, "Reports of the High Court of the Federal Territory of Lagos." The steps by which messengers climbed to the justices' bench consisted of rusted mortar containers, still marked "Explosives UK." ... Justice Mbanefo asked one of the attorneys, a bearded young man with a severe cold and with thumbprints on his glasses, whether the case might be adjourned until Wednesday. "I don't know, My Lord," he replied. "I have to come all the way from Ihiala for these appeals. The problem of transportation will be – that is, unless my learned friend

---

[124] NNAE MINJUST 115/1/1, Attorney-General/Commissioner for Justice to the Chairman, Special Tribunal, Nbawsi, November 10, 1967.

[125] NNAE MINJUST 116/1/3, in the Special Tribunal of the Republic of Biafra, no. ST/11c/69, *The State v. Stephen Mbuko*, October 2, 1969.

can ... " Finally the court did adjourn. An usher cried, "Court!" Everyone rose, and the justices left the room.[126]

As Adler's account suggests, the pace of proceedings was halting and irregular. Crime scenes could not be visited because there were "war activities" there, and alibis could not be confirmed because witnesses went missing or could not travel to a court to testify. Bailiffs found it increasingly difficult to find people in order to arrest them or to serve them with notices.[127] In one case, a bailiff was sent on a perilous journey to the front to collect three witnesses. He returned shaken and empty-handed – all three had been killed since the beginning of the trial.[128]

It was an even greater challenge to enforce the rulings that courts made. The courts could be as tough as they wished in their sentencing, but this was no guarantee that a sentence handed down would be served. This was not only because the survival of Biafra itself was uncertain but because people imprisoned in Biafra did not stay there for long. The instability of the war sometimes worked in prisoners' favor; it was easy to lose track of inmates as they were moved from prison to prison as Biafra's borders shifted. Inmates were held in schools and police stations, and the lack of fortified jails meant that it was relatively easy to escape. It was also common knowledge that wardens could be paid for an unofficial release.[129]

Biafra also commuted the sentences of many convicts who had been imprisoned prior to secession. These releases reflected both practical concerns (like the desire to ease overcrowding in Biafra's prisons) and the fact that Biafra was ambivalent about enforcing sentences that had been imposed by Nigerian courts. At the urging of the Eastern Region,

---

[126] The case was a case over land ownership, *Chief Amagwara Achonye v. The State*, which unfortunately does not appear to survive. Renata Adler, "Letter From Biafra," *The New Yorker*, October 4, 1969, pp. 77–78.

[127] NNAE 1/1/96, Deputy Bailiff, Onitsha to Court of Appeal Registry, Enugu, April 2, 1969.

[128] NNAE BCA 1/2/35, in the Court of Appeal of the Republic of Biafra, Aba, no. CA/40/68, *Kalu Njoku and Ekea Udensi v. Ukwu Eme and four others*, July 13, 1968.

[129] NNAE BCA 1/1/6, Ministry of Home Affairs, Prison Division, Okigwi to Registrar, High Court of Appeal, Aba, January 16, 1968. A description of the poor conditions of Biafran prisons can be found in the memoirs of a Mid-West civil servant who was detained for the duration of the war, Samuel E. Umweni, *888 Days in Biafra* (New York: iUniverse, 2007).

people who had been imprisoned in the north and west were transferred back to the east during the disturbances of 1966, ostensibly for
their safety. After the Eastern Region seceded, many of these people
were released. Some of them were serving terms for offenses that Biafra
considered   "political."   These   prisoners   included   Major
Chukwuma Nzeogwu, who had been jailed for his role in the assassination of the Sardauna of Sokoto in 1966. He was immediately commissioned into the Biafran Army and hailed as a "national hero."[130]
Others were ordinary criminals. This was the case with Chukwuma
Agu, who had been imprisoned for a murder committed in Benin City
in 1955 and released without trial in Biafra. His release prompted some
protest within the Ministry of Justice but he and other Biafrans serving
terms for offenses committed in prewar Nigeria – usually more trivial
than Agu's – were freed in the same general amnesty as political prisoners like Nzeogwu.[131] Similarly, men facing charges for drug use or
battery were occasionally given the choice of going to jail or joining
the army, although in the later stages of the war there was hardly a man
who appeared in court who was not already a soldier, a civil defender,
or a deserter.[132]

There was another type of law that was conspicuously absent in
Biafra. Customary law – the locally derived patchwork of "native"
laws codified by the colonial administration – had been marginalized in
the Eastern Region prior to Biafra's independence. Customary and
native courts, which city dwellers had come to see as a moribund and
despotic part of the legal system, were especially unpopular in the east.
There, the common experience of being caught up in other peoples'
customary legal systems (especially in the north) made many in the east
hostile toward the general idea of custom – even if it was one's "own."
By the time Biafra seceded, the jurisdiction of customary courts in the

---

[130] CADN 332PO/1 Box 5, Marc Barbey to Maurice Couve de Murville,
       March 31, 1967. Nzeogwu died in battle shortly thereafter.
[131] NNAE MINJUST 90/1/31, Discharge on Licence made under Section 401(2) of
       the Criminal Procedure Law, Chukwuma Agu, June 2, 1968.
[132] One defendant in a criminal case put the bargain offered to him in the following
       terms: "I am now a Biafran soldier. I decided to join the Army on the 24th
       December 1968. I resolved to join the army instead of going to prison for Indian
       hemp for ten years. So let me go to the army and fight for my father land.
       I received only one week training." NNAE MINJUST 42/1/4, in the
       Magistrate's Court of the Republic of Biafra, Awka, *Inspector General of
       Police v. Peter Nweke*, January 19, 1969.

east was restricted to a few matters of family law and chiefly succession.[133] What role it might play in Biafra was an unsettled question. When Renata Adler asked Mbanefo about the Biafran courts' attitude toward customary law, he replied that "We are still in the process of sorting it out."[134]

Biafra's mistrust of customary law was part of its larger ideology. Biafra was a profoundly modern place, at least in terms of how Biafrans understood themselves and their cause. Those who spoke for the government presented it as a technocratic and forward-looking regime, and they differentiated themselves from Nigeria by arguing that the latter was backwards, "feudal," and mired in tradition.[135] Rejecting customary law was one way to underscore Biafra's modernity. Biafra embraced a form of administration that was highly bureaucratized and, in its obsession with fingerprinting and photographing, even aspired to be biometric. "Biafra has come to stay," proclaimed a state newspaper. "Biafra is a republic of progressive people committed to survival. It is a republic for a people who see hard-work as a means of resolving their economic problems; and hardship as a challenge to be faced and conquered."[136] These ambitions would be scaled back as hunger set in, but Biafra remained committed to order and modernity until the very last days of the war – at least rhetorically, but sometimes in more tangible ways too.[137]

---

[133] After the war, customary law and the form of chiefly power that it served would return to a place of prominence in the Nigerian state. On the uses of custom to postwar military governments, see Olufemi Vaughan, *Nigerian Chiefs: Traditional Power in Modern Politics, 1890s-1990s* (Rochester, NY: University of Rochester Press, 2000). On the regionalization of the courts, see John P. Mackintosh, *Nigerian Government and Politics* (London: George Allen and Unwin, 1966): p. 56. For a more theoretical approach to custom in postcolonial Africa, see Juan Obarrio, *The Spirit of the Laws in Mozambique* (Chicago: University of Chicago Press, 2014).

[134] Renata Adler, "Letter From Biafra," *The New Yorker*, October 4, 1969, p. 78.

[135] See Anthony, "'Resourceful and Progressive Blackmen,'" pp. 41–61.

[136] *Biafra Spotlight*, June 1, 1967, p. 2.

[137] I agree with Frederick Cooper that "modernity" is mostly a cipher – a term that obscures more than it reveals, especially when used to describe African societies. Nonetheless, the pervasiveness of the idea in Biafran propaganda is worth noting. Frederick Cooper, *Colonialism in Question: Theory, Knowledge, History* (Berkeley: University of California Press, 2005): pp. 113–152.

Conclusion

A casual look at any Nigerian newspaper will reveal the important role law plays in Nigerian politics today. Highly technical questions of jurisdiction, opaque legal disputes over chieftaincy and land owner- ship, and the internal politics of the legal profession are front-page news on a daily basis, all in addition to the lurid reportage of crime that is the bread-and-butter of tabloids everywhere. This reveals something about the enduring role of law in Nigerian politics. It is now well established in African history that colonial subjects used law to their own ends, sometimes by turning the empire's rhetoric of "fair play" back on it or by carving out places for themselves in the blind spots, extremities, and gray areas of the law. Africans went to court for many reasons, including to seek protection or remedy, to secure property, to take revenge, and to make moral stands. Rarely was it a litigant's objective to participate in the establishment of a legal regime, though in the end that was the cumulative effect of their appeals.[138] Law was simultaneously a coercive force and a weapon of the weak – it could be a force of state repression "from above" or a tool to advance colonial subjects' personal interests "from below," depending on who was using it and how they did so. The historiography of colonialism in Africa has shown with great nuance how law – in all of its potential for despotism – was also the site where national, ethnic, and individual identities were produced.[139]

The possibility that law might serve a similar purpose in the *postcolony* is seldom considered. African law is usually presumed to be either corrupt or tyrannical – too unsystematic to be ideolog- ical, too weak to generate forms of subjectivity. Yet law shaped the contours of nationality in Biafra and Nigeria in many ways, both by arbitrating access to benefits and remedies and by defining

---

[138]   In a large literature on colonial rules of law in Africa, see especially
       Richard Roberts and Kristin Mann, eds., *Law in Colonial Africa* (Portsmouth: Heinemann, 1991); Martin Chanock, *Law, Custom and Social Order: The Colonial Experience in Malawi and Zambia* (Portsmouth: Heinemann, 1998); Sally Falk Moore, *Social Facts and Fabrications: "Customary" Law on Kilimanjaro, 1880–1980* (Cambridge: Cambridge University Press, 1986); Bonny Ibhawoh, *Imperial Justice: Africans in Empire's Court* (Oxford: Oxford University Press, 2013).

[139]   For Nigeria, see Bonny Ibhawoh, "Stronger than the Maxim Gun: Law, Human Rights and British Colonial Hegemony in Nigeria," *Africa* vol. 72, no. 1 (2002): pp. 55–83.

national identity through its poetics.[140] The fact that African post-colonies have emic legal orders, and that those orders can generate social dynamics (like crime) or political subjects (like Biafrans), is true beyond the aberrant setting of a civil war.[141] Even the most unruly places have rules.

---

[140] Legal historians have elaborated how legal dispute can transform people into citizens, colonial subjects, and legal persons. Works that have informed the present approach to the relationship between law and personhood include Lauren Benton, *Law and Colonial Cultures: Legal Regimes in World History, 1400–1900* (Cambridge: Cambridge University Press, 2002); Megan Vaughan, *Creating the Creole Island: Slavery in Eighteenth Century Mauritius* (Durham, NC: Duke University Press, 2005).

[141] In this I agree with Priya Lal that the tensions and contradictions within postcolonial states (and here, legal regimes) "amount to more than ideological inconsistency and material chaos." Priya Lal, *African Socialism in Postcolonial Tanzania: Between the Village and the World* (Cambridge: Cambridge University Press, 2015): p.11.

2 | Sworn on the Gun: Martial Violence and Violent Crime

A small crowd from the refugee camp was beating and kicking a young man crouched on the ground, his hands placed on his head to shield some of the blows. His trousers were splattered with holes and his collar was almost ripped off but the half of a yellow sun still clung to his torn sleeve. . . . "Stop it!" Kainene said. "Stop it right now! Leave him alone!"

"You are telling us to leave a thief? If we leave him today, tomorrow ten of them will come."

"He is not a thief," Kainene said. "Did you hear me? He is not a thief. He is a hungry soldier." The crowd stilled at the quiet authority in her voice.

Chimamanda Ngozi Adichie, *Half of a Yellow Sun*[1]

On a night in October 1969, Gabriel Nwori was awakened when fifteen Biafran soldiers broke into his compound.[2] When he confronted them, they tied him up and threatened to shoot him if he tried to escape. The soldiers ransacked the house, taking all of his paltry belongings – a length of cloth, some stockfish tails, and a packet of cigarettes. Nwori cooperated with them, and when they demanded food he had his daughter cook for them.[3] In the morning he went to the nearest military camp to file a complaint. The military police tracked down the leader of the group, who was known to the complainant. After an investigation, the Special Tribunal concluded that the robbery had been committed by a "criminal gang" of soldiers led by a private in the Biafran Army named Godwin Egbuna, who went by the *nom de guerre* Captain Blood. Even though he was on duty, Egbuna lived at home with his wife. A mobile police force was dispatched there to arrest him. Finding

---

[1] Chimamanda Ngozi Adichie, *Half of a Yellow Sun* (New York: Anchor, 2006): p. 505.

[2] NNAE MINJUST 116/1/7, in the Special Tribunal of the Republic of Biafra, Charge no. ST/21c/69, *The State v. Godwin Egbuna*, November 24, 1969.

[3] In this context, this may have been a euphemism for demanding that she have sex with them.

him missing, they arrested his elder brother instead to encourage Egbuna to present himself for questioning, which he eventually did.[4] Egbuna was tried before the Special Tribunal for subversion on the grounds that he had used his authority as a soldier to unlawfully rob a Biafran citizen.

In his defense, Egbuna claimed that he had not been on the scene the night of the robbery. A witness testified that Egbuna had passed the night in his brother's house, since the roads were too dangerous to travel after dark. When asked why he would be afraid to travel by night, Egbuna replied that he was "afraid of brigandry on the road." This was a common fear and a reasonable one given how many people – soldiers and civilians alike – were robbed or killed on Biafra's roads after dark. During cross-examination, the friend could not recall when he had met Egbuna, leading the tribunal to conclude that Egbuna and the defense witness were "comrades in crime." The fact that the Biafran soldiers had acted as a gang was particularly troubling because it violated the army's formal structure of command. "Captain Blood" was sentenced to a long prison term, and attempts were made to track down his accomplices. The military police investigated many similar events, but many more were likely never reported to the authorities. Civilians tried to avoid interacting with the military, and soldiers knew that in most cases their victims would be too fearful to lodge complaints against them.

In this case and others like it, one can see the outline of a criminological problem that would become the bane of postwar Nigeria – armed robbery. The heat of battle caused the line between combat and criminal violence to melt away. War brought firearms and the social dynamics that they engendered into areas of civic and public life where they had never been present before. Both Biafran and Nigerian soldiers used their weapons to harass their rivals, demand sex, and commandeer supplies from civilians and from one another. To civilians, the difference between these forms of violence and outright assault, rape, or robbery was unclear. In turn, civilians imitated the protocols of military conflict – which was all around them – in how they treated one another.

---

[4] Holding family members in this way was not legal, but it was a common police tactic in both Biafra and Nigeria, and it had been a mainstay of colonial policing.

Tempers flared quickly when food was short and quarters were close. Altercations also became more likely to be fatal; firearms were rarely far out of reach, allowing confrontations that might only have led to a fistfight in normal circumstances to end in death. Of course, armed violence was not invented in Biafra. People had long engaged in the kinds of crimes that brought them before Biafran courts and tribunals, and the wielding of guns was hardly unheard of in prewar Nigeria.[5] For example, a 1964 case from Port Harcourt in which a group of masked men stormed a merchant's shop in the middle of the night has all the hallmarks of the armed robberies that would become common later: the preference for face-to-face confrontation over burglary, the decision to act as a group, and especially the use of military surplus (in this case a Second World War–era handgun);[6] but the war made new opportunities for this kind of crime, and the threat of starvation pushed otherwise law-abiding people toward it.

As Chapter 1 argued, lawfulness and obedience were central tenets of Biafran ideology. In the eyes of its citizens, however, the country seemed to teeter on the edge of anarchy. Everyday life in Biafra was rife with violence and treachery. Soldiers were often the perpetrators, but civilians also threatened or hurt one another, often out of desperation. Keeping the focus on what happened behind Biafran lines, this chapter mainly describes criminal acts by Biafrans against one another. However, this is not to suggest that they had a monopoly on violence. Biafrans feared one another, but they feared Nigerian troops far more and with good reason. The massacre at Asaba in October 1967 was the starkest example of violence against civilians but it was hardly the only one.[7] The Nigerian command emphasized that they had no intent to harm local people, but several would later express remorse for abuses that transpired under their command.[8]

[5] On armed crime before the war, see Saheed Aderinto, *Guns and Society: Firearms, Culture, and Public Order in Colonial Nigeria, 1900–1960* (Bloomington: Indiana University Press, 2018): pp. 260–264.

[6] Although the case was heard on appeal in Biafra, the events took place three years before secession. ESHC uncatalogued collection, in the High Court of the Republic of Biafra, Port Harcourt, no. P/124/1964, *Ada Ube and others v. Uwanwete Alfred*, July 13, 1967.

[7] S. Elizabeth Bird and Fraser M. Ottanelli, *The Asaba Massacre: Trauma, Memory, and the Nigerian Civil War* (Cambridge: Cambridge University Press, 2017).

[8] See the interviews with the Nigerian command, especially those with Ibrahim Babangida and Baba Usman, in H. B. Momoh, ed., *The Nigerian Civil War, 1967–1970: History and Reminiscences* (Ibadan: Sam Bookman, 2000).

Martial excess was not the preserve of only one side, and the war's devastation was a coproduction between the belligerents. This is not an argument for their moral equivalence but a recognition that the war's violence was multivalent and self-reproducing. In areas recaptured by Nigeria, bloodletting took place on a large scale – but so did it in the areas of Rivers State that Biafra occupied early in the war. Biafra's command of its troops was fragile but the Nigerian Army also struggled to maintain discipline.[9] The Nigerian side of this story is equally important for understanding how violence persisted after the war's end, and the grim conditions I describe in later chapters were an outcome of the war in general – not a straightforward consequence of what one side or the other did. Biafrans were not the only ones who endured this period by cunning and violence. Nigerians did too, and the war made life precarious on both sides of the front. That said, the most extreme conditions of hardship and danger were felt in Biafra, not in federal Nigeria. In the social history of the war small places like Umuahia or Orlu, where the conflict cut directly through daily life, loom larger than Lagos or Kano where the fighting was always more distant.

The records of these events are partial, partisan, and full of interruptions. Transcripts of Biafran cases are sometimes cut off by shelling, which are jarring reminders that there was a larger context for what went on in the courtroom. There is no town or court for which I have anything like a complete record, and the partial nature of these sources makes a quantitative analysis of crime in Biafra mostly impossible.[10] I take a narrative approach instead – these are individual stories of how Biafrans and Nigerians acted and adapted to the times, mediated through law. There are many blind spots in this approach, but even a more intact legal archive would not provide a full picture of the society that produced it. The "facts of the matter" that a court transcript presents are not objectively true even though they seem

---

[9] Robin Luckham, *The Nigerian Military: A Sociological Analysis of Authority and Revolt 1960–1967* (Cambridge: Cambridge University Press, 1971): pp. 145–162.

[10] Statistics are available for federal Nigeria, although it is not clear how reliable they are. Nigerian crime rates appear to have fallen precipitously between 1967 and 1970, which is explained by the fact that the Biafran territories – and therefore all of the crimes discussed here – were not included in the Nigerian statistics. Basil Othuke Owomero, "Crime Trends and Patterns of Three African Countries, 1960–1979" (Doctoral dissertation, University of Toronto, 1986): p. 109.

unequivocal.[11] Furthermore, as Richard Roberts warns, the document available to the legal historian is only a summary, one "shaped by translations of interactions that took place in the court and by various economies of recording. These translations and summaries served to channel talk of trouble into simplified categories of dispute. These are African voices, but the voices we read are not the same as those that spoke in the court."[12] Details can be left out because they are inadmissible or altered to fit the structure and semantics of the trial. Unlike memoirs and oral histories, legal records never announce their unreliability. That does not mean they can be trusted.

There are also biases in what the legal record preserves. The cases that are most extreme, strange, or depraved are the ones that generate the thickest files and raise the complex procedural questions that lead to appeals and countersuits. In legal archives, as Wolfgang Friedmann wrote, "it is in the borderline situations, numerically small but qualitatively all important," where the true colors of law become visible.[13] For the social historian, this creates a problem; eccentric cases may be the most important ones for the law, but they are rarely the ones that most accurately reveal the character of everyday life. The priorities of courts have to be disaggregated from those of the people whom they serve. The criminal legal archive also gives the impression that the only events that happen in a given place are violent or transgressive ones. If this chapter reads as a litany of gory anecdotes, it is because that is the story that criminal records tell, not because crime was the only thing going on in Biafra. Nonetheless, these anecdotes are important. Law operates through the telling and retelling of stories, and the most gripping stories – the ones people tell one another in bars and

[11] Pablo Piccato compares criminal legal epistemology to the structure of Akira Kurosawa's film *Rashomon*, in which "each participant has a perspective, but the truth does not belong to anyone." Pablo Piccato, *City of Suspects: Crime in Mexico City, 1900–1931* (Durham, NC: Duke University Press, 2001): p. 6. See also Natalie Zemon Davis, *Fiction in the Archives: Pardon Tales and Their Tellers in Sixteenth-Century France* (Stanford: Stanford University Press, 1990); Arlette Farge, *The Allure of the Archives* (New Haven, CT: Yale University Press, 2013).
[12] Richard Roberts, *Litigants and Households: African Disputes and Colonial Courts in the French Soudan, 1895–1912* (Portsmouth: Heinemann, 2005): p. 238.
[13] Wolfgang Friedmann, *Legal Theory* (London: Stevens, 1949): p. 277.

living rooms, as well as in courtrooms – are the building blocks not only of jurisprudence but of individual and collective identities.

Despite these caveats, legal records are a valuable source for social history. Prosaic areas of law, such as property disputes and family matters, reveal that life did not grind to a halt during the war. As Mbanefo would later recall, "it was not all machet[e]s and vicious murders."[14] Even in the most trying periods of the fighting, Biafrans engaged in ordinary activities, some of which brought them to court. They married, divorced, and fought over the custody of children. They sued their neighbors over the boundaries of property and pursued debts owed to them. Land disputes, which are a constant feature of Nigerian jurisprudence then and now, continued through the mayhem.[15] Yet the war cast a shadow over everything. Even the most banal cases could erupt into violence, sometimes in the courtroom itself. The disputes that people brought to court were sharpened by famine, and nearly anything could be a matter of life and death. The war touched all areas of life, including those away from the front.

The title of this chapter refers to an aspect of legal ritual – one that illustrates how the war worked its way into everyday life. In Biafra's courts, a witness could swear an oath to speak the truth not only on a holy book or a fetish, but on a gun. The boilerplate phrase "sworn on the gun" appears as the first line of hundreds of testimonies and affidavits. This was not the first time when firearms were put to this purpose; guns have symbolic meanings everywhere, and their role in ritual (legal and otherwise) is known throughout the continent.[16] Yet gun-oathing became far more common in Biafra's courts than it had been prior to the war. In the past, only certain types of witnesses would choose to swear on a gun. Those who did so were usually hunters or ritualists, who also sometimes swore oaths on *jujus*, knives, or other power objects. Christians usually swore on Bibles, and Muslims on the

---

[14] Ekong Sampson, *Evergreen Memories of Sir Louis Mbanefo* (Lagos: Lomanc Books, 2002): p. 117.

[15] See, for example, NNAE BCA 1/3/9, in the Court of Appeal of the Republic of Biafra, Orlu, no. CA/11/69, *Ugwueze Ahamefula and other v. U. Nganagbaje and others*, August 5, 1968.

[16] In the growing Africanist literature on the technology of the firearm, see Giacomo Macola, *The Gun in Central Africa: A History of Technology and Politics* (Athens: Ohio University Press, 2015); Aderinto, *Guns and Society*. See also Joseph P. Smaldone, *Warfare in the Sokoto Caliphate: Historical and Sociological Perspectives* (Cambridge: Cambridge University Press, 1977).

Koran.[17] During the war, a broader array of Biafrans swore to speak the truth on firearms – they included people as varied as a soldier accused of rape, a Nigerian Airways stewardess testifying against her abusive husband, and a pastor who defrauded his congregants. Perhaps they meant nothing by choosing guns over Bibles; but, even if it was unconscious, this small decision was a symptom of a larger infection. A martial spirit overtook Biafra, and the violence of the battlefield bled out into daily life.

Many who lived through the war lamented that they lost their sense of security in Biafra and never regained it. Before the war it was not risky to be out at night, to travel the roads, or to keep valuables at home – all would tempt fate after 1967.[18] As a local politician recalled, "in the past the eastern part of the country hardly knew armed robbery. But when somebody is hungry it had to be done out of necessity. People were compelled by necessity. That is how crimes like that grew."[19] This chapter considers the incidence of armed robbery and other violence in the period of the Nigerian blockade, describing how the technologies and behaviors of war crossed between the battlefield and civilian life. It then moves on to analyze acts by soldiers and civilians as told through the Biafran legal record and concludes by considering how conscription and desertion fed into the war's furor. Violence in Biafra was unpredictable, and it took many different forms, but that does not mean that it was inscrutable.[20] What follows is a disquieting catalogue of

[17]   Oath-swearing on jujus and other power objects was a subject of dispute in the colonial period as well. On oaths in the Native Courts of Calabar Province, see David Pratten, *The Man-Leopard Murders: History and Society in Colonial Nigeria* (Edinburgh: Edinburgh University Press, 2007): pp. 253–257. Bastian also notes the significance of knife-swearing in the hearings following the 1929 Aba Women's War, see Misty Bastian, "Vultures of the Marketplace: Southeastern Nigerian Women and the Discourses of the *Ogu Umunwaanyi* (Women's War) of 1929," in Jean Allman et. al., eds., *Women in African Colonial Histories* (Bloomington: Indiana University Press, 2002).

[18]   Douglas Anthony cites several informants who made this connection between the war and the danger of crime as well. See Douglas A. Anthony, *Poison and Medicine: Ethnicity, Power, and Violence in a Nigerian City, 1966–1986* (Portsmouth: Heinemann, 2002): pp. 186–187.

[19]   Interview with Chief A. N. Kanu, Umuahia, March 9, 2015.

[20]   As the political scientist Stathis Kalyvas writes, violence in all of the many iterations that it takes in civil war, "is never a simple reflection of the optimal strategy of its users; its profoundly interactive character defeats simple maximization logics while producing surprising outcomes." Stathis N. Kalyvas,

transgressions – a "Part About the Crimes," to borrow Roberto Bolaño's phrase – that add up to a phenomenology of wartime violence.[21] There is nothing "African" about this violence. Many societies respond to the prospect of annihilation by consuming themselves, and what took place in Biafra says more about the corrosive effects of warfare than it does about the qualities of the society that went through it.

Martial Violence, Crime, and Vigilantism

"Gunfire," recalled a memoirist, "was the heartbeat of Biafra."[22] There was not a moment in the two and a half years of Biafra's existence when it was not at war. Violence was a fixture of Biafran life – both as an everyday reality and a discursive force. Violent crime was not unprecedented, but the forms it took in Biafra were new and disconcerting to judges and the public alike. In public memory, prewar eastern Nigeria had not been a dangerous place. The east had avoided the political violence that occurred elsewhere during the First Republic, and the general consensus was that everyday crime had not been a major problem before the war. The memory of having been subjected to violence, however, was deeply engrained in Biafrans' sense of themselves. Many experiences fed into this ethos of victimhood; the brutality of the Atlantic trade in enslaved people, the coerced labor of the palm trade that followed it, the "pacifications" of the early colonial period, and the suppression of strikes and rebellions by the British – all figured in Biafra's national consciousness.

Yet no memory loomed as large as the most recent one. Independence responded directly to the anti-Igbo pogroms of 1966, and the argument for a separate Biafran national identity was closely tied to that experience.[23] Persecution loomed in Biafra's state ideology, and its memory was one of Biafra's lodestars. Violence was ubiquitous in Biafran iconography; a series of Biafran postage stamps issued in 1968 to commemorate the victims of the pogroms of 1966 featured

The Logics of Violence in Civil War (Cambridge: Cambridge University Press, 2006): p. 388

[21] Roberto Bolaño, *2666* (Barcelona: Anagrama, 2004): p. 441.
[22] Bob Ejike, *Weapons of Biafra: A Child's Account of the Nigerian Civil War* (Lagos: Gik Communications, 2003): p. 109.
[23] Interview with Dr. Jacob Ibik, SAN, Enugu, September 26, 2014.

a graphic image of a decapitated corpse. An army officer described how he rallied his men: "I have laboured to illustrate from history a catalogue of man's inhumanity to man, series of injustices and political domination we have suffered in the past from the hands of the Hausa/Fulani vandals, and for which we have all decided together to say 'no more.'"[24] As a sign painted over the entrance to a military base near Aba optimistically read, "The secret of our miraculous military success is our innocence."[25] As conditions deteriorated, Biafra lost this sense of moral certainty. The lines between soldier and civilian, front and rear, and right and wrong faded away. Predation by Biafran and Nigerian soldiers alike, among whom "discipline is appallingly bad," as a British source reported, became unavoidable.[26] This was to say nothing of starvation and material shortages, which generated their own forms of danger.

More erratic with every passing month, the records of Biafra's disintegrating legal system show how certain kinds of crime and misconduct emerged over the course of the war. They show the lengths Biafrans went to in order to survive – and, in some cases, to turn the chaos of the war to their advantage. Intermittent Nigerian air raids disrupted life in towns and cities, and the blockade and the famine it caused drove people into situations of desperation. Many Biafran soldiers used their positions in the army to survive, but some went beyond mere self-preservation and tried to enrich themselves. Using the authority of a uniform to lay claim to civilians' belongings or labor became common, and the army's ability to control rank-and-file troops (and those to whom they loaned their weapons) diminished sharply as the war went on.[27] All of this added up to a public perception that, as a former magistrate recalled, "one could get away with anything" in Biafra.[28]

Confusion and fear set the tone for how Biafran soldiers and civilians interacted with one another. The fluid conditions of the fighting and the decentralized nature of military authority bred insecurity, especially

[24] NWM uncatalogued collection, "Tour Report on the Propaganda and the Re-Education of Troops" [1968].
[25] Fr. Ikechukwu Orjinta, *The Death of Biafra* (Enugu: Snaap Press, 2000): p. 46.
[26] NAUK FCO 38/285, M.J. Newington, British High Commission, Lagos to Commonwealth Office, January 20, 1968.
[27] As in NNAE BCA 1/2/16, in the Court of Appeal of the Republic of Biafra, Aba, no. CA18/68, *Akpan David and nine others v. The State*, February 7, 1968.
[28] Interview with anonymous informant, Enugu, September 2014.

near the fronts. The vaguely defined lines of military engagement cut through densely populated areas. Biafran soldiers often wore no uniforms and moved back and forth constantly across the lines of battle, operating in small and autonomous units that had little communication with one another. Federal "occupation" of an area often only meant patrol of the road that passed through it, with villages out of sight remaining loyal to Biafra. Guerilla warfare continued in the upstream areas of the Rivers State long after the state had ostensibly been "pacified" by federal forces. Ambushes by small cells of militia members continued throughout the war, including in areas like Nsukka that had reverted to federal control only a few months after secession. In occupied Enugu, which was deserted apart from federal troops and a skeletal Nigerian administration, sporadic attacks by Biafran snipers made the civil servants reluctantly stationed there unwilling to leave their offices in daylight.[29]

The fighting took many forms, but one of its most feared aspects was aerial bombardment.[30] Even when they missed the mark, bombings were psychologically undoing. "The best way to ignore [shelling] was to do something noisy, use the sewing machine, beat the children," recalled Rosina Umelo. "The noise of shelling was heard all over your body. After half an hour your mind ached with longing for it to stop, your limbs were cramped with nervous tension."[31] Like the blockade, Biafrans took the bombing of civilian areas as evidence of Nigeria's genocidal intent. Biafra engaged in air war as well, using a handful of bombers and repurposed civilian aircraft. Their targets included Nigerian military installations, villages near the front, and on several occasions Lagos neighborhoods, especially in the port area of Apapa. Biafran bombings rarely caused substantial loss of life – though this is probably due more to poor equipment than to moral restraint. The Nigerian Air Force's use of fragmentation bombs, which released shrapnel, suggested that the aim of air raids was not just to destroy military installations but to kill as many people as possible. They also appeared indiscriminate. Nigeria's pilots, many of them on secondment

---

[29] Interview with Jerome H. C. Okolo, SAN, Enugu, September 17, 2014.

[30] On aerial bombing generally, see Ihediwa Nkemjika Chimee, "The Nigerian-Biafran War, Armed Conflicts and the Rules of Engagement," in Toyin Falola, Roy Doron, and Okpeh O. Okpeh, eds., *Warfare, Ethnicity and National Identity in Nigeria* (Trenton: Africa World Press, 2013): pp. 126–133.

[31] IWM 6687, Papers of Rosina Umelo, "Biafra, A World of Our Own," p. 182.

from the Egyptian Air Force, usually dropped bombs from a great height in order to avoid endangering themselves. This made campaigns imprecise and unpredictably destructive.[32] A British intelligence report argued that, within Nigeria, "no-one in higher military circles appeared to be giving any thought for the future: their only concern appeared to be to secure military victory by the application of maximum force, whatever the ultimate consequences."[33] Indiscriminate aerial bombings were taken as a sign of that single-mindedness.

Dozens of bombings were described by sympathetic witnesses for the international press, which Nigeria and its allies invariably claimed were exaggerated.[34] One example among many is an Irish priest's description of a market bombing in Ozu Abam:

The market area was a complete shambles, and the buildings around the market square all shattered. Almost every square yard of the market place was covered with dead or nearly dead. Small fires were burning here and there, and I saw several bodies burning. The "walking-wounded" were staggering away from the area, dazed and bleeding. I walked around one part of the market and counted at least 35 corpses. In addition, there were literally hundreds of pieces of bodies – arms, feet, heads – lying everywhere. I gave the last rites to about 25 people who were almost dead.[35]

These grim episodes punctuated life in Biafra. That the violence of this wartime scene spilled over into other areas of life in Biafra surprised few people who were watching the situation closely.

A Biafran attack on a Nigerian detention camp near Nsukka in February 1968 – well within the territory that Nigeria ostensibly controlled – illustrates the fluidity of the military situation. The camp was filled with about a thousand displaced Igbos (Biafra called

---

[32] Foreign intelligence reports support this contention, which sympathetic journalists and Biafran sources had claimed throughout the war: "Egyptians alleged to have told [a British informant] that they did not regard their contract as committing them to any warfare where they could themselves be shot at and they conceived their role exclusively in terms of dropping bombs on undefended targets. Their rule of thumb was to select biggest building visible and to try to drop bombs on it." NAUK FCO 65/366, Extract from diplomatic telegram, March 19, 1969.

[33] NAUK FCO 38/286, E. G. Willan to Mr. L'Estrange, in re: Sam Silla, April 8, 1969.

[34] NAID 2001/43/146, "Note for Minister re Nigerian bombing" [1969].

[35] NAUK FCO 65/366, Statement of Rev. Father Raymond F. Maher on the bombing of Ozu Abam market by the Nigerian Air Force, February 27, 1969.

them "prisoners"), of whom only thirty were men of military age. It was attacked by a force of more than a hundred Biafrans who materialized from the forest, much of which remained under the control of Biafran civil defense organizations and militias. In the middle of the night, as an aid worker reported, "'peculiar' artillery began to land in Nsukka. [The informant] could not identify the weapons and was later told that they were Biafran home-made mortars. Machine guns and small arms gradually joined until there was a brisk fire fight in progress." In the course of the fight, the thirty men in the camp disappeared, leading the Nigerian commander to believe that the attack had been planned from within the camp. An eyewitness noted that some of the Biafran ammunition showed signs of having been buried, suggesting that it had been hidden nearby. The Nigerian Army concluded that the attack could not have been carried out without the cooperation of the villages around Nsukka, all of which had pledged their loyalty to Nigeria. Contrary to Nigeria's confident claims that it controlled this part of Igboland, a British intelligence report concluded that "Biafran 'militia' govern the people who are not immediately under the guns of the Nigerian army." The Nigerian military shut down the water supply in and around the camp for several days in retaliation.[36]

Over time, Biafra conceded its monopolies – both on violence and, in a sense, on officialdom. Vigilantism took off in some places.[37] Law remained important, but in rural areas where policing was thin and courts were distant, informal enactments of justice increased as the state's reach diminished. Life did not come to a halt in even the most abject villages – goods were bought and sold, people fought with one another, stole things, and made and dissolved their families just as they did in peacetime. Biafrans increasingly relied on themselves to settle these local matters. In one illustrative case, a village convened

---

[36] NAUK FCO 38/285, "Observations at Nsukka, February 5–8, 1968," February 14, 1968.

[37] The terms in which African vigilantism is broadly framed are described in Jean Comaroff and John Comaroff, "Policing Culture, Cultural Policing: Law and Social Order in Postcolonial South Africa," *Law and Social Inquiry* vol. 29, no. 3 (Summer 2004): p.515. See also David Pratten and Atreyee Sen, eds., *Global Vigilantes* (New York: Columbia University Press, 2008); Nicholas Rush Smith, *Contradictions of Democracy: Vigilantism and Rights in Post-Apartheid South Africa* (Oxford: Oxford University Press, 2019); Joseph Hellweg, *Hunting the Ethical State: The Benkadi Movement of Cote d'Ivoire* (Chicago: University of Chicago Press, 2011).

a "special tribunal" (not related to the Special Tribunal of Biafra) to arbitrate a dispute between a prominent smuggler and the chairman of the local civil defense committee. It ended with the two men going out "behind the yard to settle their grievances."[38] This was not a perfect system. As Jacob Ibik recalled,

The fear was that "jungle justice" would take over, which could lead to the same kind of situation there that had allowed Igbos to be slaughtered in the north. This happened in some places despite all of our best efforts.[39]

Some vigilante movements seemed to produce more crime than they controlled, and rudimentary enactments of justice by village "courts" fell far short of Biafra's high judicial standards. For this reason and others, lawyers and administrators were wary of this development;[40] but, as the war continued, various forms of "self-defense" came to be seen as necessary evils.

The practical and ethical dilemmas of what Ibik called "jungle justice" were evident in Umuobom, a cluster of hamlets near Orlu. A box of papers from the Civil Defence Committee from this small place offers a unique internal perspective on life in the rural, predominantly Igbo central provinces of Biafra that held out until the end of the war. By the middle of 1969, Umuobom's Civil Defence Committee was responsible for all aspects of its administration. It was effectively self-governing, but the committee's conscientious secretary dutifully sent reports of its meetings and activities to the provincial secretary at Orlu. These improbably preserved files ended up in a storeroom of the National War Museum in Umuahia. The committee's records, rich with small town intrigue and wartime treachery, show how the turn toward civil defense in the later stages of the war shaped conditions in Biafra. If there were no functional courts nearby, as was the case in Umuobom, villages were largely left to their own devices. A localized, idiosyncratic form of administration emerged.

---

[38] NWM uncatalogued collection, "Statement of C.J. Okpara, Local Civil Defence Committee in the case with the Police," December 6, 1969.

[39] Interview with Dr. Jacob Ibik, SAN, Enugu, September 26, 2014.

[40] They were not alone. Vigilantism's usefulness often does not outweigh the fear of what might happen should vigilantes be too successful in performing tasks usually reserved for governments. See the discussion of the South African organization *Mapogo A Mathamaga* in Jean Comaroff and John L. Comaroff, *The Truth About Crime: Sovereignty, Knowledge, Social Order* (Chicago: University of Chicago Press, 2016): pp. 207–217.

Civil defenders practiced an improvisational kind of justice – one that sometimes satisfied local demands, even if not everyone perceived their actions as "just."[41] They routinely investigated crimes and arrested people for theft, assault, and trafficking in humanitarian materials. They also meted out punishments. In Umuobom and elsewhere, however, the civil defense organizations were a poor substitute for a criminal justice system. Their shortcomings were especially clear when soldiers of the regular Biafran Army made trouble. In 1969, Umuobom's civil defenders begged a nearby army camp to incarcerate a sergeant named Adeodatus Echere until the end of the war. The committee complained that Echere had "his own gang who parade at night and make life and properties insecure, He possess a saboteur's tendency of parading these his gang to menace the young farm products."[42] The Biafran Army sometimes investigated claims of misconduct, but it seldom sided against soldiers.[43] In this case, the army denied the request for help, which the less charitable members of the Civil Defence Committee attributed to the fact that some of the soldiers were also members of Echere's gang.

Civil defense organizations drew their membership from women of all ages and men who were too old or infirm to be in the army. Women were often in charge of civil defense, and it is largely for this reason that many former Biafrans remember the war as a time when gender equity was advanced.[44] In many villages, older men resisted the rising profile of women in local affairs. A young woman in Okwu Nguru fought off a conspiracy to unseat her by "a group of men who paraded themselves as village elders," which entailed threats, raucous public meetings, and a scheme to frame her for treason.[45] In places where they were barred from formal leadership, women often controlled financial matters and therefore wielded indirect influence. The Biafran government generally

---

[41] NWM uncatalogued collection, "Arrest of Jonah Anyiani," September 11, 1969.

[42] NWM uncatalogued collection, "Removal or Deportation of a Criminal," November 24, 1969.

[43] NWM uncatalogued collection, "Tracking Down Soldiers' Malpractices," November 7, 1969.

[44] See Egodi Uchendu, *Women and Conflict in the Nigerian Civil War* (Trenton: Africa World Press, 2007): pp. 112–125.

[45] Angelina Ihejirika, *Escape from Nigeria: A Memoir of Faith, Love and War* (Trenton: Africa World Press, 2016): p. 111.

Figure 2.1 Young women in paramilitary training, 1967 (Priya Ramrakha, courtesy of Priya Ramrakha Foundation)

approved of women's involvement.[46] Many were proud of what they did, and some wanted a more active role than they were allowed. "I don't know why Ojukwu won't let women join the army," a female bartender in Umuahia told an American reporter. "In the old days, before the white man came, we women used to fight right along with the men. So why not now?"[47]

The Biafran Army was not the only fighting force in Biafra. There were also several militias, the most important of which was the Biafran Organisation of Freedom Fighters (BOFF), an officially sanctioned "front" that Ojukwu modeled loosely on the Viet Cong. BOFF fighters engaged in guerilla tactics and operated in clandestine cells in Nigerian territory, but they also had a mandate to keep order at home.[48] One BOFF

---

[46] NWM uncatalogued collection, "Women in Civil Defence" [December 1969].

[47] Lloyd Garrison, "In Biafra's Beleaguered Capital, War Is Just Around the Corner," *New York Times*, March 8, 1969, p. 5. Some Biafran women thought of their participation in the war effort as a continuation of the militancy that Igbo women had displayed in the *Ogu Umunwaanyi*, a major anticolonial revolt led by women in Aba in 1929. See Bastian, "Vultures of the Marketplace."

[48] A similar organization that straddled the civilian/military divide was the Land Army, which was a food production scheme established in 1969 to encourage

zonal commander recalled that the fighters also played a role in the organization of aid distribution:

Our job as freedom fighters was partly to cater for the welfare of the sick, the victims of war and the starving civilians. The international agencies had no idea they were working with Biafran guerillas. We wore no uniforms in order to blend and hide among the civilian population undetected. We protected the Relief Organizations, because our collective survival depended on their services.[49]

BOFF members had a price, and some of the less disciplined units operated in ways that had more in common with "gangsterism," as one woman who had worked in civil defense recalled, than with formal military units.[50] The employees of a feeding center at Umucheke complained that the center's administrators were embezzling funds and food:

We have no confidence in them, because we have no trust on them, therefore it is needless to allow them to feed our children and destitutes in this centre in accordance with the situation in the town. ... They failed to listen to the suggestions from the community, instead they are causing confusion and calling BOFF Army against us if we venture telling them to do things as arranged before.[51]

There were many cases where civil defenders, irregular militias, and BOFF units overstepped the boundaries of their authority – which were largely unmarked. The BOFF had an ambiguous relationship with the regular army, and there were frequent disagreements about its structure and responsibilities. The central government saw the danger in giving authority to these groups, warning "that all criminal cases

---

people (mostly women) to more efficiently produce food. Modeled on a military structure, the Land Army attempted to modernize and collectivize farming in order to stem the famine that had unfolded as a result of the blockade. Despite Ojukwu's command for people to "dispel fear from their minds and embrace the 'Land Army' scheme with enthusiasm," the initiative was highly unpopular and did not succeed in producing much food. *Biafra Sun*, March 19, 1969, p. 2.

[49] Ewa Unoke, "Biafra, Human Rights, and Memory: A Transitional Justice Perspective," in Chima J. Korieh and Ifeanyi Ezeonu, eds., *Remembering Biafra: Narrative, History, and Memory of the Nigeria-Biafra War* (Owerri: Goldline and Jacobs, 2010): p. 164.

[50] Interview with Flora Udechukwu, Port Harcourt, February 15, 2015.

[51] NWM uncatalogued collection, Fidelis Iwucha to Civil Defence Committee, Umuobom, January 9, 1969.

should be directed to the law enforcement officers."[52] In practice, there were usually no officers to be found.

Soldiers and Civilians in the Courtroom

There were many opportunities for violence in this arena, where the lines of battle were largely undefined and "the front" could be almost anywhere. Daily life came to seem like a zero-sum game of survival between soldiers and civilians, and acts of personal or private violence – some unconnected to the war – took place under the cover of battle. Confrontations took new forms, and they became deadlier in the presence of firearms. In prewar Nigeria, the most common weapons in murder and manslaughter cases were agricultural tools.[53] During the war, guns became the weapon of choice. Unsurprisingly, the presence of military-grade armaments in the hands of people who were struggling to stay alive shaped how Biafrans interacted with one another. Guns did not necessarily make people more violent, but they made acts of harassment and theft easier and more likely to end in death.[54] Although they had long circulated in eastern Nigeria, there was a substantial difference between the hunting rifles and Dane guns of the past – weapons "as dangerous to the hunters as to the game" – and modern industrial firearms.[55] These arms passed fluidly back and forth between soldiers, civilians, and those who fell somewhere on the spectrum in between.

As the war went on more and more lines blurred; did a Biafran soldier "requisition" a pail of stockfish from a market woman, or did he steal it? If a soldier wearing civilian clothes killed someone at a checkpoint, should he be considered to be on duty even though he

[52] NWM uncatalogued collection, "Meeting of Chairmen, Leaders and Instructors of Local Civil Defence Organization in the Province Held in the Provincial Civil Defence Office, Orlu," November 16, 1968.

[53] Poisons, which were associated with crimes committed by women, were also common.

[54] Judges took notice of this explicitly. See, for example, ESHC uncatalogued collection, in the High Court of the Republic of Biafra, Port Harcourt, no. P/28. c/1967, *The State v. Edwin Martin*, August 19, 1967.

[55] IWM 6687, Papers of Rosina Umelo, "Biafra, A World of Our Own," p. 94. See Samuel Fury Childs Daly, "'Hell was let loose on the country': The Social History of Military Technology in the Republic of Biafra," *African Studies Review* vol. 61, no. 3 (2018).

was out of uniform? What if he had never been issued a uniform in the first place? The Biafran Army looked increasingly like a rabble rather than a disciplined fighting force. In 1969, a soldier recorded in his journal a conversation that he overheard between two Biafran officers. "It is terrible," said one, "all these young officers commit every sort of offense. They are not disciplined at all. Why? Look, AWOL is too much." "It is because they are not well trained," replied the other. "They bring civilian life into the Army. Some of them were criminals in Onitsha. [...] All joined the Army to loot. The young officers were college boys; not very responsible. They wanted to get rich all over-night. Some are interested only in 'attack-trade.'"[56]

Factionalism in Biafra's armed forces exacerbated the situation. Strained by the same deprivations as the rank-and-file, the inexperienced officer corps was riven by internal disputes. Cleavages in the army leadership had emerged early on and were never fully resolved.[57] There were divisions over points of strategy, ideology, personality, and place of origin. Civilians became entangled in conflicts between officers, and the army did not stand outside of local politics. As an officer angrily remembered, "the problem with the Biafran Army was not that they were not gallant, but it was that they protected their own. If you were an officer in the army or responsible for recruiting men for the army you would send them to your rival village to spare your own men."[58] Another lawyer remembered that divisions within the army created "many little wars" within Biafra over rank, rights to property and labor, and other local matters.[59] Combined with the hobbling of the criminal justice system, weak military leadership destabilized daily life.

Arms could also be used to commit acts of sexual violence. Women who worked as traders were especially vulnerable to assault, since they traveled throughout Biafra and the war fronts alone, laden with goods, carrying Nigerian currency and other contraband. Women went to

---

[56] M. Angulu Onwuejeogwu, *A Study in Military Sociology: The Biafran Army, 1967–1970* (Lagos: UTO Publications, 2000): p. 95.

[57] For example, officers who had been in the east during the coup of 1966 often resented those who had come back to the east from their postings elsewhere in Nigeria. Many of the officers from elsewhere outranked their Eastern Region counterparts and felt bitter that they were not immediately integrated into the Biafran Army at the top of the ranks. Bernard Odogwu, *No Place to Hide (Crises and Conflicts Inside Biafra)* (Enugu: Fourth Dimension, 1985): p. 8.

[58] Interview with anonymous informant, Umuahia, March 2015.

[59] Interview with Barinua Moses Wifa, SAN, Port Harcourt, March 5, 2015.

considerable lengths to avoid harassment. Gloria Chuku describes how some women dressed in their finest and tried to pass themselves off as the wives of military officers. Others "painted their bodies dark with charcoal and wore ragged dresses to look unattractive to the soldiers. Some walked with a stoop or limp to make them look like old women. While some tied wads of cloth on their stomach faking pregnancy, others carried tender babies to disguise themselves as nursing mothers."[60] A few tried to wait out the war in hiding.[61] Angelina Ihejirika recalled walking many miles to Okigwe to try to obtain an exit visa in 1969 – a journey in which the possibility of being raped was very real. "Personally, I was not afraid because my strong faith in God had been the pillar on which I was always anchored, even though I still ducked out of sight whenever I heard the sound of or saw a military vehicle."[62]

Cases of sexual violence figure less prominently in the legal record than oral historical accounts of the war suggest they might. There are many possible reasons for this, including low rates of reporting, reluctance on the part of the judiciary to take on cases of sexual assault, and the fact that cases of unlawful sexual conduct were often settled informally.[63] Shame led many women to conceal their experiences of sexual violence, and others were likely pressured into silence by men who felt that the rape of "their" women reflected poorly on them as husbands, brothers, and fathers.[64] In the few extant records of sexual violence by soldiers, Biafran courts rarely doubted women's claims of assault but imposed low penalties on the men charged, especially if the guilty party was "a useful man in the society" or was on active duty.[65] In one high court case, two members of a civil defense militia were

---

[60] Gloria Chuku, "Biafran Women Under Fire: Strategies in Organising Local and Trans-border Trade During the Nigerian Civil War," in Eghosa E. Osaghae, Ebere Onwudiwe, and Rotimi T. Suberu, eds., *The Nigerian Civil War and Its Aftermath* (Ibadan: John Archers, 2002): p. 222.

[61] AdaOkere Agbasimalo, *The Forest Dames* (Milton Keynes: AuthorHouse, 2012).

[62] Ihejirika, *Escape from Nigeria*, pp. 130–131.

[63] Comparatively, see Mary Louise Roberts, *What Soldiers Do: Sex and the American GI in World War II France* (Chicago: University of Chicago Press, 2013); Elizabeth Thornberry, *Colonizing Consent: Rape and Governance in South Africa's Eastern Cape* (Cambridge: Cambridge University Press, 2019).

[64] Bird and Ottanelli, *The Asaba Massacre*, pp. 118–122.

[65] ESHC uncatalogued collection, in the High Court of the Republic of Biafra, Achina, no. O/102c/69, *The State v. Simeon Onuasoanya and Peter Mbaetaka Alias Ikonkwu*, July 11, 1969.

found to have illegally arrested a group of female students. On the pretext that they had violated a curfew, the women were

detained at the check point for three hours and then were taken on a night patrol into the bush at about 1 a.m., a most ungodly hour. There all alone with a complete stranger, and far out in the bush where no one can hear her shouts, there and in those circumstances 2nd P.W. was alleged to have consented to an act of sexual intercourse with the 1st accused.

The case turned on whether the women had consented to having sex with their captors. Justice Oputa found that they had not consented, ruling that "the whole atmosphere of this case is to my mind designed to breed fear and alarm."[66] To the Biafran judiciary, this and other cases were evidence that public order was collapsing. Misconduct by soldiers and militia members was becoming uncontrollable.

Biafran society seemed to be coming apart at the seams. Of all the forms of violence that took place there, the one that most denoted the breakdown of order, and provoked the most horror, was cannibalism. Talk of it far outpaced its actual incidence, but the legal record reveals that a handful of people traded and ingested human flesh in the depths of famine. All were motivated by hunger. Even though it was more rumor than fact, cannibalism became a rallying point for anxiety about the collapse of order and an emblem of the dehumanizing effects of the Nigerian blockade. The fear of unwittingly buying human remains in the marketplace was a topic of frequent, wary discussion in the enclave.[67] The Biafran government did not wish to publicize stories of cannibalism abroad, but it made no attempt to suppress them in the local press.

In December 1969, a sergeant in the Biafran Army gave a gruesome deposition before a tribunal near Aba.[68] He and a group of five others stood accused of fatally shooting a woman loitering near the front at Abayi and selling her remains as food to starving villagers nearby. The charge was first brought by his horrified brigade commander before being transferred to the Special Tribunal. Implicating his comrades in the hope of receiving a lighter sentence, the sergeant described how he got some friends to cut the woman's body into pieces

of various sizes, I gave Irondi two pieces, about eight pieces to Nwafor, two pieces to Onyedinma and Emmanuel was given about twenty pieces . . . The

---

[66] Ibid.   [67] NAUK FCO 23/182, extract from the *Irish Press*, May 23, 1968.
[68] NNAE MINJUST 116/1/11, Charge Against BA/148304, [1969].

main reason why Onyeuma and Silas reported me to our 2IC [deputy commander] is because I did not share the flesh of the dead woman equally with them. I usually give Emmanuel a flesh to eat whenever I return from oppressions in the bush. I am a rocket launcher and master of many types of instruments and weapons. After launching rockets, we usually collect kits and if a nice flesh is seen we invite civilians to take such flesh for eating.[69]

The sergeant told them that, if anyone asked, they should claim it was a Nigerian soldier's flesh – consuming the enemy was marginally less repugnant than a compatriot (which the deceased in fact was).[70] Like many Biafran trials, this one was disrupted by unspecified "war activities," and it was left unresolved. The fragment that remains of the trial is an extreme example of how military conflict, humanitarian crisis, and violence wove together. Perhaps more than any of the other cases described here, it illustrates the desperation to which the Nigerian blockade drove people.[71] The judges and administrators involved found this case extremely repulsive, but they followed due process nonetheless.

Shocking crimes like this were not unthinkable. Courts recognized that abhorrent acts were committed out of desperation – and even the most brutal of them could be crimes of survival. The war was a major extenuating circumstance, and there was no use pretending that conditions were normal. This is especially clear in post-conviction statements of allocutus, where those found guilty of crimes could appeal to the court for mercy in the hope of receiving a lenient sentence. In these statements, Biafrans explained that they acted from desperation; starvation, fear, and madness from grief all feature prominently in them. Courts and tribunals often sympathized with people accused of assault, as in the case of a schoolteacher who became involved in a tussle over some black market food because he and his pregnant wife had been "dying of starvation." He had already been detained and beaten by the army, and the tribunal recommended his release in recognition of his hardship, despite finding him guilty.[72] In a similar case, a young

[69] NNAE MINJUST 116/1/11, Deposition of Ude Chinedu, Exhibit 1 in *State v. Ude Chinedu and five others*, December 16, 1969.

[70] NNAE MINJUST 116/1/11, "Translated statement by Nwafor [illegible]," December 7, 1969.

[71] Later, Nigerian courts would express repulsion about the consumption of human flesh during the war. See, for example, Supreme Court of Nigeria Law Reports 166/1971, *U. Nwokoronkwo v. The State*, January 20, 1972.

[72] NNAE MINJUST 19/2/3, in the Special Tribunal of the Republic of Biafra, no. CX/267A/69, *The State v. Samuel Arokewe and four others*, January 24, 1969.

woman who brandished a gun at a market seller to steal a bag of spoiled grain was acquitted despite clear evidence of her guilt. Gesturing to the conditions outside the courtroom, the judge remarked that "her senses have been driven low by our current state."[73]

Both the practice of property crime and the ethics attached to it changed over the course of the war. In addition to being a criminal offense, armed robbery was a touchstone for broader conversations about morality. In the early stages of the war, Biafran courts tended to see theft as a function of greed, leading them to impose harsh sentences.[74] This moral opprobrium waned as the war went on, as judges and tribunals imposed lighter sentences and acquitted accused armed robbers. Biafra's judges appreciated that the conditions of war made people desperate, and the law could not ignore that fact. Humanitarian crisis undid the bright-line moral order that Biafra's leaders had hoped to establish.

That said, not all crimes were crimes of survival. The war was also an opportunity to settle old scores, and Biafrans used the presence of soldiers in their towns and villages to advance their personal interests. Soldiers could be hired to guard a disputed piece of land, sent to conscript a rival, or be paid to harass a competitor. In one case, a landowner claimed that his neighbor had recklessly shot off a prohibited gun and then planted ammunition on the landowner's property and reported him to the police. The Biafran attorney general remarked that "it has become a common practice for people here to make false reports to the Army Authority against their opponents with the result that their opponents are brutally manhandled and at times kidnapped by soldiers."[75] In another case, Georgina Eke conspired with a Biafran soldier to beat, detain, and rob her sister of a large sum of money that she claimed was owed to her. The sister complained to the military police, and the Special Tribunal of Biafra charged the soldier with robbery. Since he had committed the crime in uniform, he was also charged with offenses "against the public welfare of the

---

[73] ESHC uncatalogued collection, in the High Court of the Republic of Biafra, Owerri, no. OW/43/69, *The State v. Marjorie Ifedigbo*, July 10, 1969.

[74] See for example, ESHC uncatalogued collection, in the High Court of the Republic of Biafra, Port Harcourt, no. LOW/4.3.c/66, *The State v. Benson Okopoafor*, June 19, 1967.

[75] NNAE MINJUST 123/1/1, *In re: Inspector General of Police v. Ben Eneregbu and another*, December 16, 1967.

inhabitants of this Republic." Georgina Eke was imprisoned and her soldier accomplice was officially reprimanded.[76] The most common cases like this were attempts to evict rival claimants to agricultural land. In one, a farmer took the opportunity of the chaos following a Nigerian bombing to fence in part of his neighbor's plot and plant it with cassava. He then paid two Biafran soldiers to threaten the neighbor to discourage him from taking the matter to the police. He did so anyway, and in the case before the local magistrate it emerged that the land had long been in dispute between the two farmers. The magistrate ruled in favor of the complainant, though no judgment was made with regard to the soldiers who had hired themselves out.[77]

Soldiers played an important role in the life of villages, and their actions were not limited to causing disorder and requisitioning goods. They became deeply embroiled in civilian affairs, sometimes acting as self-appointed agents of the law. In June 1968, Stella Amanaso accused a neighbor of sexually assaulting her five-year-old daughter. When she threatened to complain, he hired a group of soldiers to beat her up. "But when they came," she testified in Igbo, "I showed them what had happened to my daughter. The soldiers then took me, my daughter and the accused to the police station. The police then took us to hospital where my daughter was examined." The civilian defendant, Sunday Agwu, said that he was falsely accused by Amanaso, whom he claimed was a prostitute who had given him gonorrhea and was now trying to get rid of him. He testified that a meddling neighbor had "told Stella last night to enter [break her daughter's hymen] so that I will saffar de consequence."[78] Amanaso admitted to prostitution but not to the rest of it. The magistrate believed her, and Agwu was sentenced to prison. The soldiers emerged as the heroes of the day. The magistrate commended them for turning against the man who had hired them, overlooking the fact that they had accepted payment to assault a woman in the first place. In this setting, matters that might otherwise have been

[76] NNAE MINJUST 116/1/3, in the Special Tribunal of the Republic of Biafra, Nbawsi, no. ST/11c/69, *The State v. Philip Mbuko*, November 25, 1969.
[77] NNAE MINJUST 42/1/4, in the Magistrate's Court of the Republic of Biafra, Aguata, no. MAW/118e/69, *Inspector General of Police v. Ofojebe Okpala*, March 20, 1969.
[78] NNAE MINJUST 1/5/19, in the High Court of the Republic of Biafra, Aba, no. A/45c/6a, *The State v. Sunday Agwu*, August 19, 1968.

clear – here, that all parties except the child had broken the law – became murky.

Other forms of nonviolent crime added to the sense that things were falling apart. Drug use, although not common in matter of fact, was a source of much public concern. Biafra stringently enforced drug laws and continued to do so even after resources had become very limited. One lawyer argued that trading morphine and other pharmaceuticals "would have been easy" given that the state was preoccupied by other concerns, but most people had no interest and few would have had the money to buy them anyway.[79] A few Biafrans depended on marijuana to escape the hardships of wartime life. When a jobless deserter in Agba was turned in by his aunt for growing marijuana, he was unrepentant:

The reason why I smoke it "gay" [marijuana] and cultivate it is because I know myself and I do not misbehave as other people. ... I have snuffed it, smoked it, used the leaves in making soup, porridge and drank it with wine. I wanted to see what effect it would have in me but I still discovered no bad effect except goodness.[80]

The court was unmoved by this defense. To judges, cannabis was a sign of a broader social malady and a symptom of unemployment, alienation, and the anomie of warfare.[81]

Conscripts and Deserters

Biafra is often remembered as a war between mercenaries. Indeed, in the first eighteen months of the conflict the Biafran government experimented with the use of mercenaries, including Europeans, Americans, South Africans, and Rhodesians.[82] Yet Biafra's military leadership soon became disenchanted with them; a series of tactical failures and acts of insubordination, together with the high cost of using foreign "soldiers of fortune,"

---

[79] Interview with Anthony Mogboh, SAN, Enugu, October 2, 2014.

[80] NNAE MINJUST 42/1/4, "Statement of Accused – Cletus Okeke," April 29, 1969.

[81] For a more extensive discussion of cannabis in independent Nigeria, see Matthew M. Heaton, *Black Skins, White Coats: Nigerian Psychiatrists, Decolonization, and the Globalization of Psychiatry* (Athens: Ohio University Press, 2013): p. 169.

[82] A personal recollection of this impetuous group of men can be found in Al J. Venter, *Biafra's War 1967–1970: A Tribal Conflict in Nigeria That Left a Million Dead* (Solihull: Helion and Company, 2015): pp. 212–222.

made it clear that the war could not be won by an army led by a handful of foreigners – at least some of whom were reckless and impulsive.[83] In November 1968, Ojukwu abruptly dismissed the mercenaries working for Biafra, telling reporters that "it cuts across everything we believe, to find our struggle for survival led by white mercenaries."[84] Perhaps the real reason, as one journalist surmised, was that "their contribution to the Biafran war effort has been marginal, and they have cost a great deal of money," or, as was widely rumored, that one of them had drunkenly berated Ojukwu over a point of strategy.[85] Colorful as their behavior was, journalists exaggerated the importance of foreign fighters.[86] This over-stated role has carried over into many histories of Biafra. Far more important for the story of the conflict were the experiences of ordinary Biafran soldiers, most of them conscripts, who seldom caught the attention of the international press.

Conscription was a matter of life and death. In the early months of the war, a piece of propaganda circulated in Biafra featuring a picture of a ten-year-old child dressed in a baggy uniform. It was captioned: "there is none too small or too big for the important job of defending the Fatherland. The young 'officer' above has sworn to bring back ten heads of Nigerian soldiers in strict obedience to the charge made to the nation."[87] This was not meant to be taken literally at the begin-ning of the war, but by its end the Biafran Army counted both children and the elderly among its ranks. Press-ganging adolescents, old men, and the physically or mentally incapacitated was not legal, but it was widespread. Churches and government agencies could petition the Biafran government to exempt their employees from military service, but that did not prevent them from being drafted (or "kidnapped" – it was a fine line) by militias and rogue units of the

---

[83] The justifiable fear that their allegiance could be bought by Nigeria was also probably behind the decision to stop using them. South African National Defence Force Archive, Pretoria [hereafter SADF] MIL INT GP6, Box 28, "Discussion Between Brig. Palmer, Maj. Fortuin and Zeederberg," September 22, 1967.

[84] NAUK FCO 65/362, Quoted in transcript of BBC African Service, November 28, 1968.

[85] NAUK FCO 65/362, Clipping from *The Economist*, February 15, 1969.

[86] The fixation on white mercenaries has had a similarly occluding effect on the history of Katanga. See Erik Kennes and Miles Larmer, *The Katangese Gendarmes and War in Central Africa: Fighting Their Way Home* (Bloomington: Indiana University Press, 2016): p. 190.

[87] *Biafra Sun*, July 12, 1967, p. 5.

Biafran Army.[88] Conscription was similarly chaotic on the Nigerian side; one officer tasked with raising the Second Infantry Division "recruited" his men from Kirikiri Prison in Lagos. When the poorly trained men tried to desert from their first military engagement, he staged a mock execution to whip them into shape.[89]

Conscription gave soldiers unchecked authority to seize or detain people, but soldiers were not the only ones who captured people. Recruitment became, as one Biafran bureaucrat complained, a "free-for-all," and it became hard to parse it from abduction and extortion.[90] Rosina Umelo related how two stragglers posed as soldiers, kidnapped a passerby, and demanded a bribe from him. The ploy backfired, and the man ended up trying to extort his would-be kidnappers. In the end, all of them were conscripted by real Biafran soldiers.[91] As the war went on the process became increasingly arbitrary, and it was unclear who was empowered to draft men and who could be drafted. In practice, any man of almost any age could be pressed into military service, and it meant an immediate and irreversible loss of liberty. The conscription of women, while uncommon, occasionally took place. When a group of young women turned up among the recruits brought to an army camp near Orlu, an officer dismissed them but only after asking his superiors whether they were fair game.[92] The labor of able-bodied men was also requisitioned for tasks like digging trenches, which reminded people of the forced labor policies of the colonial period.[93] By the middle of 1968, there were no uniforms given out and almost no training given to new recruits, and a soldier was lucky if he was issued a gun before being sent to the front.

Conscription sometimes took the form of a communal exercise. Villages were told to collect a certain number of men – sometimes more than were present – and bring them to the nearest army base.

[88] NWM uncatalogued collection, H.E. Meniru, B.G.C. Ltd. to Chairman, Civil Defence, Orlu, July 30, 1969.
[89] Bird and Ottanelli, *The Asaba Massacre*, pp. 14–15.
[90] NNAE MINJUST 21/1/2, M.O.I. Idigo to Solicitor-General, Enugu, March 17, 1969.
[91] Her account is fictionalized, but it was drawn from real experience. Rosina Umelo, *The Man Who Ate the Money* (Ibadan: Oxford University Press, 1978): pp. 69–77.
[92] NWM uncatalogued collection, "Recruitment into BA" [1969].
[93] NWM uncatalogued collection, "Provincial Zone F Defense," November 27, 1969.

The consequences for failing to produce them were serious, which led to raid-like attacks on neighboring villages if enough men could not be found. An administrator wrote to a province that had fallen short of its recruitment targets that "neglect and carelessness in dealing with the problem is suicidal. You can well understand why any village which defaults in making full contribution to troop requirement is regarded as working against the interest of Biafra. This warning will not be repeated."[94] The collection of "taxes" for the war effort often accompanied conscription drives. The largest were the "jet levies," which required villages to raise funds in cash and in kind, theoretically to purchase fighter planes but in fact mostly to keep the Biafran government afloat. Villages that failed to raise the money were singled out for especially brutal recruitment drives as punishment.[95] In the later stages of the war, as a lawyer recalled, "the only time you would see a man in uniform is if he was trying to conscript men or collect money."[96]

Conscripts were both the victims and the perpetrators of violence, and conscription overlapped with crime in complicated ways. In November 1969, Abraham Daniel testified before the Special Tribunal that he was robbed by Biafran soldier Simon Atulobi and two of his accomplices in the village of Okpuala Ngwa.[97] He claimed that his home was invaded in the middle of the night by a group of men, who accused him of harboring deserters. The soldiers threatened to "take him to the war front or shoot him" if he did not reveal where he was hiding them. All of this was a ploy to extort him for money, which Daniel eventually gave them. To add insult to injury, the soldiers demanded that his daughter provide them with "drinks and chicken pepper soup." As the food was being prepared, a second, larger group of soldiers – who were *also* on a mission to round up stragglers in the area – showed up and began to question Atulobi and his men. Atulobi lied that he was the man's brother and that he was dealing with a family matter, but the second group of soldiers did not believe him. Seeing that he had been severely beaten, and finding no evidence that Abraham

---

[94] NWM uncatalogued collection, "Recruitment into the Biafran Army," November 15, 1969.

[95] NWM uncatalogued collection, Civil Defence Committee, Umuobom to Provincial Secretary, Orlu, September 26, 1969.

[96] Interview with Mike Onwuzunike, Enugu, September 14, 2014.

[97] NNAE MINJUST 116/1/14, in the Special Tribunal of the Republic of Biafra, Nbawsi, no. ST/17c/1969, *The State v. Simon Atulobi, Edward Offong and Shem Emereole*, November 26, 1969.

Daniel had harbored deserters, the second group of soldiers turned around and arrested Atulobi and his men instead.

The accused soldiers testified that, although they had originally come looking for deserters, they beat Daniel because they found ammunition in his possession. Finding ammunition, sometimes after planting it, was a common ruse for soldiers to demand food and money from civilians. The possession of ammunition by civilians was theoretically a treasonable offense in Biafra, but soldiers knew that many people had bullets and gunpowder for peaceable reasons.[98] Atulobi also testified that Daniel had paid them to not turn him in to the police. He indignantly argued that, if the second group of soldiers had not turned up, the matter would have been resolved – Daniel had paid off the soldiers and they had confiscated the ammunition and beaten him up as punishment. In their minds, justice had been done. It is telling that the soldiers, who had no legal counsel, thought this would be a reasonable defense. By this late stage in the war, violence of this type had become so common that the defendants could admit to it with no fear of the consequences. Indeed, they were right – the tribunal ultimately ruled that Daniel's actions, especially giving the soldiers food and drinks after they demanded it, were "inconsistent with what a victim of a robbery would do." Daniel was convicted of subversion for the ammunition, and the soldiers were unconditionally released. Even though the decision confidently asserted that justice had been done, this case and others like it challenged the idea that soldiers were bound by law. Here, the court turned a blind eye to what the Biafran Army did to replenish ranks depleted by death and desertion.

The complement of conscription was desertion.[99] The need for new conscripts was so great not only because men were dying in battle but

[98] In addition to hunting and ritual uses, gunpowder was commonly used as a medicine to treat deformities. There were a few cases before the Special Tribunal where people who used gunpowder in this way were charged with treason. NNAE MINJUST 116/1/10, in the Special Tribunal of the Republic of Biafra, no. ST/31c/1969, *The State v. Pte. Job Anyim*, November 13, 1969.

[99] The incidence of desertion from the Biafran Army was high. A survey of Biafran courts martial conducted in the 1980s (from records which are no longer extant) found that more than 40 percent of the offenses investigated by the Biafran Army were for desertion and absence without leave. Acts of theft were the second most common at 13 percent, followed by false statements at 8 percent. The methodology for this study was suspect, but its broad conclusion that these were the most common forms of indiscipline in the Biafran Army is

because many deserted the Biafran Army as things went from bad to worse.[100] Acts of desertion were harshly punished when they went before tribunals – early on by execution but later by sending deserters for hard labor at the front where, as one memoirist recalled, "they never had a chance of ever returning."[101] In the chaos of the collapsing state, however, most deserters could be confident that they would not be caught. Falling morale and the army's growing inability to monitor its troops – let alone compel them to fight – encouraged many men to simply walk away from their units and return home. Abandoning duty did not attract much stigma, and villages went to great lengths to conceal deserters so that when the anti-stragglers units arrived they would not be able to find any young men.[102] Few of these deserters were exactly "hiding" – most of them were known to village administrators, and the Biafran government accepted that soldiers went to live at home when their bases could no longer support them; but most men would rather that their whereabouts not be known.

Even though Biafra was a highly militarized society, military service carried little prestige. As the refrain of a popular song from the era went, "the parents of a solider are childless."[103] Honor was not much of a lure, and neither were the more tangible things that the army might have offered. Rations dwindled to nothing, and "going to fight in the battle field was like going to be tied up for the firing squad," as a Biafran infantryman recalled.[104] Morale declined precipitously

---

corroborated by oral sources. Onwuejeogwu, *A Study in Military Sociology*, p. 101.

[100] There were sporadic desertions from the Nigerian side as well. In December 1968, for example, a group of approximately 800 soldiers deserted in and around Asaba. Where they went and what they did with their arms was not clear. NAID 2000/14/ 24, Paul Keating, Ambassador of Ireland to Nigeria to Department of External Affairs, Dublin, December 6, 1968.

[101] Ernest N. Onuoha, *Biafra: The Victims* (Enugu: Alliance Publications Nigeria Limited, 2012): p. 37.

[102] NWM uncatalogued collection, "Recruitment and Stragglers Drive" [September 1969]. See also Dulue Mbachu, *War Games* (Lagos: New Gong, 2005): pp. 140–143.

[103] Odogwu, *No Place to Hide*, p. 249. Colonel Joe Achuzia of the Biafran Army later recalled that, in Asaba, "the highest insult that can be bestowed to a family is to say that one is a soldier." When his mother saw him in uniform, she vowed never to speak to him again. "Chief Joe Achuzia," in Momoh, *The Nigerian Civil War*, p. 252.

[104] Thomas Enunwe (Omenka), *The Biafran War: The Story of an Orphan* (Ojo: Teg Commercial Enterprises, 2005): p. 159.

when the hunger of the blockade set in and Biafra was no longer on the offensive. Shortages made soldiers raucous, and the pride that Biafrans had in their army in the first year of the war gave way to fear.[105] Sometimes the structure of command broke down entirely. In Aba, a division of the Biafran Army came under the sway of a spiritualist calling himself "Doctor Wise" and would follow orders from no one but him.[106] The commander of an army camp near Orlu lamented the "dismaying panic that ensues in this camp whenever the Air Raid alarm is sounded," and officers constantly found fault with enlisted men for running from battle.[107] In the early years of the war, as one employee of the propaganda directorate remembered,

it was easy to get everyone in the war mood. But when "sabotage" found its way into our war dictionary, the morale of the troops crashed down to the very bottom. . . . In many locations we found troops who had grounded their arms and refused to move again. In some we found those who were insisting on the blood of their commanders.[108]

The presence of so many deserters in Biafran towns – some of them armed – had serious implications for crime.

Checkpoints had been set up all over Biafra to find deserters (of whom there were many) and Nigerian spies (who were far fewer). At these checkpoints, fugitives, soldiers, and civilians encountered one another, sometimes with violent results. In October 1968, a group of seven palm tappers between the ages of six and twelve had their bicycles and palm knives seized while fleeing Okigwe after it fell to "the Hausas." One of the children testified before the Special Tribunal that the soldiers manning the checkpoint told them that "we should take oath that we are not enemies."

He took me to a place where he said I was to take oath. 1st accused told me to undress. I did as I was told. He asked me to kneel down, and raise my hands to the heavens and then place my hands on the ground. I did so as he said this was the method of taking oath in their village. One man wanted to hit my head with a stick. I dodged but it hit my right shoulder.

---

[105] Interview with Comfort Chukwu, Owerri, July 22, 2014.
[106] Alexander Madiebo, *The Nigerian Revolution and the Biafran War* (Enugu. Fourth Dimension, 1980): p. 358
[107] NWM uncatalogued collection, "Anti-Aircraft Drill," October 5, 1968.
[108] NWM uncatalogued collection, "Re-Education Team – Functions," June 8, 1968.

One of them, a six-year-old boy, was killed in the course of the "oathing." The rest of the children managed to run away, and they reported the soldiers at a nearby army post. After being brought before a military tribunal in Umuahia, the soldiers defended their actions by saying that the palm wine tappers were deserters from the Biafran Army. One testified that he saw the children abandon their uniforms in the bush, which two of the three tribunal members did not believe. The tribunal sided with the prosecution, believing that the child "had never been in the army before and could not have been because of his tender age. If he could not, it is very unlikely that the deceased, could have been in the army at the age of six years." The Special Tribunal concluded that the children could not have been deserters, but the fact that there was even a debate about whether the six-year-old might be a soldier suggests that the presence of minors in the Biafran Army was plausible. Addressing the spectators crowded at the back of the room, the lead judge issued a warning of what would happen if behavior like this went unchecked:

No one has a right to kill another Biafran on the mere pretext that the person being killed is an enemy infiltrator. The burden becomes heavier on the accused to explain how he can be justified for killing an unarmed boy of six years of age, and who produced a pass showing that he had come from Okigwe as a refugee. . . . If persons are at liberty to kill at random no one will be stopped. What will stop a person killing his enemy on the pretext that the enemy is either an infiltrator or a straggler?

The soldiers were found guilty and executed.[109] This was a demoralizing trial, and it was a stark illustration of how far the reality of life in Biafra had fallen from the ideal that led it to independence.[110]

Conclusion

In 1968, Ojukwu gave a speech in Aba, where several civilians had turned against the Biafran soldiers quartered in their houses. In a rage, he accused the people of Aba of being murderers and cannibals,

---

[109] NNAE MINJUST 116/1/1, in the Special Tribunal of Biafra, *The State v. Emmanuel Eke Onwuachimba and six others* [1969].

[110] The case also illustrates the fuzziness of jurisdictional questions in the context of the fighting. In his decision, the tribunal's chair remarked that a case like this would have been better tried before a High Court but that, given the circumstances, a hearing before the Special Tribunal would have to do.

"produced from behind a screen four persons who had been caught and had confessed to the killing and eating of Biafran soldiers," and burst into tears as he stormed off the dais. Ojukwu declared the entire city a military area and ordered that those responsible for having killed Biafran soldiers "should be rounded up and publicly shot or hanged."[111] The crackdown was swift and vindictive, but by this point conditions in Biafra were too far gone for it to have much effect.[112] Ojukwu's speech was typically hyperbolic – probably no soldiers had been eaten – but he was correct that theft and violence were rampant. The state had little capacity to administer places like Aba, and soldiers and civilians harassed one another with impunity. If Biafra ever had been a "real" state, it looked much less like one after the midpoint of the war.

These cases about violence, firearms, and excessive military force show how security frayed over the course of the war. The Special Tribunal and other legal institutions tried to maintain some semblance of public order and to contain the excesses of men in uniform; but, as its records show, the war jammed the machinery of law. The wide availability of weapons, the hardship of the blockade, and the diminishing ability of the Biafran government to keep the peace – through a civilian judiciary or otherwise – conspired to create a situation where acts of violence were increasingly unavoidable and even normal. It was at this point that armed robbery came into focus as a criminological phenomenon.[113] In postwar Nigeria, it would become a national problem; but even after armed crime had become common, it never lost its capacity to shock and disturb.

Godwin Egbuna (alias Captain Blood), the ringleader of the gang described at the beginning of the chapter, disappears from the public

---

[111] Ntieyong U. Akpan, *The Struggle for Secession, 1966–1970: A Personal Account of the Nigerian Civil War* (London: Frank Cass, 1971): p. 195.

[112] This crackdown, entailing summary trials, public executions, and the implementation of strict curfews, is also described by Aba Province's administrator in his memoir of the war. See Ben Gbulie, *The Fall of Biafra* (Enugu: Benlie Publishers, 1989).

[113] Under military rule, social scientists tended to stay away from studies of crime and policing, but the handful of quantitative analyses of armed robbery from the time broadly corroborate this account. For an overview of this literature, see Tekena Tamuno, "Trends in Policy: The Police and Prisons," in Tekena Tamuno, ed., *Nigeria Since Independence: The First Twenty-Five Years*, Vol. 4 (Ibadan: Heinemann, 1989).

record with his conviction. He may have died toward the end of the war, or changed his name, or perhaps like many former Biafrans he simply chose to keep a low profile after 1970. The archive gives no indication of what happened to Egbuna himself, but for many soldiers like him the acts of violence that they committed in uniform would not be their last. These men grew accustomed to the authority they enjoyed as soldiers, and, as several veterans told me, one never forgets how to shoot a gun. After the war, they would struggle to find a place in the new order. Returning to their prewar work was almost impossible. There was certainly no place for them in the Nigerian military, though few of them would have wanted one; and so, they buried their guns and made their way as best they could in the lean conditions of the postwar. For the most part, their buried arms were not a promise that they would one day resume the fight for Biafra's independence but a guarantee that they would be able to provide for themselves if things took a turn for the worse.[114] Keeping their weapons turned out to be a prescient decision – but it was also a self-fulfilling prophecy.

[114] Interview with Mike Onwuzunike, Enugu, September 14, 2014. See also Patrick Ediomi Davies, "Use of Propaganda in Civil War: The Biafra Experience" (Doctoral dissertation, London School of Economics, 1995): p. 255; "Captain Elechi Amadi," in Momoh, *The Nigerian Civil War*, p. 294.

3 | Counterfeit Country: Fraud and Forgery in Biafra

In February 1969, in one of Biafra's darkest months, Arnold Akpan found his calling in life. Akpan had been a high school student in Uli until being press-ganged into the Biafran Army. His parents had disappeared in the first months of the war, and when he deserted he had nowhere to go. Alone and unprotected, he feared that he would be conscripted again. Mustering what he had learned in school, he forged a document for himself saying that he was exempt from military duty. The pass worked, and Akpan realized that he had a valuable skill. He began making passes for others. He stole a sheaf of letterhead from the Mkpat Enin Divisional Office, carved a rubber stamp reading "Officer of the Commander-in-Chief, Aba – Para-military Operations," and sought out other young men who were threatened by conscription. This led him to Emmanuel Imoh, to whom he hoped to sell forged exemption papers. Akpan prepared Imoh a set of papers that claimed that the bearer was ineligible for conscription because he was a qualified stenographer "engaged in para-military activities." Imoh was unsatisfied by Akpan's work, and, when Akpan insisted that he pay anyway, Imoh told a nearby soldier that Akpan was a saboteur. He tried unsuccessfully to swallow the passes, and the partially chewed papers were presented as evidence against him in a trial before the Special Tribunal. He was found guilty of theft and subversion.[1] Like most of the people who engaged in fraud in Biafra, Akpan had no prior criminal record. His file does not reveal what happened to him next. Eighteen years later, however, long after Biafra had been defeated, he makes another appearance – this time in a court registry from Onitsha, where he had been arrested for forgery again, this time of school certificates.[2] I do not know the particulars of this later arrest, but it

---

[1] NNAE MINJUST 116/1/8, in the Special Tribunal of Biafra, Nbawsi, no. ST/24c/69, *The State v. Arnold Akpan*, November 18, 1969.
[2] Imo State High Court, Owerri, uncatalogued collection, "Return of cases to registry from Anambra State," February 1, 1991.

confirms something that lawyers and judges knew to be true anecdotally; skills that ordinary people like Arnold Akpan used to survive the war would long outlast the fighting.

By the middle of the war, fraud and forgery were no longer the preserve of professional criminals or con men. The danger of the war obliged Biafrans to survive by deception, and nearly everyone was engaged in some form of subterfuge. The circle of people who knew the mechanics of fraud widened, and the Biafran state's relationship with truth became looser. This chapter analyzes how techniques of fraud developed over the course of the war and what conditions they responded to. Passes became fetishized in Biafra, and they had great value both as tools and as totems. Since carrying the correct papers was sometimes a matter of life and death, knowing how to forge them became immensely valuable. Biafrans like Arnold Akpan – educated, literate, and with some experience of state bureaucracy – had a knack for it for reasons related to the longer history of colonial administration. As a result, the demand for forgeries was high, and there was a supply to meet it. Both the courts and the public came to accept fraud as a fact of life.

Hunger, fear, and desperation drove people to fraud, just as it propelled them to armed crime. It was easy to be dishonest in the circumstances. The rackets that proliferated in Biafra took advantage of the fact that the war split up households and villages, breaking the bonds of trust that had structured social and economic life in peacetime. A sociologist who studied the Onitsha market noted that prewar commerce had worked "without the slightest precautionary measures either by receipting or by the formal witnessing of a third party."[3] "Everybody in your village would know who you were and if you were a man of standing," recalled Ejike Ume. "That was how everything worked – trust."[4] This economy of trust broke down as untruth and concealment became survival tactics. The legal record is full of false identities, confidence artists, and embezzlers – and these are only the ones who were caught.

Wartime forgery and fraud laid the groundwork for the postwar crisis of trust that would become known by the menacing number "419." Most of the Biafran cases that follow are not "419" in the

---

[3] J. O. C. Onyemelukwe, "Some Factors in the Growth of West African Market Towns: The Example of Pre-Civil War Onitsha, Nigeria," *Urban Studies* vol. 11, no. 4 (1974): pp. 7–59, 54.

[4] Interview with Ejike O. Ume, SAN, Onitsha, March 12, 2015.

technical meaning of the term – that of advance-fee fraud as defined by section 419 of the Criminal Code; but they bear a strong resemblance to 419's colloquial meaning – the practice of everyday deception for the purpose of survival or advancement. They mobilized similar skills, took similar rhetorical forms, and instrumentalized uncertainty in similar ways. For this reason, the forms of fraud and forgery that developed in the context of the war provide part of the genealogy for 419 as we know it today. The fraud and forgery discussed here – which I consider together, as overlapping criminal practices – did not merely go away when the war ended, and in postwar Nigeria they would reemerge in the elaborate mechanics of 419. The war had instructed people in the art of deception and muddled standards of truth and lines of authority. Postwar crime would feed on those ambiguities.

Warfare involves double crossings, forgeries, and the assumption of false identities, all of which are normal and even honorable behaviors when survival and victory are the orders of the day. What happens if these behaviors do not come to an end with the fighting? If they continue in peacetime, activities that are cast as patriotic duties during war (like espionage), or tolerated as ways of "getting by" in moments of crisis (like forgery), are revealed for what they are at heart – fraud. This is what happened in Nigeria after the war, and Chapter 6 will analyze how forgery, impersonation, and other wartime métiers persisted in postwar Nigeria. The objective of this argument is not to draw a straight line between wartime fraud and the contemporary phenomenon of 419 but to suggest that the war made certain forms of untruth necessary, and even acceptable, in a way that they had not been before. It cannot be explained solely by the colonial inheritance, by technological factors, nor by any sort of "native mendacity" inherent in the Nigerian character, as the British had often ascribed to their colonial subjects.

Lying and Surviving

Paperwork and bureaucracy were extremely important in Biafra. As John de St. Jorre wrote in his war memoir, "the Biafrans love the formalities and ritual of government; no matter how desperate and crazy the situation is, things must be done properly."[5] The new

---

[5] John de St. Jorre, *The Brothers' War: Biafra and Nigeria* (Boston: Houghton Mifflin, 1972): p. 409.

country's leaders tried to conjure sovereignty through bureaucratic tasks – by enumerating and registering its population, using Biafran postage and letterhead, and issuing Biafran passports, for example. By and large, they did not succeed; no postal service would deliver a letter with Biafran stamps, and Biafran passports were almost always turned away, even by its handful of allies.[6] Yet, to ordinary people, paperwork was important for a more immediate reason. Documents were helpful in navigating a world full of risk.

In the first year of the war, the Biafran government made public statements that it would not tolerate fraud, and the large number of prosecutions for that crime under the emergency measures and section 419 of the criminal code suggest that this was not just rhetoric. Biafra was indeed hard on fraud, and judges were confident that they could tell a real document from a fake one. In the course of a fraud case, Justice Nkemena threatened the accused that he could not be lied to:

Lying is difficult; it is an art which is very tricky. A lie forces the blood into the head, and produces a tremor in the voice comparable to the faint rattling of a window-pane responding to almost inaudible gunfire. It should not be imagined that a man can say with ease "no" when "yes" has once leaped into his mind.[7]

As the war drew to a close, his judicial intuition would be challenged by the sheer scale of mendacity. Forgers would prove that they could make more convincing documents than their government. Biafran judges, ever confident in their abilities, thought that the rules of evidence would allow them to sort out truth from falsehood. Modern forensic science, for example, continued to be part of criminal procedure. Crime scene photography, autopsy reports, and the testimony of handwriting experts appeared in trials until the very end. Yet no amount of proceduralism could make order out of the war's chaos.

---

[6] Portugal frustrated Ojukwu by turning away Biafran passport holders when they arrived in Lisbon, or only admitting their bearers on their Nigerian documents. Portuguese firms doing business with the Biafran government regularly refused to accept Biafran currency, a problem that took an absurdist turn when the Portuguese company hired to print Biafra's stamps and banknotes refused to accept payment in the Biafran pounds that they had just minted. For a general history of Biafran currency, see Peter Symes, "The Bank Notes of Biafra," *International Bank Note Society Journal* vol. 36, no.4 (1997).

[7] NNAE MINJUST 117/1/7, in the Special Tribunal of the Republic of Biafra, no. ST/15/c/69, *The State v. Joseph Nwabueze*, March 10, 1969.

The State v. Catherine Nwabunike, a Special Tribunal case from 1969, demonstrates how law-abiding people were driven to desperate measures by the situations that the war created.[8] Karina Anasoh, a Finnish woman married to a Biafran physician serving a prison sentence for subversion, was duped into giving a large sum of money to a Biafran acquaintance, Catherine Nwabunike. In what the tribunal found to be a premeditated attempt to gain her confidence, Nwabunike came to Anasoh and appealed to her on the basis that their husbands were being held in prison together (which was true) and insinuated herself in Anasoh's household over a period of a few weeks. At one point, Anasoh helped Nwabunike track down her children, who had been sent to safety in a remote village. After some time, Nwabunike came to her friend and said that, if she could give her 200 pounds, Nwabunike would be able to bribe the prison warden to let both of their husbands out of jail. Anasoh agreed immediately and cadged the money from her friends. Nwabunike absconded with the money and tried to sell the car that Anasoh had loaned her to travel to the prison at Umuahia. Nwabunike then used the money to try to get her own husband – a British expatriate – out of jail. The fact that the two husbands – one Biafran, one British – had shared a cell gave Nwabunike the idea that the foreign wife of her husband's cellmate might have the money she needed to buy her own husband's release. When it became clear that Nwabunike was not coming back, and had done nothing to help her own husband, Anasoh reported the whole matter to the police.

There were two main questions at hand in *The State v. Catherine Nwabunike*. The first was whether attempting to bribe a prison official to secure the release of a detained person constituted an act of subversion under the Law and Order (Maintenance) Edict of 1967. Arguing for the prosecution, the state counsel implored that "this country is in a state of war. Persons are detained to protect the safety and security of the state. That being so if any person takes any step to effect the release of a detainee that act militates against the safety and security of the state." He urged that the court should make an example of Nwabunike. The tribunal took it for granted that the prison warden could be bribed, placing the onus of the crime entirely on the woman who offered the

---

[8] NNAE MINJUST 116/1/6, in the Special Tribunal of the Republic of Biafra, no. STC/21C/69, *The State v. Catherine Nwabunike*, April 10, 1969.

bribe rather than the state official who accepted it. That prison wardens could be bought was common knowledge and not worth the tribunal's time to investigate. The second question was whether Nwabunike's defrauding of the Finnish woman was an offense against the welfare of the Biafran state under the emergency measures of 1967 or merely a violation of section 419 of the Nigerian Criminal Code (still in force in Biafra), which prohibited obtaining money under false pretenses with fraudulent intent. The tribunal decided that the consequences of the case were larger than one woman being defrauded, and it ruled that Nwabunike's actions were an offense against the welfare of the Biafran state. She was given twenty years' imprisonment – although her sentence was suspended indefinitely. The case shows how people like Catherine Nwabunike, who were far from being confidence artists, devised ways to dupe one another in response to the crises that the war created. It foreshadows the form of postwar confidence scams, including the fact that Nwabunike targeted a foreigner, the way she bound them together in a shared illegal enterprise, and the heightened emotional tone of her pitch, replete with danger and corruption. Unlike in later 419 cases, however, in embattled Biafra the scam's emotional urgency was not manufactured – it was very real.

Deception became ethically abstruse. There were no clear victims or villains in this case; it is hard not to be sympathetic to both Nwabunike and Anasoh given the strains that they were under. In part, the growing acceptance of fraud was a consequence of the legal system's diminishing capacity. Although prosecutors continued to pursue fraud cases, they could only go after a small percentage of them; but it was not just a problem of enforcement. The ethics surrounding deceit changed in light of the crisis. The lawyer Jerome Okolo described how the shame of crime fell away during the war:

In the past, if your relative went to jail the entire family would be tainted by that fact and would be shunned. Before the war your community would never speak to you again when you got out of prison – in Biafra, they would throw you a party when you got out. The sense of shame that went with being a criminal diminished, perhaps because so many people had been through shameful experiences. Having been in prison was no longer seen as shameful perhaps because so many people had been imprisoned arbitrarily. As a result, the stigma attached to it diminished and crime rates rose.[9]

[9] Interview with Jerome H. C. Okolo, SAN, Enugu, September 17, 2014.

There was even a note of begrudging respect in Biafran reportage about purveyors of fraud. The newsmagazine *Biafra Time* reported extensively on crime, including a complicated fraud case against real estate magnate James Osuji, who was accused of forging power of attorney documents. Despite the war going on all around it, the case proceeded; but, as the tabloid reported, "despite all his troubles, the pot-bellied, sharp and ferret-eyed [Osuji] still feels ebullient enough to show up himself in Port Harcourt streets in elegant swagger, with his eyes enclosed by a pair of grotesquely large and tinted glasses."[10] Osuji was a wealthy, high-profile person, but he was hardly alone in having been dishonest in a situation where there were many opportunities to do so. The fact that so many otherwise law-abiding people – rich and poor, and in places high and low – survived through "criminal" means would ensure that few people felt they were in a position to condemn others for breaking the law. People like Osuji, whose actions went beyond mere survivalism, could cloak themselves in moral ambiguity.

The imperative of "survival" did not just pertain to individuals. It was also how the Biafran state understood itself, and deceit could be tolerated or forgiven if it was done in the service of victory.[11] In certain circumstances, forgery could even serve the Biafran cause, as the Court of Appeal found in *Oscar Oti and two others v. The State*. In this case, the court acquitted three men who had been arrested before secession for possessing paper, ink, and printer's plates to forge Nigerian currency, which was a clear violation of both the federal and the regional criminal codes of Nigeria, the latter of which remained in force in Biafra. The decision was made on the dubious grounds that it was not illegal to possess these materials, because to forge specifically *Nigerian* bank notes was not specified as a crime in the Eastern Region's criminal code (presumably because that wording would have been taken for granted). This was a decision calculated to give oblique legal sanction to forgery – as long as it was Nigerian currency being forged.[12] Impersonation could be patriotic too; a propaganda

---

[10] HIA, Nigerian Subject Collection XX787, Box 7, *Biafra Time*, April 30, 1968, p. 11.

[11] See Douglas Anthony, "'Ours is a war of survival': Biafra, Nigeria and Arguments about Genocide, 1966–70," *Journal of Genocide Research* vol. 16, nos. 2–3 (2014): pp. 205–225.

[12] NNAE BCA 1/1/15, in the Court of Appeal of the Republic of Biafra, Aba, no. CA/15/67, *Oscar Oti and two others v. The State*, February 2, 1968.

piece in the *Biafra Sun* celebrated an Igbo refugee from Katsina who "used to don the dirty Hausa gown and speak the gruffy language. I did so well in my Hausa affectations that most of them thought I was their member." In the story, he steals money from the Bank of the North, "which was provisionally open since the northerners, in their inborn stupidity, had deserted the bank in their frenzy to kill Easterners," and then takes the money back to Biafra, where he uses it for "patriotic purposes."[13] These anecdotes are not indicative of the Biafran courts' attitude toward forgery, impersonation, and theft in general, but they suggest how the broader social meanings of crime changed during the war. Actions that are normally criminal can become patriotic in wartime.

Splintered Authority and Slippery Identities

Writing one of many letters of complaint to his increasingly unresponsive superiors in Biafra's capital, the head of the civil defense force in Umuobom described how his village had been "abandoned by God" in mid-1969:

It is Umuobom again, where anything can happen unchecked, where any crime can be committed in the name of keeping Umuobom one, where people live by the Law of the Jungle where the strong overpowers the weak, where stragglers are bribed into beating people who are not on the good books of the Chief and his gangsters, where the law of the Military Government is replaced with that of [local administrators]. [...] We are human beings. We have been oppressed, we have been kicked and we have noticed all sorts of unspeakable degradation and have witnessed the most inhuman atrocious calamity perpetuated on us. We are human beings who should be handled with delicate hand. We have endured enough.[14]

Umuobom was not alone in feeling that it had been abandoned by Ojukwu (to say nothing of God). The state fractured into many competing authorities, begging the question of which if any of them constituted the "real" Biafran government. They operated with varying degrees of formality and had different claims to be "official." What

---

[13] This piece is not unique among Biafran propaganda in its stridently anti-Hausa language. *Biafra Sun*, Sam Nwachukwu, "It Was Quite a Perfect Nose-Dive," July 16, 1967.

[14] NWM uncatalogued collection, Chairman, Local Civil Defence Committee, Umuobom to Divisional Officer, Nkwerre, June 15, 1969.

follows is a description of how Biafra's legal system came apart in the later stages of the war and how communities policed and defended themselves in the absence of a cogent government. Biafra's decline forced people to develop new ways of getting by and getting along, while also giving them leeway to misrepresent themselves to one another. Matters of identity became slippery, and it became both easier and more necessary to pretend to be someone else.

Power was diffuse and malleable in these conditions. Civil defenders blurred into guerilla "freedom fighters," police blurred into soldiers, and with a baton and a loud voice almost anyone could claim the mantle of authority.[15] Individuals, in addition to civil defense organizations and militias, were ordered to be vigilant in protecting the Biafran state.[16] A case from a magistrate's court in Nnewi illustrates how civilians interpreted that order. While sitting on the porch of the hotel where she worked, a middle-aged woman witnessed a young man stealing a drum of oil from a cart across the street. She ran over to the man, wrestled the drum away from him, and held him to prevent him from running away while she called other people over. Applauding her bravery, the magistrate ruled that "in exercise of her civil right [she] on seeing accused committing an offence was justified in arresting him." He further observed that the "stealing of petrol and diesel has been rampant since the shortage of fuel in the Country. This sort of thing must be checked. A gallon of diesel sells up to 5 pounds and even more. It is big easy money and attractive. The diesel was for supply of water to already suffering people of Biafra." He was sentenced to a lengthy prison term. This kind of "citizen's arrest" was legal, but it had seldom been carried out before the war.[17] It was a sign of the broader moment; people were learning to fend for themselves and to dispense "justice" without waiting for the state to do it.

---

[15] Later, Amina Mama would memorably describe the imitative quality of authority in military Nigeria: "Street children and madmen can be seen acting out the roles of soldiers: they march, salute, and gesticulate frantically in a bid to convey their wholly imaginary authority." Amina Mama, "Khaki in the Family: Gender Discourses and Militarism in Nigeria," *African Studies Review* vol. 41, no. 2 (1998): pp. 1–17, 4.

[16] NWM uncatalogued collection, "Beating up of Civil Defenders and Allegation of Conspiracy with the Artillery Soldiers," October 20, 1969.

[17] NNAE MINJUST 127/1/74, in the Magistrate's Court of the Republic of Biafra, Nnewi, no. MO/715c/68, *Inspector-General of Police v. Joshua Okezie*, July 19, 1968.

The number of militias grew as the territory that Biafra controlled shrank. Some were the stubs of Biafran Army units that had deserted or been cut off from their superiors, while others emerged organically in small communities. In some cases, the distinction between "militia" and "criminal gang" was hazy.[18] The proliferation of authorities allowed people to lay claim to powers usually reserved for governments. An embarrassed official at the clandestine headquarters of the Biafran Organisation of Freedom Fighters (BOFF) outside Enugu wrote to the Civil Defence Committee in Umuobom that

> It has come to our notice that stragglers and other civilians in Umuobom come to the market and commit any irresponsible acts and claim that they are "BOFF boys." This happens especially on stragglers' drive days. As from now, inform those who come on stragglers' drive that people claiming BOFF identity should be reported to Civil Defence Committee for identification. In such cases get the person's name and his number and if possible demand his pass and then inform us.[19]

In Orlu, small militias and even the occasional individual attempted to collect war levies for themselves, which the main Civil Defence Committee and the Biafran Army tried to punish.[20] Similarly, militias, "ambulance corps," and an array of paramilitary organizations demanded money and payment in kind from the communities where they operated. All of them claimed to act under the aegis of the state.

Attempts to draw clear lines between soldier and civilian were unsuccessful. In late 1968, Biafra began issuing identity cards to civilians as part of a larger attempt to crack down on desertion and impersonation, but by this late stage in the war the damage had been done.[21] It also tried to impose a system of identity cards for civil defenders, complete with fingerprints and photos.[22] It too came to nothing, and the few cards that were issued were used fraudulently. Uniforms did little to clarify the difference between soldier and civilian.

---

[18] Comparatively, see Jonny Steinberg, *Thin Blue: The Unwritten Rules of Policing South Africa* (Johannesburg: Jonathan Ball, 2008).

[19] NWM uncatalogued collection, "Identification of Soldiers claiming 'BOFF,'" September 18, 1969.

[20] NWM uncatalogued collection, Circular from Civil Defence Committee, Umuobom, "Stay Clear of Our Activities," September 14, 1969.

[21] NWM uncatalogued collection, "Identity Cards," September 30, 1969.

[22] NWM uncatalogued collection, "Identity Cards," September 5, 1969.

In the early stages of the war, the Biafran Army went to some lengths to ensure that only soldiers wore the emblem of the rising sun, the image on Biafra's flag, on their uniforms.[23] Over time, militias adopted the insignia as well, blurring the visual line between soldier and militia member. This ambiguity was compounded by the fact that not all regular soldiers wore uniforms – mostly due to shortages rather than tactical considerations – whereas some of the better organized militias did.

Biafran soldiers expressed shame at having to fight in civilian clothes, and the danger of using boots made from tires and milk tins hammered into the shape of helmets was immediately apparent. Troops, as one military historian writes, "became obsessed with trying to capture uniforms from the enemy almost to the exclusion of other objectives, stripping the dead and any prisoners and adding their own insignia if available."[24] Umelo described how military authority dissimulated in the later part of the war:

Now we were seeing Biafran troops all the time, not the well pressed and starched officers at their ease in the back of commandeered cars or the stoical wounded but the fighting men. They wore uniform shirts and lappas, or khaki green trousers with cotton shirts, captured steel helmets ornamented with leaves or streamers of green baize, heavy cartridge belts, knives or matchets. An automatic rifle was slung over one shoulder while their rosary beads were worn around the neck or looped around the wrist.[25]

People with no claim to military authority – formal or informal – made use of the confusion. They included criminals like Christopher Nwokocha and Godson Onunekwu (alias Captain Marvel), who donned Biafran uniforms and made a small fortune searching cars and requisitioning valuables from their drivers before they were arrested.[26] This kind of deception became very common.

Sensing that the Biafran government had little leverage, vigilante groups began to act under their own orders. A minor crisis emerged in Umuobom in late 1968, where "the civil defenders who have just been trained are claiming full authority of themselves and refused to

[23] NWM uncatalogued collection, "Armed Forces Identification Sign: The Biafra Sun," November 4, 1967.
[24] Philip S. Jowett, *Modern African Wars (5): The Nigerian-Biafran War 1967–1970* (Oxford: Osprey, 2016): p.41.
[25] IWM 6687, Papers of Rosina Umelo, "Biafra, A World of Our Own," n.p.
[26] *Biafra Sun*, July 25, 1968, p. 8.

take orders from the existing committee. They are misled by some
elements who are at the verge of dissolving our committee."[27] They
managed to suppress the insurrection, but it was clear that civil defenders increasingly answered only to themselves. In some places, multiple
militias claimed authority. Writing to complain that he was being
harassed by two separate militia organizations, one of which was
allegedly the "personal army" of a local chief, the manager of
a marketplace outside of Umuobom wrote to his local Civil Defence
Committee, asking "as the leaders of local affairs here are you [serving]
your own interest or that of the Government of the Republic of
Biafra?"[28] Another wrote to a local administrator to complain that
"we have been seeing a lot of soldiers whom use to harass civilians over
this our area" and asked "whether their coming is official or not."[29]
The bureaucrat did not know, and he wrote to his superior to see who
was formally in charge. He did not receive a response.

Militias and civil defenders bullied local people and refugees into
giving up their belongings. They insisted that aid given to their regions
pass exclusively through their hands, and they commandeered food
and seedlings from refugee camps in the name of their "absolute
authority to transact all matters" of town administration and refugee
affairs.[30] The checkpoints that civil defenders set up along roads could
easily become devices to shake down people passing through, intimidate neighboring communities, or punish rivals.[31] Civil defenders came
up with many ways to harass civilians, often invoking poorly understood edicts to justify what looked like simple theft to most people. One
such tactic was to claim that it was illegal to possess Nigerian coins in
Biafra. While Nigerian notes had in fact been banned, Nigerian coins
were entirely legal to own and use. Civil defenders routinely arrested

---

[27] NWM uncatalogued collection, Civil Defence Committee, Umuobom to
Chairman, Rehabilitation Committee, Orlu, September 28, 1968.

[28] NWM uncatalogued collection, A. O. Anyikila to Secretary, Civil Defence
Committee, Umuobom, November 20, 1969.

[29] NWM uncatalogued collection, Paulinus [illegible] to Charles Okwara,
December 18, 1969.

[30] NWM uncatalogued collection, "Overstepping bound of authority," May 14,
1968.

[31] This took place not only at the level of everyday transactions between
individuals but between communities. An easy way to tar an enemy was to say
that they were not being sufficiently vigilant in the operation of checkpoints,
which could lead to heavy fines for the accused. NWM uncatalogued collection,
David Irechukwu to Civil Defence Committee, Umuobom, August 28, 1968.

people for possessing coins and confiscated the money or used its possession as an excuse to demand larger sums.[32]

Civil defenders also came into conflict with what remained of official administrative structures. At a market near Arondizuogu in late 1969, a BOFF militia arrested members of the local police after the police told the men to stop demanding money from people. "They seize people with even a cup of corn meal and on their way to the station they release them after paying sums of money from ten to twenty pounds," one witness complained. In turn, the BOFF men "mercilessly beat up" the local police and civil defenders, and the situation quickly developed into "uncontrollable combat," leaving local leaders stunned at how "two arms of the military authorities should fail to cooperate" so dramatically.[33] Markets were among the most dangerous places one could be. In addition to being targets for Nigerian bombs, they were the sites of conscription campaigns, combing missions, and general harassment by groups ranging from Biafran Army units to criminal gangs posing as militias.[34] The Oye Market near Umuobom was "menaced" frequently by both stragglers organized into militias and by the soldiers who were sent in to collect them.[35] Once a unit of men had settled into a marketplace, it was hard to convince them to move on.[36]

The problem of indiscipline was not unique to civil defenders and paramilitary organizations. Discipline in the regular Biafran Army, too, was low by the war's midpoint and only grew worse after that. Soldiers were not always the ones aggravating civilians, and, in some war-weary towns, army units were harassed by local people. A delegation from the Biafran Army's Re-Education Unit reported that "in the course of our trips to the various fronts, we notice that the personnel of the Armed Forces are often cajoled and subjected to a great deal of molestation

---

[32] See Diliorah Chukwurah, *Last Train to Biafra: The Memoirs of a Biafran Child* (Ibadan: Constellation Publishers, 2015): p. 94; NWM uncatalogued collection, "Meeting of Chairmen, Leaders and Instructors of Local Civil Defence Organization in the Province Held in the Provincial Civil Defence Office, Orlu," November 16, 1968.

[33] NWM uncatalogued collection, "Statement of C.J. Okpara, Local Civil Defence Committee in the case with the Police," December 6, 1969; "Victimisation of civil defenders," November 16, 1969.

[34] NWM uncatalogued collection, Rangers office, Orlu to Chairman, Local Civil Defence, Umuobom, September 7, 1968.

[35] NWM uncatalogued collection, "Soldiers menace in mkt.," August 19, 1969.

[36] NWM uncatalogued collection, "Victimisation of civil defenders," November 16, 1969.

from the civilians in many areas. All armed forces personnel carry passes and this is not often known to the civilians who often beat up soldiers on official trips."[37] Many outside observers commented on the erratic pace of combat. A British intelligence source at the front in Asaba wrote in 1968 that "I have never seen any war fought in quite the leisurely fashion of this one. . . . Even as near the war front as this, Star Beer is the order of the day and the acting C.O. is in civvies (as were most officers on the other side of the river)."[38] The pace of the war was not generally as relaxed as this suggests, but it was true that the fighting took place in fits and starts.[39] Both armies were undisciplined, and it became especially difficult to control the behavior of soldiers who were stationed near towns. Soldiers used their authority to commandeer goods, demand money, and in some cases to settle personal scores. Such was the case with Lieutenant Mark Ebbeh of the Biafran Army, a "broken elementary teacher with the most objectionable reputation, [who] was forced to join the army after committing a lot of crimes for which he was punished by the military police." He returned to his home town in June of 1969 to take revenge on the town leaders who had made him join the army:

For the four days he was at home [he] caused a lot of panic. He paraded [with his band of] stragglers in the streets and illegally conscripted so many people whom after giving him some sums ranging from three to five pounds each he released them. There was a lot of indiscriminate shooting by him with the hard-paid-for Biafran bullets bought for the vandals [Nigerians].

Following their brief "reign of terror" in Umuobom, Ebbeh and his band of deserters kidnapped the chairman and secretary of the local Civil Defence Committee and held them ransom for fifty pounds. After the ransom was paid, they released their captives and left town.[40]

---

[37] NWM uncatalogued collection, "Troops Re-Education Unit, Fourth Interim Report," April 9, 1968.

[38] NAUK FCO 38/286, Tony Ingledow to British High Commission, Lagos, April 5, 1968.

[39] A graphic description of battlefield experience can be found in the memoirs of a Biafran officer who later became governor of Imo State. Achike Udenwa, *Nigeria/Biafra Civil War: My Experience* (Ibadan: Spectrum, 2011).

[40] NWM uncatalogued collection, "Kidnapping of some members of the Civil Defence Committee by Lt. Peter Ebbeh and Umuobom Stragglers," June 10, 1969.

The Biafran government claimed that there were saboteurs everywhere, which a handful of well-publicized incidents seemed to confirm. Biafrans were admonished to be skeptical of anyone whom they had not known personally before the war. In October 1968, a Biafran officer encountered a man wandering along the road between Umuahia and Okigwe, "black in complexion, quite stark naked or in his birth-day suit with minor rashes over the body standing. As people were jeering at him as a mad-man, I became apprehensive as to assess him." The officer questioned him, and after being fed and clothed the man revealed that he was Corporal Frederick Nwagwu, alias Areawire, of the Nigerian Army. In return for clemency, he offered to lead the Biafran officer to the place where his men were in hiding in the bush. Areawire's story turned out to be a ruse, and the Biafran soldiers were ambushed when they reached the place the infiltrator was leading them to.[41] Stories like this circulated widely, and they made Biafrans both in and out of uniform wary of anyone they did not recognize; but the Biafran government's warnings about saboteurs and infiltrators were undoubtedly exaggerated – not every refugee was a Nigerian agent, as militia leaders and administrators seemed to fear. The Civil Defence Committee in Umuobom reported in January 1970 that "after a whole week we were unable to comb out any strange faces. Some few passerby we got were interrogated and identified by some people and then we had to release them."[42] The civil defenders were told by the Ministry of Justice to look harder.

The number of spies and revolutionary plots in Biafra was exaggerated, but the number of "strange faces" was not. By late 1967, humanitarian organizations estimated that there were half a million "refugees for a second time" wandering in the forests around Orlu – so-called because they had been displaced first from the north and then from other parts of Biafra.[43] There are no reliable figures for how many displaced people traversed Biafra later in the war, but it would have been a far greater number than half a million. Searching for unfamiliar faces became a kind of national obsession. Colloquially called

---

[41] NWM uncatalogued collection, "Secret OP Torch – Need for Extra Vigilance," November 5, 1968, "Report on Extra Vigilance by BA/18150416 WOI Peter Iwueke – DHQ," November 5, 1968.

[42] NWM uncatalogued collection, "Report of Combing," January 2, 1970.

[43] SOAS Christian Aid Collections, CA/A/6/5, "Involvement of the World Council of Churches in the Nigeria Crisis," November 8, 1967.

"combing," this practice empowered Biafrans to harass their neighbors, enter houses, and challenge the presence of anyone they deemed a "stranger." Everyone was expected to participate in combing expeditions, and women were preferred for leading them because they were thought to be less inclined to accept bribes or grant favors to friends. Combing was a mass activity, which created confusing situations where everyone in a given village was out looking for everyone else.[44] It gave wide latitude for abuse by soldiers and violence by civilians against one another, all under the banner of an official, patriotic activity.

These chaotic conditions made deceit easier, and impersonation became rife. The war disturbed the mechanisms of recognition and face-to-face interaction that had fixed people to their identities, and Biafrans took advantage of the holes that had formed in the social fabric to become someone else. Like other forms of fraud, assuming another identity was most commonly a survival tactic – it was a way to throw off the scent for one's enemies, creditors, or the state. The availability of forged documents and the general confusion of the situation made this possible; while impersonation was not a new kind of crime, in the chaos of the war it became far easier to pull it off.[45] Multiple informants recalled that they spent stretches of the war pretending to be someone else – not because they had something to hide but because they felt that creating ambiguity about who they were would keep them safe. Many had taken refuge in their home villages, in the hope that a small and remote place would be safest when Biafra was overrun, as seemed increasingly inevitable. When outsiders came looking for a particular person or family – whether those outsiders were Biafran officers, emissaries from Nigeria, or fellow refugees in

---

[44] NNAE MINJUST 1/5/5, in the High Court of Biafra, Enugu, *The State v. Nwadiko Ajaogu* [1968].

[45] One can find many examples of impersonation and acts like it in the history of the prewar east, the most richly told of which is the complex story of the British eccentric known as Odeziaku, described by Stephanie Newell in *The Forger's Tale: The Search for Odeziaku* (Athens: Ohio University Press, 2006). False identities and the problems they create were also stock plots of prewar Onitsha market literature. See, for example, "Counterfeit Policeman Runs Away," in J. O. Nnadozie, *Beware of Harlots and Many Friends: The World Is Hard* (Liechtenstein: Kraus Reprint, 1970). Impersonation had also been a worry for the colonial government, suggesting that it was something more than a plot device for pulp fiction. See Steven Pierce, *Moral Economies of Corruption: State Formation and Political Culture in Nigeria* (Durham, NC: Duke University Press, 2016): pp. 3–4.

search of shelter – the safest thing was to pretend not to be around. In a few cases, villages closed ranks and gave a wanted person the identity of someone who had already been killed. A junior officer who deserted from the Biafran Army recalled how one day, while he was in hiding, a childhood friend came looking for him in an unmarked car. Suspicious of the visit, when the man in the car stopped him on the road, the officer looked his friend in the eye and told him that he was someone else. He was so gaunt and disheveled that the man failed to recognize that he was speaking to the very person he was looking for. The officer still wonders if his schoolmate came as friend or foe, but in the moment it seemed safest to pretend to be someone else.[46]

The cultivation of uncertainty was about survival. "I resolved never to be lulled into any false sense of security and to always keep the bad times in view," wrote a child survivor of what the war had taught him.[47] Surrounding yourself with doubt – about who you were, where you were from, or how you supported yourself – allowed you to easily abscond if a situation turned dangerous, and it built plausible deniability into every interaction and relationship. This reflex to obscure, I argue, was born in wartime. It was an impulsive, instinctual response to uncertainty, and it applied to all sorts of people, not just "criminals." People who had nothing to hide did it too, since in these perilous times one never knew exactly whom one was dealing with. The injunction to trust no one would long outlast the fighting.

The Genuine and the Counterfeit in Biafra

In early 1969, a small-town politician in Biafra tried to get rid of his rivals once and for all by framing them for treason. Joseph Nwabueze, the unpopular head of the Civil Defence Committee in Isuikwuato, forged a letter purporting to come from the Nigerian Army command addressed to various town elders, all of them Nwabueze's political opponents and enemies. The spurious letter thanked them for their dedication to the Nigerian war effort, assuring them that their payment for services rendered to Nigeria was on its way. The typist who prepared the letter was alarmed to see that some of his relatives were named among the collaborators, and he asked Nwabueze why he was

---

[46] Interview with anonymous informant, Enugu, September 2014.
[47] Dulue Mbachu, *War Games* (Lagos: New Gong, 2005): p. 172.

not going straight to the police. Thinking quickly, Nwabueze told him that it was all part of a high-level mission he had been given by Ojukwu himself and that "the persons named therein were 'spoiling' their town, and if he told anyone and the soldiers came to arrest these persons and found them absent he [the typist] would be shot to death by the soldiers."[48] Nwabueze slipped the note into a shipment of pots bound for the (then) Biafran capital at Umuahia and waited for the army to come and arrest his rivals. Unluckily for Nwabueze, the note was discovered by the wrong person, and a local man connected the dots and reported him to the military police. He was found guilty of treason before the Special Tribunal of Biafra. Treason was a capital offense, but Nwabueze was given a prison sentence in recognition of the fact that he had turned in many deserters to the military police.

Sophisticated schemes to defraud, steal, and smuggle took advantage of the Biafran government's murky relationship with truth. The growing sense that crimes that had been harshly punished in peacetime were now treated with a lighter touch made Nwabueze and others like him confident that they could get away with nearly anything. His case also illustrates how fraud could be turned not just to bare survival but to personal advantage. Over the course of the war, it grew easier and more necessary for Biafrans – from petty traders to chiefs like Nwabueze and even further up the political hierarchy – to deceive one another. The documents that they produced survive as exhibits in the trials against their producers or bearers. Most of them are amateurish, full of misspellings and obviously faked stamps; but material shortages could cover up a lack of skill. It was not hard to pass off a document written by hand or on scrap paper as genuine, since shortages ensured that *real* Biafran papers were usually little more than handwritten scraps.[49] In

---

[48] NNAE MINJUST 117/1/7, in the Special Tribunal of the Republic of Biafra, no. ST/15c/69, *The State v. Joseph Nwabueze*, March 10, 1969.

[49] The passes that were of the highest value were those signed by Ojukwu himself, which were reserved for high-level government employees and members of the Research and Production Directorate tasked with producing armaments. Chikwendu Christian Ukaegbu, "War and the Making of an Organic Scientific and Technological Intelligentsia: The Case of Biafran Scientists in the Nigeria-Biafra War," in Apollos O. Nwauwa and Chima J. Korieh, eds., *Against All Odds: The Igbo Experience in Postcolonial Nigeria* (Glassboro, NJ: Goldline and Jacobs Publishing, 2011): pp. 73–94, 89. See also M. Angulu Onwuejeogwu, *A Study in Military Sociology: The Biafran Army, 1967–1970* (Lagos: UTO Publications, 2000): p. 114. Several real Biafran passes and other

fact, a genuine pass, issued under the spurious authority of a self-appointed civil defense organization, or by a bureaucrat whose only remaining trace of officialdom was the stamp that he carried, often looked *less* convincing than a forgery. The scale of forgery was unprecedented, as was its variety. Most common was the counterfeiting of government documents – evidence files overflowed with forged passes, vouchers, qualifications, certificates, and deeds.[50]

This had implications for how Biafrans viewed their government. It became difficult to distinguish a forged document from a genuine one, which begged a larger question – how genuine was the Biafran state itself? Just as Biafra's existence was a matter of its recognition by other sovereign states, the validity of Biafran documents was largely in the eye of the beholder. Often, those who made their own passes did not see what they were doing as fraudulent. Given the general sense of confusion about who was in charge, people with only a tenuous connection to the state (like civil defenders or militiamen) could appropriate the responsibility to produce and endorse documents. Although few of these cases were taken to court, civil defense committees routinely complained that the passes they issued to their members were not honored by soldiers, tax collectors, and policemen.[51] They took great umbrage at being accused of forgery by the central government, considering their passes and documents to be as real as any issued "by Ojukwu himself."[52] It was not clear who counted as a government official, and to many Biafrans the distinction was unimportant. Some of the people who became "forgers" in Biafra had not long ago been legitimate bureaucrats elsewhere in Nigeria. When they returned to the east, they continued to issue documents even though they no longer had posts. As one lawyer recalled, "the mass of the people [in Biafra] thought that any man who possessed a stamp was as good as a civil

documents are reproduced in S. Elizabeth Bird and Rosina Umelo, *Surviving Biafra: A Nigerwife's Story* (London: Hurst, 2018).
[50] Currency counterfeiting was less common. It was illegal to possess or use Nigerian notes, and Biafran pounds were of little value even at home. Biafran currency would have been difficult to forge, since it was professionally printed in Portugal. José Duarte de Jesus, *A Guerra Secreta de Salazar em África* (Lisbon: Don Quixote, 2012): p. 179.
[51] Thomas Enunwe (Omenka), *The Biafran War: The Story of an Orphan* (Ojo: Teg Commercial Enterprises, 2005): p. 122.
[52] NWM uncatalogued collection, "Umuobom Civil Defence Committee Minute Book," 1968–1969.

servant."[53] The main consideration was not whether a document was real but whether it worked.

Forged passes were made and traded briskly throughout the enclave, and buyers included men like Akpan who hoped to avoid conscription and women who conducted trade along the front. Ben Gbulie recalled how a former schoolmate came to him and asked him for a pass to avoid being harassed by soldiers. He indignantly refused, recognizing that "although he did not actually spell it out for me, the pass was to help him dodge conscription. By then I had realized that many Biafran youths had taken to evading military service; and that words were already being passed around, albeit covertly, to the effect that there is no such thing as death with honour – just death."[54] It was not only would-be conscripts who had something to fear; checkpoints had been set up every few miles on Biafran roads, and those who manned them were distrustful of everyone who passed through. Even a short journey could be difficult without an official-looking chit or pass, and soldiers harassed anyone who did not appear to be on military business. Umelo described how critical the pass she had been issued was in her daily life:

This simple document proved quite invaluable as it answered all the regular checkpoint questions, at least when I was returning to school. "Who are you? Where from? Where are you going? Why?" A permanent post was mounted at the main gate. At each checkpoint the car would stop at the barrier, usually a pole laid out across empty oil or paint drums. The militia, police, or at really important road blocks the army would come up and take a look at the car and occupants. Often everyone would be told to get out of the car which was quickly searched, bonnet, boot and glove compartments. Any briefcases, handbags, shopping bags were inspected, the driver and passengers questioned. "Who are you? Where are you going? Where have you come from?" And after that usually "You can go," even if it was only on to the next check, just along the road perhaps within sight of the last.[55]

Traders found that carrying papers – of almost any provenance – could help them both within Biafra and when they went behind enemy lines to buy goods clandestinely from Nigerians. Moving freely within Biafra

---

[53] Interview with Mike Onwuzunike, Enugu, September 14, 2014.
[54] Ben Gbulie, *The Fall of Biafra* (Enugu: Benlie Publishers, 1989): p. 56.
[55] IWM 6687, Papers of Rosina Umelo, "Biafra, A World of Our Own," pp. 40–42.

Figure 3.1 Biafran soldiers at a checkpoint, 1968 (Keystone-France/Gamma-Rapho, via Getty Images)

was especially difficult for members of ethnic minorities, who were looked on with mistrust in the Igbo-majority regions.[56] As one Delta trader testified in his trial for having forged a pass, "the villagers used to molest us because they felt we brought in the Hausas [Nigerians]. They did not molest those with passes."[57]

There was much confusion in Biafra over who was authorized to issue passes, who could exempt someone from military duties, and what kinds of private business were "essential" to the war effort. Forgers took advantage of these ambiguities by creating fakes that purported to come from real administrators. They could trust that the authority named in a forged pass would not be able to disavow it, since communication problems made it

---

[56] On this mistrust and the position of minorities in Biafra generally, see Kingdom E. Orji and Uebari Samuel N-Ue, "Nigerian Civil War and Refugee Crisis: The Fate of the Minorities in the Former Eastern Region," *IOSR Journal of Humanities and Social Science* vol. 16, no. 2 (2013): pp. 45–57.

[57] NNAE MINJUST 117/1/8, in the Special Tribunal of the Republic of Biafra, no. ST/16c/69, *The State v. Benson Isaac Jaja*, April 10, 1969.

difficult to check.[58] The war had thrown government offices into disarray, and there was no gazette that a registrar or bank teller might consult to see which signature an official document should bear. A depersonalized bureaucracy could not work in these circumstances. Knowing that stamps and seals were less and less trustworthy, Biafran courts and businesses turned to other proofs of authenticity. A hard-to-reproduce signature by a known individual was the only proof some judges would accept, and banks began to require that all transactions be carried out in person.[59]

The forgeries that circulated in Biafra were rudimentary, but this did not mean that no skill went into making them. Mastering the language of state bureaucracy, toeing the line of how much latitude a pass should offer to its bearer, and being able to cite the appropriate government agency or individual were all considerations that the forger of even the most basic handwritten document would have to make. These skills were not obvious, and they entailed various kinds of learning and transmission. It is difficult to reconstruct how the technical skills associated with forgery were passed from person to person and to account for how people with no experience of fraud mustered the ability to con one another. Many former Biafrans remember the war as a time of trickery, but few can recall the specifics of how it came to be that way. Press accounts and criminal cases like the ones discussed here provide some sense of how this happened, but they do not tell a complete story – and at any rate they only tell about those who were discovered. Oral history only helps so much; many interviewees had no qualms about admitting that they had used forged documents, but few remembered the minutiae of where and how they obtained them.

---

[58] Postwar fraud would take the same form – many 419 letters purported to come from real people in the Nigerian government. The harder those people were to contact, the better they served as lures into a scam.

[59] Similarly, Ojukwu himself managed the affairs of the state in an increasingly face-to-face way. Ojukwu often spent his mornings in audiences with individual members of the public, who came to make personal requests or ask him to intervene in small disputes. He regularly did so. See, for example, Angelina Ihejirika, *Escape from Nigeria: A Memoir of Faith, Love and War* (Trenton: Africa World Press, 2016): pp. 134.

The 1969 Special Tribunal case *The State v. Benson Isaac Jaja* gives a sense of how this happened.[60] In the course of the proceedings, the accused described how he came into possession of his forged pass:

> On the 30th October 1968, I came back from Umuahia main market and on my way home along Uzuakoli Road I saw my friend an army man by name Friday Ekpenyong. He asked me whether I do still trade, I said to him yes. He wanted to know how we trade I told him that we do trade well, but that the only trouble we encounter on the way is the worriness from the natives of the place we go to buy things. They continue to ask one where he comes from and if one says from Umuahia they will demand paper from Umuahia. I asked him where he works and he told me that he works at the State House, Umuahia. He then asked whether I need any paper, I then told him that if he would get me any good paper which I will carry with me wherever I go that I will be happy. I mean pass when I talk of paper. [...] This pass makes me to move freely and especially whenever I go to the village to buy things. I cannot do trade without am and I am sure I would be dead [by] now without paper.

The soldiers who arrested him denied that they had demanded the bribe, but, having little faith in them as witnesses, the tribunal decided to believe Jaja. Ekpenyong, the soldier who had provided the forged pass, and who was reportedly serving in Owerri, was nowhere to be found despite a long search by the tribunal's bailiffs.

Jaja's defense challenged what constituted a "genuine" pass in Biafra. The pass was marked as having come from the statehouse, but it was signed by someone from the Divisional Headquarters of the Biafran Army. Both the stationery and the signature looked real, and its convincing appearance led the tribunal to believe that perhaps the pass *was* real despite the seemingly fraudulent way Jaja had come to possess it. The tribunal wanted to "get to the bottom of the racket," and it tried to investigate the Biafran Army to find out who might have been issuing these fraudulent passes; but the inquiry came up against a wall of silence, suggesting that perhaps someone powerful was protecting those responsible for the racket. The investigation stopped there, and the tribunal moved on to other matters. The possibility that a high-level bureaucrat might be involved in forgery was alarming, but it was not surprising. The state was falling apart, and administrators had

---

[60] NNAE MINJUST 117/1/8, in the Special Tribunal of the Republic of Biafra, no. ST/16c/69, *The State v. Benson Isaac Jaja*, April 10, 1969.

great autonomy. If they sold "genuine" passes to people who needed them, no one would stop them. The difference between real and fake was paper thin in these circumstances.

The tribunal ruled that "the police failed to investigate thoroughly the origin of the pass so as to disprove the claim of the accused that the pass is a genuine one. [. . .] In any case there is no evidence before us that the pass is not genuine, there being no evidence from an official of the DHQ to say so." Effectively, the ruling suggested that a document must be assumed to be genuine until it is conclusively proven otherwise – which was quite a liberal notion of authenticity. Whether it was genuine or not, the tribunal found that

the accused reasonably believed that the pass is a genuine one. That honest but mistaken belief makes him not criminally liable. The accused is merely an innocent agent. He did not now that the person who signed was defrauding the government. This argument arises even if the pass is not genuine. The accused had no intention to harm the Republic of Biafra.

He was acquitted. This decision illustrates how permissive the Biafran courts had become toward forgery by the end of the war – a permissiveness born out of both administrative collapse and the knowledge that this kind of crime had become a necessity of survival.[61] Fraud and forgery attracted less scorn as the fighting wore down Biafra.

Nigerians also blurred the boundary between real and fake documents. Refugees who crossed into Nigeria reported that most Biafrans believed they would be killed immediately if they surrendered. To assuage this fear, Nigerian planes dropped packets of "safe conduct passes" printed in English, Igbo, and other eastern languages along the front. These were not meant to work as passes in a literal sense – they were propaganda leaflets made to look like "official" documents, which they hoped would embolden Biafrans to defect to the camps awaiting them on the Nigerian side. They were printed at the suggestion of a British diplomat, who believed that a "psychological weapon" of this sort would be effective in a Biafra gripped by apprehension. "While truth is perhaps not a prime ingredient for documents of this sort, one has a feeling that the promises made in the leaflet relate more

---

[61] NNAE MINJUST 117/1/8, in the Special Tribunal of the Republic of Biafra, no. ST/16c/69, *The State v. Benson Isaac Jaja*, April 10, 1969.

to the benevolence of Federal intentions than to their ability to carry them out in present circumstances."[62] It is unclear how successful this initiative was, but Nigeria was right to think that passes had become fetishized in Biafra.

Biafrans' turn to forgery was not inevitable, and some explanation is in order of why this survival tactic became so common, and not something else. Part of the explanation for the rapid spread of fraud in Biafra can be traced to the longer history of bureaucracy in Nigeria. Eastern Nigerians had played a disproportionately important role in Nigeria's state bureaucracy up to secession. Eastern Nigerians, and especially Igbos, had been favored for administrative positions by the colonial government, and their presence in other parts of the federation was often as civil servants, clerks, teachers, and technicians.[63] A large proportion of the 4–5 million refugees who came to Biafra from elsewhere in the federation were literate, and many of them had worked in the formal economy. Some of the Biafrans arrested for forgery and fraud had been government clerks or bureaucrats before the war, although it is hard to gauge how many.

The experience of having been administrators in Nigeria – or at least having a bureaucrat in the family, as many eastern Nigerians did – meant that a disproportionately large part of the Biafran public was familiar with the intricacies of producing documents, giving affidavits, and other bureaucratic procedures. The common experience of having lived outside of the east as migrants also meant that eastern Nigerians were more likely to carry official identity documents than Nigerians who spent most of their lives in one place. Living as "strangers" in the north and elsewhere had taught them that carrying an official pass could offer some protection from both the state and their

[62] NAUK FCO 38/288, G. D. Anderson to P. D. McEntee, Commonwealth Office, August 15, 1968
[63] Many, but not all, of these people were Igbo. A significant proportion of the civil servants and clerks who worked in the north and elsewhere were members of eastern minorities and not Igbo – a nuance that is often ignored in administrative histories of Nigeria. Although it was Igbo people who gained the reputation for being administrators, and who were most frequently singled out as the face of state authority, in fact that face was often Efik, Ijaw, or Ibibio rather than Igbo. In the eyes of their northern neighbors, many of these people were lumped in with Igbos, but the proportion of Igbos who worked in government service has been somewhat exaggerated. As noted in Chapter 1, it is important to note that "Biafran" is not the same thing as "Igbo." That national category conceals a considerable amount of diversity.

neighbors.[64] People from the east, and especially Igbos, were more likely to have inscribed themselves in government records. They had a higher rate of enrollment in government schools, and they were more likely to have traveled abroad (for purposes ranging from agricultural labor in Spanish Guinea to elite education in England) and therefore carry passports. All of these experiences gave them a long acquaintance with bureaucracy, both under British rule and after independence. The Igbo experience in Nigeria challenges the notion that the bureaucratic cast of mind was unknown to African colonial subjects.

Biafra was a nation of bureaucrats. It is therefore not surprising that paperwork was important there and that knowledge of what an official document would say and look like was largely *common* knowledge. Bureaucratic processes carried much weight in Biafra, even as they became increasingly decentralized and idiosyncratic – or, in other words, fraudulent. The mechanisms of bureaucracy ticked along, even as their movements became warped. To courts, the resulting confusion over who was legitimately empowered to issue documents or passes resulted in practices indistinguishable from fraud.

Trust, Commerce, and Ambition

In most cases, deception was about survival, but for a handful of Biafrans it was also a means of personal transformation. The war could be a time of possibility, and in all its hardship there were opportunities to reinvent oneself or at least to improve one's lot in life. This resonated with one of Biafra's grand narratives; propaganda argued that it was not only a protector of the Igbo people but a new country for a new type of person. Some Biafrans took this as license to remake themselves through impersonation. The general turmoil made it easier to become someone else, and a forged identity card, a borrowed uniform, or a pilfered nun's habit could be used to start a new life.[65] In a way, Biafra's overtures to the world and its citizens' cons of one

---

[64] Protective documentation had its limits. Passes had not protected the Igbos killed in the pogroms leading up to the war. Interview with A. M. O. Onukaogu, Umuahia, March 9, 2015.

[65] The military's broad powers meant that impersonating a soldier was a particularly powerful form of identity theft. For example, a civilian who impersonated a Biafran soldier to steal some valuables from his former mistress made the defense that he was "requisitioning" them. *Biafra Sun*, August 4, 1967, p. 5.

another were both acts of guile – statements of untruth that their speakers hoped would be believed and might even *become* true through repetition.

"You have many more chances of winning a fortune," proclaimed an advertisement for the Biafrapools betting agency, offering to its winners the chance to gain "Amazing Advantages Over All Others."[66] One might imagine that gambling would be far from anyone's mind in April 1968. The war was going badly, and hunger was beginning to creep into the countryside. Yet crisis made the promise of easy money more potent, not less. Chaos and constant displacement made Biafra fertile ground for confidence scams, racketeering, and impersonation. Some Biafrans used disorder as a cover for criminality. The informal mechanisms that allowed people to buy and sell goods, loan out capital, and entrust money to collective enterprises were all corrupted by the war. Biafrans were cut off from their homes, properties, and investments as they fled the constantly shifting fronts, making them vulnerable to the avarice of friends and strangers alike. New, opportunistic forms of fraud emerged in these conditions. Ojukwu's political advisor Akanu Ibiam described how "in some areas Biafrans masquerade and fleet around, evidently in glee, and cause unpleasantness. In this connection, I get the unhappy impression that some Biafrans could care less whether Biafra burns to ashes or not."[67]

Michael Ajogwu remembers that "people were trying to survive by forging certificates and the like to be accepted here and there. They were frustrated by how stultifying some of the requirements had been in Nigeria, and so some of them simply made their own and passed them off."[68] The Biafran press was full of reports about people who forged credentials or claimed fictive pedigrees for themselves, knowing that in the midst of the war no one would check them. A common ruse was to use forged diplomas to obtain jobs that required qualifications, like police work or engineering.[69] One young woman was sentenced to a long prison term by a magistrate in Aba for having pretended to be a nun. Claiming to be a nurse in a local hospital, she bought controlled

[66] HIA, Nigerian Subject Collection XX787, Box 7, *Biafra Time*, April 30, 1968, p. 20.
[67] HIA, Nigerian Subject Collection XX787, Box 7, "We Are One in Biafra," 1967.
[68] Interview with Michael Ajogwu, SAN, Enugu, March 19, 2015.
[69] *Biafra Sun*, June 17, 1967, p. 4.

medicines from a distributor in bulk, which she then sold on the black market at a brisk profit.[70] Forging a school certificate or taking on another person's identity was not always about enduring the war – sometimes it was to start a new life.[71]

The most well-known instances of this problem were in Port Harcourt, where Igbos who fled the city after it fell to Nigeria in May 1968 would have an exceedingly difficult time reclaiming their property after Biafra's defeat.[72] Yet the question of who would care for houses and land left behind applied to refugees within Biafra as well. The evacuation and reoccupation of towns was usually fairly orderly; a Swedish aristocrat who fought on the Biafran side described the "calm atmosphere" of the retreat from Umuahia in April 1969, in which "there were little padlocks on the doors of the empty houses and the floors had been swept clean."[73] Despite the tidiness and the locks, there was much room for deception in abandoned towns and villages.

Owerri had been evacuated in a similarly orderly manner prior to its fall to Nigeria, but when the town was recaptured by Biafra in March 1969 many people found that their land and houses had been occupied by whoever was first to reach them.[74] In some cases, squatters buttressed their claims by adopting the identities of the people who had owned them. This act usually could not be kept up for very long. One officer stationed elsewhere in Biafra begged his rivals to not take advantage of his absence to make a spurious claim to a piece of land:

I will not be happy to hear that you and my people are [still] quarrelling within these crucial hours of our young Republic. Please, please fathers I know that before you and my people, I am nothing but as son I will be able to find out when something is wrong between you and as such, I humbly beg you to cool your minds and reconsider the matter once more and make things better for me, yourselves and my people as well.[75]

---

[70] *Biafra Sun*, July 14, 1968, p. 8.

[71] The use of forgery for the purpose of self-making was not unique to the Biafran episode, even if the war made more opportunities for it. Most pointedly, see Newell, *The Forger's Tale*.

[72] This will be discussed in Chapter 5.

[73] SOAS Nigerian Civil War Collections MS 321463 vol. 68, Manuscript, "Biafra – As I See It," Carl Gustaf von Rosen, 1969, p. 144.

[74] Interview with A. M. O. Onukaogu, Umuahia, March 9, 2015.

[75] NWM uncatalogued collection, "Appeal for Clemency Against Land Law Contrivance," September 19, 1969.

They did so anyway, precipitating a long and involved dispute.

Biafra's prisons offered particularly rich opportunities for impersona-tion. People accused of sabotage, treason, and ordinary crime were detained in makeshift cells, often for months before they were formally tried. Being incarcerated made one especially susceptible to identity theft. This is what befell the politician Effiong Okon Eyo, who attempted to sue the Bank of West Africa in 1968 from prison, where he was serving a term for political charges against Biafra. Someone imperson-ated him while he was incarcerated, withdrawing all of his money by presenting forged identity papers at a distant bank branch, giving the plausible story that he was a refugee who could not make the withdrawal at his local branch because the area was "disturbed." The bank discov-ered the fraud and closed the now empty account, leaving Eyo unable to support his family while he was in jail.[76] The impersonation only suc-ceeded because Eyo was in prison – in normal circumstances, the bank would have insisted that a large withdrawal be done at the home branch, where the teller would have known what Eyo looked like.

When asked if fakery was present in Biafra, Cyprian Ekwensi was unequivocal: "it was there alright."[77] Fuel, medicine, and food were unobtainable through normal means, and commerce became furtive. Counterfeiting took off shortly after secession, and one could find cigarettes filled with sawdust and tea being sold as whiskey in Biafra's marketplaces.[78] A British intelligence report found that, in spite of the blockade, "surprising things went in and out of Biafra, [including] elephant tusk carvings, ball-point pens and cocoa in bags marked 'Cocoa Nigeria.'"[79] It is difficult to gauge the scale of commerce, but this and other sources suggest that much trade in commercial goods took place across the war front – often at great risk to those who carried it out. The porous, shifting nature of Biafra's borders made it possible for traders to travel back and forth between Biafra and Nigeria for commercial purposes. This trade in salt, agricultural products, drugs, and other portable goods was carried out mostly by women using

[76] The case's outcome is unclear. NNAE BCA 1/1/45, in the Court of Appeal of the Republic of Biafra, Aba, no. CA 56/67, *Bank of West Africa, Ltd., Uyo v. Effiong Okon Eyo*, June 24, 1968.

[77] "Chief Cyprian D. Ekwensi," in H. B. Momoh, ed., *The Nigerian Civil War, 1967–1970: History and Reminiscences* (Ibadan: Sam Bookman, 2000): p. 510.

[78] *Biafra Sun*, June 8, 1967, p. 8.

[79] NAUK FCO 65/231, "Record of Mr. Foley's meeting with Ambassador Ferguson on Friday, 21 November" [1969].

barter or illicit Nigerian currency. It came to be known in Igbo as "*ahia attack*" – attack trade. It was a dangerous business that exposed women to the risk of assault by both Biafran and Nigerian soldiers. It usually provided only enough for a trader's immediate family to survive. Although it was tactically risky (and a clear violation of Biafran law), the Biafran government recognized that *ahia attack* was essential to civilian livelihoods, and little was done to suppress it.[80]

To make matters worse, regulations intended to keep down the prices of essential goods ended up producing a large black market. The Biafran courts sometimes pursued violations of wartime price controls, but they did so in a way that created more confusion than clarity. The line between essential commerce and war profiteering was almost impossible to police.[81] In one case, a good Samaritan was sentenced to a year in prison for selling four gallons of petrol to an army officer who had run out of fuel and asked him for help. The state counsel wrote to express his disappointment that the Special Tribunal was going after acts like this while leaving major acts of profiteering, some of them carried out by prominent people, uninvestigated.[82] Other types of profiteering, like renting accommodation to refugees returning from the north at exorbitant rates, were technically legal but attracted public scorn.[83]

The scale of commerce in Biafra was considerable given the circumstances, much of it in aid materials and goods smuggled from Nigeria. Deception was inherent in this kind of trade, including when it involved Biafra's biggest institution – the army. Ben Gbulie recalled that "in [that] day and age, many an unscrupulous contractor had taken to submitting for settlement bills which, on scrutiny, appeared out of all

---

[80] On "*ahia attack*," see Egodi Uchendu, *Women and Conflict in the Nigerian Civil War* (Trenton: Africa World Press, 2007); pp. 139–146; Axel Harneit-Sievers, ed. *A Social History of the Nigerian Civil War: Perspectives from Below* (Hamburg: Lit. Verlag, 1997); Gloria Chuku, "Biafran Women Under Fire: Strategies in Organising Local and Trans-border Trade During the Nigerian Civil War," in Eghosa E. Osaghae, Ebere Onwudiwe, and Rotimi T. Suberu, eds., *The Nigerian Civil War and Its Aftermath* (Ibadan: John Archers, 2002). Chimamanda Ngozi Adichie also describes the trade in *Half of a Yellow Sun* (New York: Anchor, 2006): p. 504.

[81] The journalist Renata Adler would recall that her flight out of Biafra was full not with refugees but with a shipment of used refrigerators. Longform podcast, episode 156, "Renata Adler," [2015].

[82] NNAE MINJUST 117/1/3, in the Special Tribunal of the Republic of Biafra, Umuahia, no. ST/10c/69, *The State v. Ohalete Chijioke*, December 17, 1968.

[83] *Biafra Sun*, August 6, 1967, p. 5.

proportion to the actual bulk of the food items physically delivered to us in the Biafra Army Service Corps."[84] Infrastructure projects and large government contracts were also sites of graft, most notably the construction of the Ikem–Calabar highway. An investigation was opened when Biafran representatives of the construction company found imported iron rods intended for the road for sale in nearby markets. It emerged that Biafran soldiers were using forged chits to requisition iron, concrete, and gravel by the truckload and then selling it to the public. The construction was halted when Nigeria captured Calabar, but most of the concrete had disappeared by this point anyway. One witness testified that there was hardly a house built in Biafra that did not use material intended for the road in its construction.[85]

A series of good harvests did not produce enough to feed the many people crammed into Biafra's shrinking borders, and famine conditions prevailed from the fall of Port Harcourt in May 1968 to the end of the war. An airlift, conducted by foreign aid organizations and the Biafran Air Force, became the only way to bring humanitarian aid into the country. Nigeria's attitude toward the flights was inconsistent; they were allowed so long as Nigerian officials were allowed to inspect their cargo, but this did not guarantee safe passage through Nigerian airspace. Flights that originated in ports where Nigerian inspectors were not allowed, especially Portuguese São Tomé, were regularly shot at. Planes arrived in Biafra at a small, rough-hewn airstrip outside of Uli – sometimes dozens per night, with no radar and no landing lights.[86] Since the aperture that aid came through was so narrow, controlling its distribution became lucrative. Theft, corruption, and fraud at all levels of the humanitarian project multiplied. The distribution of aid was poorly supervised, allowing food and medicine to find its way into public markets, where it could be sold at exorbitant prices.[87]

[84] Gbulie, *The Fall of Biafra*, p. 28.
[85] NNAE MINJUST 19/2/1, in the Special Tribunal of the Republic of Biafra, no. CX/132/68, *State v. Benjamin Egbuna Amaluize and two others*, October 31, 1968.
[86] On the airlift to Biafra, see Michael I. Draper, *Shadows: Airlift and Airwar in Biafra and Nigeria 1967–1970* (Aldershot: Hikoki Publications 1999); Sydney Emezue, *The Last Flight Out: Reminiscences of a Biafran Air Force Pilot (The Alfred Anowai's Story)* (Enugu: Moorhen Books, 2011).
[87] "Chief Cyprian D. Ekwensi," in Momoh, *The Nigerian Civil War*, p. 510.

In a few cases, officials of organizations like the Red Cross used their positions to enrich themselves or channel aid to their clients. The Special Tribunal went after this kind of misconduct with particular energy. For six months in 1968, Casimir Ige embezzled relief materials from the stores of the Biafran Red Cross in his capacity as a regional manager. The case against him includes a lengthy description of how he and his accomplices used forged documents to repackage and sell relief materials at a considerable profit:

It is clear that the accused has been using his position in the Red Cross to carry on spurious deals with relief materials. [...] the modus operandi in this case is this: the accused who is a Red Cross official is in a position to know which contractors supply the Red Cross gari in exchange for stockfish. He uses one of these contractors as a camouflage to carry out his criminal designs, to wit, stealing relief materials to which he has access. Whenever he is caught he already has an answer, which is that Mr. Kalu, a contractor to the Red Cross, brought them to his house for safekeeping. Of course Mr. Kalu will then produce an authority like exhibit 5 to confuse everyone into believing the story of the accused.

Exhibit 5 was a forged pass printed on "Comité International de la Croix-Rouge" letterhead stating that "the bearer, Mr Nathan Ofoma is authorised to transport and sale 5 bags of stockfish of the ICRC foodstuff in exchange for 20 bags of Gari contracted on the 2nd November 1968" and signed by the defendant. The tribunal went on:

these relief materials are distributed to needy Biafrans free of charge. They are sent to us without any charge whatsoever. It is wicked therefore for these relief materials to be diverted for the sole purpose of making money in the midst of suffering of many. Anyone who does that does an act against the welfare of the inhabitants of Biafra. It is subversion because of the present state of affairs in the Republic. [...] We would like to deplore the action of the accused, particularly when he is supposed to be an officer of the Biafran Red Cross now engaged in a praiseworthy humanitarian work.

In controlling Biafra's food, individuals like Casimir Ige wielded the power of life and death. For those who abused that power, the penalty was usually execution.[88]

---

[88] Ige, however, had a shrewd lawyer. He got a long prison sentence. NNAE MINJUST 117/1/6, in the Special Tribunal of the Republic of Biafra, no. ST/13c/69, *The State v. Casimir Ige,* February 19, 1969.

Figure 3.2 Biafran soldiers and an aid worker, 1968 (Rob Burton/Mirrorpix, via Getty Images)

The line between duty and self-interest was not always so clear. In another embezzlement case, an employee of the Transportation Directorate forged a payment voucher to purchase petrol for the vehicles he was responsible for maintaining. After a long discussion about whether it was possible for a legitimate government official to "forge" a document coming from his own office (they decided it was), the tribunal ruled that "the accused, who is a professional engineer, was given a position of trust in the Transport Directorate. He abused the trust reposed in him. At this critical period of the life of this young Republic of Biafra every simple penny embezzled is an act which tends to disturb the economy of the Republic. Such acts amount to subversion."[89] The employee argued that he could not keep the vehicles under his care running without forging a voucher to pay for their fuel, since obtaining it through official channels was impossible. Fulfilling his duty required him to engage in forgery – an entirely plausible defense (fuel shortages were constant, and not even essential services

---

[89] NNAE MINJUST 116/1/5, in the Special Tribunal of the Republic of Biafra, no. ST/20C/69, *The State v. Auguatine Meniru*, June 6, 1969.

were immune from them). The tribunal did not doubt his word, but they gave him a long prison sentence anyway.

Deception in the Statehouse

Ordinary civilians were not the only ones engaged in fraud for the purpose of survival. The Biafran state itself often employed practices that might be considered fraudulent, and an advisor who worked closely with Ojukwu recalled that it was full of "untruth" and intrigue from top to bottom.[90] Corruption and fraud overlapped in Biafra's administration from the beginning. Not long after secession, Justice Aniagolu (of later fame for a postwar armed robbery tribunal that bore his name) convened a public tribunal to investigate reports of forgery and fraud by employees of the Biafran Development Corporation. Dozens of payment vouchers had been forged by multiple employees of the parastatal, suggesting to Aniagolu that forgery was in danger of being a normal part of state business.[91] The tribunal was plagued by indiscretions and irregularities; one of the accused threatened to kill a witness on the stand, leading to a further charge of contempt. No further high-level inquiries were made into acts of corruption. As the Biafran government dissipated, more opportunities for government officials to engage in fraud or corruption presented themselves, while the chances of being caught diminished. Oblique evidence of this only survives in the records of foreign governments and in Biafra's press – which was mostly a propaganda device. Yet, even in the absence of records, inferences can be made about the state's complicated relationship with the truth.[92]

Deception had an important place in the war effort, especially when it came to purchasing arms. Since Biafra was not broadly recognized as a sovereign state, procuring weapons was a convoluted affair. Biafra's weapons came from many places, and obtaining them required cunning and ingenuity. Biafra's best-known weapon was the *ogbunigwe*, an improvised artillery device made from repurposed oil barrels. Yet homemade artillery was not enough to wage a modern war, and Biafra went to great

[90] Interview with anonymous informant, Enugu, September 2014.
[91] *Biafra Sun*, July 13, 1967, July 28, 1967.
[92] This affinity between warfare and "trickery" is not unique to Biafra. See James Q. Whitman, *The Verdict of Battle: The Law of Victory and the Making of Modern War* (Cambridge, MA: Harvard University Press, 2012): pp. 199–201.

lengths to import munitions from abroad.[93] International regulations controlling the transport of armaments forced the Biafran state to regularly use forged or illegitimately obtained "end-user certificates."[94] Biafran arms buyers sometimes became ensnared in other people's schemes. In one case, Biafran agents were hoodwinked by a group of arms merchants who offered them a black market "torpedo" at an exorbitant price, with which they hoped to sink a Nigerian destroyer. The torpedo turned out to be a fake – a prop created for the occasion by a film company.[95] As Ojukwu would later write, the Biafran cause attracted "all the adventurers of the world [...] Some [were] honest, while most were not."[96]

Munitions were brought to Biafra through shadowy routes. A British internal investigation shed light on one; an employee of the Indonesian Embassy in London, with assistance from business-men in Germany, had used forged documents to purchase guns from a dealer, which were brought by Portuguese agents through the Azores, to Gabon, and then to Biafra.[97] It was never discovered who in the Biafran government had orchestrated the purchase, but it was likely someone at a very high rank. Biafran agents made many such transactions, using forged documents purporting to come from the United Arab Republic, Czechoslovakia, and elsewhere.[98] In 1969, the Irish government discreetly investigated a charter company retained to fly weapons for Biafra from Prague to Lisbon on the grounds that it

[93] Nigeria, too, fought with a jumble of weapons from many places, including the Soviet Union, which Nigeria tried to use as leverage to demand greater support from the United Kingdom. NAUK FCO 65/163, B.A.M. Adekunle to Rt. Hon. Lord Shepherd, House of Lords, November 19, 1968.

[94] In practice, as a "gunrunner" in London told a British journalist, this entailed "buying yourself an ambassador so you can get your end-use certificates." Timothy Green, *The Smugglers: An Investigation into the World of the Contemporary Smuggler* (New York: Walker and Company, 1969): p. 132.

[95] The following account does not offer a source for this story, but it was related to me in slightly different form – as a set of fake landmines rather than a torpedo – by an informant who had worked for the Biafran representative office in Portugal. George Thayer, *The War Business: The International Trade in Armaments* (New York: Simon and Schuster, 1969): p. 168.

[96] "Chief Chukwuemeka Odumegwu-Ojukwu," in Momoh, *The Nigerian Civil War*, p. 755.

[97] NAUK FCO 24/768, Foreign and Commonwealth Office to M. P. Preston, British Embassy, Jakarta, May 6, 1970.

[98] The use of fraudulent documents to obtain arms was reported as early as 1966, before Biafra formally seceded. See Ogechi E. Anyanwu, "Understanding the Causes of the Nigeria-Biafra War," in Toyin Falola and Ogechukwu Ezekwem, eds., *Writing the Nigeria-Biafra War* (Woodbridge: James Currey, 2016): p. 60.

had contravened Ireland's ban on the use of nationally registered aircraft for the transport of armaments. The investigation revealed a long path of forgery and obscuration. The shipment officially contained food and "sporting goods," but in fact it contained several thousand Czechoslovak small arms, purchased with a forged end-user certificate.[99] An Israeli intelligence source claimed that consignments of Chinese-manufactured arms paid for by Tanzania had come into Biafra, and rumors circulated that France was providing arms from Bulgaria, Albania, and elsewhere.[100] Tanzania denied these allegations, and Biafra's supporters claimed that the arms were from Tanzania's national arsenal and had been given as a gesture of support.[101] Wherever they came from, arms were transported to staging grounds, especially São Tomé, where they were packaged along with relief materials and loaded onto planes bound for Biafra. Aid agencies may have known about this, including Joint Church Aid and the Catholic charity Caritas, although the extent of their involvement is unclear.[102] It is hard to be confident about anything regarding the arms trade. Who forged the certificates? Who bought the weapons? How complicit were international organizations in transporting them? Unlike the more everyday forms of deception that went on in Biafra, these transactions were never scrutinized by courts; but weapons reached the front somehow, and they would never have gotten there without subterfuge.

---

[99] Fearing that this news would confirm the already common public perception that Ireland was covertly supporting Biafra, the investigation was kept out of the press. NAID 2000/14/25, Paul Keating, Ambassador of Ireland to Nigeria to Department of External Affairs, Dublin, December 6, 1969.

[100] NAID 2000/14/24, Paul Keating, Ambassador of Ireland to Nigeria to Department of External Affairs, Dublin, March 1, 1969.

[101] NAID 2000/14/25, "Tanzania News Bulletin," November 15, 1968. Tanzania would be one of the few countries to go beyond the provision of aid and recognize Biafra diplomatically. The Tanzanian government justified its recognition of Biafra by arguing that Igbos were an oppressed people in Nigeria – the fact that Nigeria was "free" of colonialism did not make it a free country for all. Nyerere drew comparisons to the experience of European Jews in the Second World War and invoked Israel in describing Biafra's cause. "Fortunately," he noted, "Biafrans do not want someone else's country; they have their own." East Africana Collections, University of Dar es Salaam, "Maelezo ya Serikali ya Tanzania Kuhusu Kuitambua Nchi ya Biafra," 1968; Austine S. O. Okwu, *In Truth for Justice and Honor: A Memoir of a Nigerian-Biafran Ambassador* (Princeton: Sungai, 2011): p. 226.

[102] On the airlift, see Draper, *Shadows*; David L. Koren, *Far Away in the Sky: A Memoir of the Biafran Airlift* (Oakland, CA: Peace Corps Writers, 2016).

Biafra also had a corps of roving envoys who tried to cajole other countries into extending diplomatic recognition. Eyoma Ita Eyoma, the unofficial Biafran "ambassador" in Stockholm, spent considerable energy lobbying the Icelandic government to recognize Biafra, invoking its experience as "a small country using all its resources of blood and treasure to achieve independence."[103] Pius Okigbo went as far as Paraguay and Argentina to make the Biafran case, and he spent months traveling to the newly independent states of the Caribbean to drum up support. He came closest to securing recognition from Guyana, but he was foiled when Nigeria sent a larger and more impressive delegation as a "prophylactic operation."[104] To the foreign ministers of these small states, the Biafran "diplomats" with hastily drafted credentials and canceled Nigerian passports who tried to meet with them seemed suspicious. When they consulted the British High Commission for guidance (or a Nigerian representative if there was one), they were advised to treat Biafra's representatives as imposters.

Other forms of deception served the war effort as well, although only glimpses of them are visible in the record. Espionage, for example, played a part in Biafra's strategy. Memoirist Diliorah Chukwurah described the Biafran Boys Company, which was recruited from Biafran children between the ages of ten and thirteen who understood other Nigerian languages. Posing as abandoned children, they would infiltrate Nigerian camps to gather intelligence and slip back across the front into Biafra to report what they heard.[105] Biafra had more conventional spies as well, including women. In occupied areas, they would enter into relationships with Nigerian soldiers to gather information about the movements of Nigerian troops or pose as traders and move surreptitiously through markets behind the front lines, gathering information about public sentiment and the rumors that circulated on the other side.[106] Although spying on Nigeria was not "fraud" as the law defined it, spies made use of similar skills to those of confidence artists, including impersonation, sexual entrapment, and the

---

[103] FCO 65/246, British Embassy, Reykjavik to Foreign and Commonwealth Office, June 18, 1969.
[104] FCO 65/246, British High Commission, Georgetown to Foreign and Commonwealth Office, August 7, 1969.
[105] Chukwurah, *Last Train to Biafra*, p. 48.
[106] Interview with anonymous informant, Lagos, June 2019.

manipulation of affect.[107] To the Biafran government, of course, acts of deception conducted in diplomacy, reconnaissance, or arms buying were not only analytically distinct from fraud – they were acts of high patriotism. Yet to those on the wide spectrum between soldier and civilian – boys' brigades, civil defenders, and *ahia attack* traders among them – the difference would have been murky. What did it mean to be a spy in the service of a state like Biafra, which, especially in the later stages of the war, did not look very much like a state? In the haze of war, it was hard to tell espionage for the national cause from lying for personal survival.

The argument that Nigeria was committing genocide against Igbos was an important part of Biafra's international struggle for recognition. Several committees of "impartial" foreigners convened by the United Nations and the Organisation of African Unity – Swedish, British, American, and Yugoslav observers among them – had found that there was no evidence that Nigeria's actions were genocidal.[108] The Biafran government decided to stage its own "independent" report on Nigeria's actions, which was completed in 1969.[109] The report, compiled by a jurist only ever described as "Dr. Mensah of Ghana," recounts the events of the pogroms of 1966, the Asaba massacre, and other acts committed by Nigeria and Nigerians against Igbos. The events described in the report can be corroborated elsewhere, and there is little reason to doubt that what it records is broadly true. Its contents were probably derived from the judicial commission of inquiry into the 1966 killings that the Eastern Region had convened immediately before Biafra's secession, conducted under the leadership of Justice G. C. N. Onyiuke.

Yet Dr. Mensah himself seems to have been a smokescreen. The international body to which the Biafran government allegedly appealed to conduct the investigation, the International Committee for the Study of the Crimes of Genocide, was invented for the moment. Despite its

---

[107] On the roles of "sex witches" and "diabolical voodoo machination" in espionage, see Obi N. Ignatius Ebbe, *Broken Back Axle: Unspeakable Events in Biafra* (n.p.: Xlibris, 2010): pp. 135–137.

[108] Chima J. Korieh, "Biafra and the Discourse on the Igbo Genocide," *Journal of Asian and African Studies* vol. 48 no. 6 (2013): pp. 727–740.

[109] International Committee on the Investigation of Crimes of Genocide, "Nigeria/Biafra Conflict: An International Commission of Jurists Find Prima Facie Evidence of Genocide." The School of Oriental and African Studies holds a mimeographed copy in its general collection.

official-looking seal and its Paris headquarters, I can find no record of an organization by this name, other than citations of this report.[110] If Dr. Mensah was a real person, it is not clear why no further identifying information was given about him in the report that he purportedly produced.[111] The report itself does not seem to have circulated widely – only a handful of typecopies are extant. Perhaps its creators realized that it might do the Biafran cause more harm than good, but it is telling that it was drafted in the first place. Making up an international organization, while not synonymous with the fraud of day-to-day survival, shows that Biafra's complicated relationship with the truth extended to its leadership. The country had been founded in the name of law and order, but the pressures of the war compelled people – in positions both high and low – to forge their own passes, pretend to be people they were not, and lay claim to things that were not their own.

Conclusion

In May 1969, Biafran commandos stormed an oil platform in federal territory and took eighteen foreign workers hostage. They were charged with spying and brought before a tribunal, which sentenced them to death. Their sentence caused international outcry, and the Pope made a personal appeal for their release.[112] Ojukwu was furious. "For 18 white men, Europe is aroused," he said over Radio Biafra. "What have they said about our millions? Eighteen white men assisting in the crime of genocide. What do they say about our murdered innocents? How many black dead make one missing white? Mathematicians, please answer me. Is it infinity?"[113] A lawyer who

---

[110] The fullest account of the organization is by the journalist Suzanne Cronje, who emphasized the report's connection to figures in the Soviet intelligence community. Suzanne Cronje, *The World and Nigeria: The Diplomatic History of the Biafran War, 1967–1970* (London: Sidgwick and Jackson, 1972): p. 277.

[111] A possible candidate is the jurist Thomas Mensah, although since his specialization was maritime law it would be unusual for him to have taken an interest.

[112] CADN 332PO/1 Box 4, "Le Saint-Siège et les techniciens de l'ENI libérés du Biafra," June 11, 1969. In the end, the hostages were released after protracted negotiations with the Italian and French governments and the payment of a ransom, which did damage to Biafra's reputation. See Roy Doron, "Biafra and the AGIP Oil Workers: Ransoming and the Modern Nation State in Perspective," *African Economic History* vol. 42, no. 1 (2014): pp. 137–156.

[113] "Biafra: Reprieve for eighteen," *Time*, June 13, 1969.

Figure 3.3 Nigerian soldiers in Owerri, 1970 (A. Abbas/Magnum Photos)

served as their state-appointed defender recalled that this was "theatre, not law," but by this point he had lost faith in Biafran justice.[114] Many people were losing faith in the cause of independence too. Biafra's global position was untenable, its population was starving, and its internal order was unraveling faster than ever.

   The last months of the war were punctuated by bombings, sieges, and counterattacks in the East Central State, where Nigeria chipped away at what remained of Biafra through a combination of assault and starvation. Biafran troops succeeded in retaking Owerri in April 1969, briefly galvanizing the cause and creating a temporary stalemate. The same month, Nigeria captured Biafra's capital at Umuahia, forcing what remained of the government to retreat to Owerri. In January 1970, Nigerian troops under the command of Obasanjo, Muhammad, and Adekunle launched Operation Tailwind, which surrounded the remainder of the Biafran Army and moved on the airstrip at Uli. When it fell, Biafra lost its only link to the outside world. The war was over.

---

[114]   Interview with anonymous informant, Enugu, September 2014.

Ojukwu hastily handed over power to his chief of staff, Philip Efiong, and fled with his entourage to Ivory Coast. After being escorted to Lagos, Efiong and the belligerents' chief justices – Mbanefo for Biafra and Adetokunbo Ademola for Nigeria – drafted an instrument of surrender, which was signed on January 15, 1970.[115] "The soul of Biafra," Chukwuemeka Ike wrote, "ascended into the heavens in full military regalia."[116] Millions of "ex-Biafrans" – now Nigerians again – made their way home and tried to resume their lives. Ben Gbulie described the road from Udoh in the final days of the war "strewn with refugees: a handful of them sitting and squatting, shivering all over with cold, too fagged out to continue their flight to safety; the rest of them lying huddled up in family pockets, snoring. The scene was fraught with pathos."[117]

The reconciliation process began at this point, but the tenor of that process had already been established in the Biafran territories that Nigeria occupied early in the war. Nigeria's capture of Rivers State and the South-Eastern State had been followed by a long process of settling scores. Emboldened by the Nigerian occupation, people in Calabar and Port Harcourt had turned against their Igbo neighbors. The end of the fighting had played out less violently in the Enugu–Nsukka corridor, but this region too had suffered as the war raged on elsewhere. By the end of the war, Enugu was more like a garrison than a working city, and the federal university at Nsukka was a shell pock-marked by bullets. For the central territories that held out the longest, peace would not come until Biafra's final surrender in 1970. Some of its towns had changed hands multiple times during the war. Many were in ashes. Others were physically intact but crippled by hunger and gripped by fear. Crime would thrive in these broken places.

---

[115] Philip Efiong, *The Caged Bird Sang No More: My Biafra Odyssey, 1966–1970* (Pinetown: 30 Degrees South Publishers, 2016): p. 225.
[116] Chukwuemeka Ike, *Sunset at Dawn: A Novel About Biafra* (London: Collins and Harvill, 1976): p. 246.
[117] Gbulie, *The Fall of Biafra*, p. 183.

4 | *Burying the Hatchet: The Problems of Postwar Reintegration*

In February 1970, less than a month after Biafra surrendered, Jerome Okolo returned to his house in Enugu for the first time since the city had fallen to Nigeria. The lawyer and his wife found their house looted and shot up, his large collection of books ruined from exposure. They slept unprotected on the lawn, but they felt safe for the first time in three years. "It was oddly peaceful," he recalled. "Everyone was too tired go on, and all anyone wanted to do was to go home." In the following months, crime and insecurity would become endemic in the reconstituted East Central State, "but for the first weeks the feeling of shock and exhaustion was so great that no one would molest you." Okolo's first order of business was to drive what remained of his car after three years of running on homemade petrol to Lagos to be serviced. The journey was dangerous, long, and littered with checkpoints manned by soldiers who treated him with suspicion. When he reached Lagos, he went straight to the home of a Nigerian friend from university. When they came face-to-face, Okolo was so emaciated that he was unrecognizable. It was only when he could recite personal details about their studies together in Dublin that the friend believed he was who he claimed to be. A photograph from that day shows him with his friend, sunken and prematurely aged. Looking at the photo fifty years later, Okolo could barely recognize himself.[1]

The war's wake was a time for reconstituting broken lives, settling scores, and finding ways to get by. Accomplishing these things almost always involved dispute and often involved lawbreaking. This took place in the context of a dense military occupation. The press published photos of Nigerian and Biafran soldiers embracing at the end of this "brothers' war," but they concealed a deep bitterness. Civilians took victory as license to extort or harass Igbo Nigerians, and the people who had recently called themselves Biafrans responded with defensive, wounded

[1] Interview with Jerome H. C. Okolo, SAN, Enugu, September 17, 2014.

aggression. The war's fallout touched practically every area of life in the former Biafran territories, and most court cases heard in the East Central State in the 1970s followed on from the war in some way. Surplus firearms were used in armed robberies, family relationships made or broken in Biafra filled the dockets of magistrates' courts, and grudges dating from the war played out in complicated ways. A common defense in criminal cases was that a witness for the prosecution had "lied to put [the defendant] in trouble" as comeuppance for "some part played against his people during the civil war."[2] Statements of allocutus pleaded that convicted criminals were "young and just rehabilitating after the deadly civil war," which moved judges to impose light sentences.[3] Old rivalries that had been set aside were taken up again in its stead. In one case from Port Harcourt, a Nigerian Army veteran brutally killed an old adversary when he came back to Rivers State in the weeks after the war's end. He later defended himself by arguing that the deceased had been an officer in the Biafran Army – he was taking his victim's "treason" into his own hands. The court was unconvinced by this defense, and he was sentenced to death.[4]

Biafra's reintegration into Nigeria took place under the banner of a policy that Gowon called "no victor, no vanquished."[5] This philosophy of national reconciliation promised that ordinary Igbos (and others) who had fought for Biafra's independence would not be punished for having done so. "Gowon was quite good," recalled a local politician in Umuahia. "He showed some maturity. He warned soldiers not to molest our people. Some obeyed him, some didn't."[6] Bringing

[2] ESHC uncatalogued collection, in the High Court of the East Central State of Nigeria, Aba, no. A/2c/72, *The State v. Festus Alozie*, February 23, 1972.
[3] ESHC uncatalogued collection, in the High Court of the East Central State, Owerri, no. HOW/5c/1970, *The State v. Innocent Uhuegbulam*, December 15, 1970.
[4] Rivers State Law Reports, High Court of Port Harcourt, *The State v. Jesse George*, September 30, 1971.
[5] NNAI CWC 1/2/12, "Blueprint for Post-War Reconstruction" [c.1970].
[6] Interview with Chief A. N. Kanu, Umuahia, March 9, 2015. A historian who visited Gowon in London after he was overthrown by General Murtala Muhammed in 1975 was one of many who observed Gowon's graciousness toward his former opponents: "While Gowon was driving Elaigwu and me from the Chalk Farm tube station in his little British car, he joked about the irony of history. He pointed out that the Igbo he had defeated were among the few Nigerian friends he had in London in 1978. I replied that they were friendly to him now because of the magnanimous statesmanship he had shown them in their darkest hour; in fact, I asserted, the Igbo were not as bad as opponents made them

Biafra back into Nigeria involved a drawn-out process of reconciliation, reconstruction, and rehabilitation, commonly called the "three
Rs." For many individual "ex-Biafrans," the question of where they
would fit into Nigeria was murky. Lieutenant Ejiofor Oteka of the
Biafran Army was wounded in battle and taken to Switzerland by the
Red Cross, where he received treatment and eventually found work in
a factory. Stranded in Geneva, he wrote to a British friendly association
that "since the sudden collapse of Biafra, I have been confused and
don't really know what to do. The glorious sun has set unduly and the
resplendent colour has become dim. Merchants of death have achieved
their long-sought for aim. Imperialist materialism has conquered natural brotherly love."[7] He shared this malaise with many of his compa-
triots, who were dubious of Nigeria's promises of fair treatment in the
war's aftermath.[8]

The political order that emerged in the East Central State was
repressive, paranoid, and capricious. Emergency rule remained in
place; and, like in the rest of Nigeria, tribunals worked alongside
common law courts. Some aspects of civilian administration were left
intact, while others were remade in the image of the military. The state
arrogated to itself new powers in the name of maintaining public order,
which it justified by invoking the danger prevailing there at the end of
the war. This did little to improve public security, and it further
hollowed out what remained of Nigeria's civilian legal culture. All of
this took place while insecurity spread uncontrollably. This chapter
analyzes how the end of the fighting sustained conditions where insecurity and violence could thrive. The first section describes how the
former Biafra was administered immediately after surrender and how
its residents experienced the military occupation. The chapter then
considers reintegration as a political problem. Finally, I examine the
postwar period through the lens of a case about police brutality, which
illustrates how Nigerians came to see the state itself as criminal.

out to be. Gowon responded that he knew this to be true." G. N. Uzoigwe,
"Forgotten Genocide: The Igbo People and Genocide Studies," in Chima
J. Korieh, ed., *The Nigeria-Biafra War: Genocide and the Politics of Memory*
(Amherst, NY: Cambria Press, 2012): p. 71.
[7] NAUK FCO 65/818, Ejiofor Oteka to Margot Parish, December 2, 1970.
[8] For a comparative analysis of the disruptive capacity of veterans in postwar
societies, see Gregory Mann, *Native Sons: West Africa Veterans and France in the
Twentieth Century* (Durham, NC: Duke University Press, 2006).

Making Law and Order in the Former Biafra

The courts were briefly closed after Biafra's surrender, but reopening them was one of the East Central State's first orders of business. In large part, reintegration was a legal process. "The problem of Nigerian unity," wrote the political scientist Anthony Oyewole during the difficult early years of reconstruction, "is not the task of the legislative and the executive branches alone, it is, in a special way, that of the courts also."[9] The preponderance of violent crimes and thefts also made it imperative to get the courts up and running as quickly as possible. In March 1970, the East Central State's judges – nearly all of them erstwhile Biafrans – were called back to the bench without ceremony. There was discussion within the Federal Ministry of Justice about removing judges and magistrates who had served in Biafra, but for practical reasons it was decided not to do so.[10] Moreover, the Biafran judiciary counted among its members some of Nigeria's best-known and most respected judges. To suspend the judges who had sat in Biafra would create both a personnel shortage and a crisis of confidence in the federal government's promises of reconciliation.[11] Biafra's judges, magistrates, and legal administrators returned to their posts, now as loyal (if somewhat wary) Nigerian citizens. Most made a seamless transition back into their prewar positions, thanks both to their personal connections and to the fact that their services were desperately needed. Judges who had served Biafra just a few months before, and had been among its main architects, were tasked with liquidating it.[12]

---

[9] Anthony Oyewole, "The Role of the Courts in the Process of National Integration in Nigeria," *Journal of Administration Overseas* vol. 12, no. 2 (April 1973): pp. 136–143, 143.

[10] True to form, the British High Commission suggested that the administration of the East Central State after the war might best be done by expatriates. NAUK FCO 65/213, "Expatriate Recruitment for East Central State," November 22, 1969.

[11] Interview with Anthony Mogboh, SAN, Enugu, October 2, 2014.

[12] HIA, Nigerian Subject Collection XX787, Box 6, "Re-absorption of former Civil Servants and the appointment of Central-Eastern State Indigenes in the Federal Public Service and other Public Services of the Federation," Federal Public Service Commission, 1970. In the South-Eastern State it took until August for the state Ministry of Justice to resume operations. Owing to political infighting it took another full year for a chief justice to be appointed – a West Indian whose status as an outsider the state government hoped would restore public faith in the legal system. Peter Odo Effiong Bassey, *The Nigerian Judiciary: The Departing Glory* (Lagos: Malthouse Press, 2000): p. 43.

The former Biafra was full of crime and dispute – "a good place to be a criminal, or a lawyer, or especially a criminal lawyer," as one barrister recalled.[13] There was a glut of filings in the East Central State, as people took actions to secure property and initiated torts that they had set aside during the war. Lawyers went back into practice immediately. Unlike most former Biafrans, they found that there was no shortage of work for them. "We private practitioners didn't suffer," one recalled, noting that the Nigerian government made no requirement that former Biafrans officially register their loyalty before returning to work in the private sector. "After the war the only people who had anything to fear from the federal government were those who wanted to carry on with Biafra."[14] As Enechi Onyia recalled of his practice in the early 1970s,

it was almost entirely criminal cases, and there were a lot of them – everything else was pushed to the side. People came out of the woodwork after the war to bring criminal charges against others that they had been afraid to start when the war was going on. There were more criminals because of the war and the problems that it had brought to ordinary people.

Representing armed robbers, especially, could be a brisk business for lawyers in the East Central State, "if one could stomach it."[15]

The letter of the law did not change much after the war, and the East Central State continued to use the prewar criminal code. Tellingly, a copy of the 1960 code used in an Owerri court has had its title page altered twice, first to print "Republic of Biafra" over "Eastern Region of Nigeria" and subsequently to scribble out "Republic of Biafra" and replace it with "East Central State of Nigeria."[16] When the military government made changes to the law, it did so through edicts and decrees. Biafra's decrees were annulled in 1970, and a new set of directives were enacted.[17] The Public

---

[13] Interview with Kola Babalola, SAN, Port Harcourt, March 5, 2015.
[14] Interview with Anthony Mogboh, SAN, Enugu, October 2, 2014.
[15] Interview with Chief Enechi Onyia, SAN, Enugu, September 29, 2014.
[16] The East Central State would later be further subdivided, but the content of the law remained largely the same despite the shifting of political boundaries.
[17] In 1970 the administration of the East Central State issued the Enactments (Revocation) Edict, which declared that "all enactments of the illegal regime are hereby declared void and of no effect. All existing laws which were revoked or suspended either expressly or by necessary implication by the enactments affected by section 3 of this Edict are hereby re-enacted and shall have effect as if they were never revoked or suspended as the case may be." With regard to legal decisions from Biafra, however, the attitude of the postwar government was more mixed. Some decisions made by lower courts were allowed to let stand,

Figure 4.1 A group of lawyers in Enugu celebrating the end of a session, 1971 (A. Abbas/Magnum Photos)

Law and State Security Edict of March 1970 gave the East Central State government broad authority to detain people suspected of harboring fire-arms or plotting against the state, and it dramatically expanded what constituted breach of public order. The state executive reserved for himself the right to define "any act which is capable of damaging the friendly relationship existing between the State and any other State within the Federation of Nigeria." Anyone critical of Nigeria could be detained indefinitely "in the interest of the security of the State or of peace."[18] Taking a page from colonial rule, the East Central State used laws prohibit-ing vagrancy, begging, and solicitation to control movement. The demar-cation of civil and military jurisdiction was unclear, just as it had been in

---

while decisions made by the Court of Appeal were declared void. Supplement to Central Eastern State of Nigeria Gazette no. 3, vol. 1, March 12, 1970. Edict no. 3 of 1970, Judicial Acts (Validation) Edict; Supplement to Central Eastern State of Nigeria Gazette no. 3, vol. 1, March 28, 1970. Edict no. 5 of 1970, Public Law and State Security Edict.

[18] See Isabella Okagbue, "Wither the Wanderer: An Examination of the Vagrancy Type Provisions in Nigerian Criminal Law," in M. Ayo Ajomo, ed., *New Dimensions in Nigerian Law* (Lagos: Nigerian Institute of Advanced Legal Studies, 1989).

Biafra. There was no consensus about what was the responsibility of the common law courts, the military's own tribunals, and the special tribunals that the state established for civilians. Cases that bridged military misconduct and criminal law, like a 1972 theft of a civilian's personal items by a soldier in Aba, were usually heard in the East Central State High Court;[19] but there were no firm guidelines.

Judges in the East Central State could do no right in the public eye. If they were harsh in their sentencing, they were accused of picking off the state's population one by one as retribution. When they showed leniency in violent crime cases, especially if the defendants were Nigerian soldiers, they were accused of letting anarchy reign – again in order to punish the east.[20] In this politicized context, very few people believed that justice was a neutral process. One important case from shortly after Biafra's defeat concerned a group of Nigerian soldiers who commandeered a car and shot its driver with an automatic rifle as he ran into the forest.[21] The trial that followed was intended to restore public faith in the legal system and to convince the eastern Nigerian public that soldiers were not above the law. Yet the final ruling seemed to make the opposite point; the unreliability of a key witness led to their acquittal, which confirmed the already widely held idea that no ex-Biafran could obtain justice in a Nigerian court.

Public, televised executions of soldiers found guilty of violent crime were intended to reassure Igbos of Nigeria's good intentions.[22] In occupied Benin City, two Nigerian officers were executed in front of a large crowd after being convicted of the murder of two employees of Barclays Bank, a prison warden, and a police inspector, all four of whom were West Niger Igbos. The accused men were Bini and Urhobo. The ethnicities of the victims and perpetrators made the execution into

---

[19] ESHC uncatalogued collection, in the High Court of the East Central State of Nigeria, Aba, no. A/3C/72, *The State v. Francis Okwujie and Anthony Ezeji*, March 13, 1972.

[20] It is difficult to gauge public reaction with much confidence, but editorialists who wrote to the newspaper *The Renaissance* often reacted to prominent convictions and acquittals in this way. This was a state-sponsored publication, but these editorials likely reflected some degree of genuine public opinion.

[21] ESHC uncatalogued collection, in the High Court of the East Central State of Nigeria, Aba, no. A/4c/70, *The State v. Francis Odijie and Oseni Alimi*, November 20, 1970.

[22] Lloyd Garrison reported on some of these executions. "Old Enemies Slowly Building New Lives in Nigeria," *New York Times*, February 11, 1970, p. 12.

an object lesson. Dignitaries were invited, and speeches were made as the men were tied up before the firing squad. The British Deputy High Commissioner described the event to his superiors:

The crowd was strangely quiet, both before and after the executions. Apart from the expected pushing by those at the rear, striving for a better view, which caused the front ranks of spectators, mainly women, to be severely belaboured by both police and military, there was very little movement or noise. Curiosity and apathy were the only feelings displayed. Generally speaking the executions have been welcomed. The civilian population is getting very tired of the high-handedness of the military and they hope this will teach them a lesson.[23]

As an Irish diplomat present wrote, "the murders committed by these two men would probably have passed without disciplinary action, like hundreds of others, were it not for the fact that news of the atrocities leaked out and could not be suppressed."[24] The white barrels that the soldiers had been tied to were left standing in the square as a reminder that the Nigerian government would not tolerate any challenge to its authority. Capital punishment, especially in armed robbery cases, was as much about the performance of control as it was about "justice."

The former Biafran territories chafed under the Nigerian occupation. A Nigerian administrator described how "a thin air of psychological defeat" hung over the east, afflicting both those who had embraced the Biafran idea and those who had been "Biafrans" against their will.[25] Nigerian troops were feared, even in places where they had been welcomed as liberators. Anxiety was common across the areas they occupied, whether they had only been "Biafran" for a few months (like Benin City) or had held out until the very end. The occupying forces were blamed for crime and other social ills, especially in the East Central State. Although they were indeed responsible for much of the armed violence that took place there, Nigerian soldiers were also made scapegoats for unsolved crimes and for the growth of disturbing social phenomena like drug use and child marriage. Not every problem in the postwar east

---

[23] NAUK FCO 38/287, G. d'Arnaud-Taylor, British High Commission, Benin City to M.J. Newington, British High Commission, Lagos, June 28, 1968.

[24] NAID 2000/14/22, Confidential report by Joseph Small, Embassy of Ireland in Lagos, July 1, 1968.

[25] Samuel Osaigbovo Ogbemudia, *Years of Challenge* (Ibadan: Heinemann Education Books, 1991): p. 111.

could be pinned on Nigerian soldiers, but the legal record shows many instances of harassment, violence, and theft against local civilians.

The concentration of soldiers in the East Central State was dense; out of about 240,000 troops in the Nigerian armed forces, about 130,000 were stationed there in 1970.[26] Although most were housed in barracks, soldiers were still highly visible in the "military villages" and urban camps that adjoined civilian settlements. The Rivers, Mid-West, and South-Eastern States still hosted large populations of soldiers from when they had been recaptured earlier in the war, though none as large as the East Central State. A British diplomat described the

increasingly bitter feelings against the army, its excesses at road blocks, its demanding of money, its "purchase" of goods without payment, its general air of swaggering, domineering insolence. [...] Women are particularly "anti": they want more and more severe action taken against soldiers who abuse their authority. It is the French Revolution all over again, but modified for the occasion. They want to see heads roll, or more accurately, more bodies crumple at the stake.[27]

Most people resented soldiers, but traders liked that they spent money with profligacy – their business was especially welcome given the shortage of Nigerian currency. Many women supported their families by selling food, alcohol, companionship, and herbal medicines or charms to Nigerian soldiers, but men tended to avoid the occupying army if they could.[28] The closure of army camps was greeted with relief by most Igbo men and dismay by women who feared losing their livelihoods. "I feel sad that army headquarters is being moved," wrote a civilian to an Enugu newspaper in 1972. "Army spending has helped to brighten up the pockets of market and petty traders. Those who will lose heavily are the party girls and other camp followers. They will have to engage themselves in other forms of labour to be able to keep up their psychedelic attractions."[29]

The Nigerian soldiers who occupied the former Biafra included men of all ethnic backgrounds and places of origin, along with some women

---

[26] NAUK FCO 65/1195, R.E. Parsons, British High Commission, Lagos to Foreign and Commonwealth Office, April 20, 1972.

[27] NAUK FCO 38/287, G. d'Arnaud-Taylor, British High Commission, Benin City to M.J. Newington, British High Commission, Lagos, July 3, 1968.

[28] Egodi Uchendu, *Women and Conflict in the Nigerian Civil War* (Trenton: Africa World Press, 2007): pp. 150–155.

[29] *The Renaissance* [Enugu], January 30, 1972, p. 4.

in administrative positions.[30] No unit was entirely homogeneous, though most were divided by region of origin. The largest contingents were Hausa northerners, Yoruba westerners, and men from the Rivers State. There were many soldiers from minority groups interspersed in these units, including a small number of West Niger Igbos. Some soldiers were remembered as more violent than others, but criminal acts and indiscipline cut across the army. As one former Nigerian officer recalled, the Nigerian forces had become difficult to control: "Corruption and abuse of power was rampant and all were attributed to the exigencies of war."[31] War-weary soldiers disrupted life wherever they were stationed.

Urban Property Disputes

City life in the former Biafra in the 1970s was jumpy and dangerous, including in the "minority" areas that had fallen to Nigeria early in the war. For the first time since the advent of the transatlantic slave trade, Calabar and Port Harcourt had no significant Igbo community. Although some Igbos returned in the late 1970s, Calabar never fully recovered its prewar Igbo population. Recaptured Port Harcourt was physically intact but a ghost town, with more than half the population missing, Igbo-run businesses shuttered, and a new military occupation – this time by Nigeria – stalking the streets. "[It] was a lonely city," recalled the writer Elechi Amadi of the tense months that he spent there after its fall. "There was no doubt about that. The streets were for the most part deserted. Sometimes one found oneself the only person on a street, and this could be dangerous."[32] The siege mentality outlasted Biafra's defeat. Two years after the war's end, a British intelligence source described how "the motor park was completely empty. It used to be a busy 24-hour park where goods and passengers

---

[30] Godwin Alabi-Isama, *The Tragedy of Victory: On-the-Spot Account of the Nigeria-Biafra War in the Atlantic Theatre* (Ibadan: Spectrum, 2013): pp. 10–25.
[31] Major General Ibrahim B. M. Haruna, "The Nigerian Civil War: Causes and Courses," in A. E. Ekoku and S. O. Agbi, eds., *Nigerian Warfare Through the Ages: Proceedings of a Seminar Published by the National War Museum Committee* (Lagos: State Printing Corporation, 1987): p. 159.
[32] Elechi Amadi, *Sunset in Biafra: A Civil War Diary* (London: Heinemann, 1973): p. 142

Figure 4.2 Nigerian soldiers on patrol in Port Harcourt, 1970 (A. Abbas/ Magnum Photos)

were conveyed to the different parts of Eastern Nigeria."[33] As a lawyer who practiced there recalled, "the place was just very scanty."[34]

After 1970, Igbos began to return quietly to Port Harcourt. Igbo managers and technicians in the oil industry, who were sorely needed, came back under the condition that they be given protection by private security guards. Some were enticed into returning from exile by promises of large salaries and secure housing within company compounds. Oil companies put pressure on the Nigerian government to guarantee the safety of their Igbo employees, and heavily guarded reserve areas for oil workers cropped up around the city.[35] Port

[33] NAUK FCO 65/1195, "Report of tour of Rivers and East Central States," Mayo O. Osime, British High Commission, Lagos, October 16–22, 1972.
[34] Interview with Kola Babalola, SAN, Port Harcourt, March 5, 2015.
[35] CADN 332PO/1 Box 4 Dp. 45, "Compte rendu de déplacement à Port-Harcourt," November 30, 1971. These reserve areas are not dissimilar from the ones that house the thousands of foreign workers who work in the oil industry today. The garrison-like cities within a city where oil workers live were first introduced in Port Harcourt to house Igbo technicians in the early 1970s. Today their occupants are more likely to be Filipino or American, but the preoccupation with protecting them from danger remains much the same. On the architecture of the oil economy, see James Ferguson, "Governing Extraction:

Harcourt was consequently a very closely watched place in the 1970s, but Igbos were still at risk there. A French envoy found that, in the months after the end of the war, "Ibos working in factories in the city were obliged every night to return home out of Rivers State to escape the reprisals of what were effectively 'commandos' organized to hunt them and lynch them in the streets."[36] The fear of returning to Port Harcourt, long a center of Igbo commercial and cultural life, was greater than returning to Lagos or even to the north.[37] Igbo commercial activity resumed fairly quickly there, but in Rivers State it never returned to prewar levels.[38] To local people in Port Harcourt, the sudden departure of the Igbo professional and commercial class was an opportunity. Ijaw locals who had welcomed the Nigerian occupation scrambled to fill vacated positions and lay claim to property. The French diplomat predicted that the replacement of Igbos in leadership positions would be permanent: "This urban mass seems to have the satisfaction of having finally conquered Port Harcourt, and seems determined not to leave."[39] In nearby Uyo, local authorities established a system of identity cards for residents, which a local administrator admitted was an attempt to prevent Igbos from resettling there.[40]

One of the most persistent postwar problems was over the ownership of buildings that Igbos had "abandoned" when they fled to Biafra in 1966. The military government guaranteed that those who had left property behind in Nigeria would be allowed to reclaim it. Houses and

---

New Spatializations of Order and Disorder in Neoliberal Africa," in *Global Shadows: Africa in the Neoliberal World Order* (Durham, NC: Duke University Press, 2007): pp. 195–210; Hannah Appel, Arthur Mason, and Michael Watts, eds., *Subterranean Estates: Life Worlds of Oil and Gas* (Ithaca, NY: Cornell University Press, 2015).

[36] CADN 332PO/1 Box 4 Dp. 45, "Visite à Port-Harcourt: place et rôle de la France dans la Sud-Est de la Fédération," December 17, 1971.

[37] Though fears of returning to Lagos remained acute. Many who did so in the early 1970s lived solitary lives there, keeping to themselves for fear of being perceived as politically active or too commercially successful. See Sandra T. Barnes, "Voluntary Associations in a Metropolis: The Case of Lagos, Nigeria," *African Studies Review* vol. 18, no. 2 (1975): pp. 75–87.

[38] On the north, see Kate Meagher, "The Informalization of Belonging: Igbo Informal Enterprise and National Cohesion from Below," *Africa Development* vol. 34, no. 1 (2009): pp. 31–46.

[39] CADN 332PO/1 Box 5, "Visite à Port-Harcourt: place et role de la France dans le Sud-Est de la Fédération," December 17, 1971.

[40] SADF CSI GP 15, Box 26, "Nigeria: Soviet Penetration and News from the Interior," March 1970.

businesses owned by Igbos had been held in trust for them, and commissions had been set up to manage the properties. In theory, the state
governments had collected rent on behalf of their Igbo owners, who
would be free to return to them at any time. In practice, that money
usually did not materialize, and renters were reluctant to leave the
properties they occupied. When the war ended, a deluge of property
claims by Igbo landlords and their agents followed. In the north, the state
governments largely kept their promise to return abandoned properties,
which came as a happy surprise to their owners. Most who returned to
Kano and other northern cities in the 1970s got their houses back with
minimal hassle, although only a few received the rent that had been
collected on their behalf.[41] In the south, it was a different matter.

In Port Harcourt, where Igbos owned large amounts of commercial
and residential property, the Rivers State government defied the federal
government by refusing to help Igbos reclaim their real estate.[42] The
state's refusal to evict local people who had moved into abandoned
Igbo houses developed into a legal and political crisis. The state courts
sided with the renters-turned-squatters; in one case, a Port Harcourt
judge awarded substantial punitive damages to a squatter, ruling that
a federal agency had acted "stupidly and outrageously" when it tried to
evict him.[43] These decisions exasperated Igbo landlords, who saw the
state government's refusal to comply with federal policy as an act of
retribution against them. A lawyer who represented squatters in the
early 1970s argued that Igbo grievances were overblown: "Their worries were psychological and financial rather than for their physical
safety. Many sold their property to willing buyers. They did in fact
receive their due rights."[44] Very few Igbos had actually sold their
houses – under duress or otherwise – and the Rivers State government
actively discouraged them from trying to take repossession
themselves.[45] The abandoned property issue was not limited to Port

---

[41] A. M. O. Onukaogu, in his chambers in St. Finbarr's St., Umuahia, March 9,
   2015.
[42] See Howard Wolpe, *Urban Politics in Nigeria: A Study of Port Harcourt* (Berkeley:
   University of California Press, 1974); Grace Malachi Brown, "Abandoned
   Properties in Nigeria: The Effect of the Civil War in the Nigerian State," *Icheke:
   Journal of the Rivers State University of Education* vol. 4, no. 2 (2016).
[43] *Nigerian Tide* [Port Harcourt], January 8, 1972, p. 1.
[44] Interview with anonymous informant, Port Harcourt, March 2015.
[45] CADN 332PO/1 Box 4 Dp. 45, "Crise politique de l'Etat du Sud-Est,"
   August 13, 1971.

Harcourt. In the South-Eastern State, the state government was similarly recalcitrant. In Calabar, a prominent high court judge was dismissed from the bench for returning a cinema to its Igbo owner against
the governor's wishes.[46] Most abandoned property cases were ultimately settled by federal interventions, first under the Murtala
Muhammed regime in 1976 and again in the 1990s, but others remain
unresolved.[47] The debacle made Igbos wary of buying property in other
parts of the country, at least until building a house in the east.[48]

There were property disputes in the East Central State as well,
although there both parties were usually Igbos.[49] In one representative
case, two people released from a Red Cross camp came to blows over
the ownership of a small piece of land near Onitsha. When Ezekiel
Okoye saw an emaciated woman erecting a makeshift tent on the plot
of land that he had demarcated to build his own house, he confronted
her. The altercation culminated with him striking her with a piece of
bamboo, and, in her weakened state, she died from internal bleeding. In
the subsequent trial, it emerged that the woman's husband had
arranged for the plot of land to be left to her and their daughter, so
she had not been "trespassing" on it. The court sentenced Okoye to

[46] He was later rehabilitated. Bassey, *The Nigerian Judiciary*, p. 91.
[47] Even Ojukwu became embroiled in an abandoned property case over a house in
Lagos. Ojukwu's case did not resolve the larger abandoned property question, but
the lengthy Villaska Lodge case did have the effect of limiting executive power in
a later period of military rule. Supreme Court of Nigeria Law Reports 241/850,
Chief Emeka Odumegwu Ojukwu v. Military Governor of Lagos State, 1985. See
also Yemi Akinseye-George, *Legal System, Corruption and Governance in Nigeria*
(Lagos: New Century Law Publishers, 2000): p. 25; Gloria I. Chuku, "Quest for
National Purification: Murtala Mohammed's New Vision, 1975–1976," in Levi
A. Nwachuku and G. N. Uzoigwe, eds., *Troubled Journey: Nigeria Since the Civil
War* (Lanham, MD: University Press of America, 2004): p. 89.
[48] Daniel Jordan Smith, *To Be a Man Is Not a One-Day Job: Masculinity, Money,
and Intimacy in Nigeria* (Chicago: University of Chicago Press, 2017): p. 110.
This anxiety is found in many accounts of property ownership. Notably, see
Nkem Liliwhite-Nwosu, *Divine Restoration of Nigeria: Eyewitness Account of
Her Trials and Triumphs* (Lagos: CSS Books, 2004).
[49] The small number of northerners who had lived in the east before the war
generally found that they were no longer welcome there. Aside from northern
soldiers whose right to be there was backed by force, the handful of northern
herdsmen, butchers, and moneychangers who tried to reestablish their
businesses in the east were run out of town. They only returned permanently
years later. See, for example, ESHC uncatalogued collection, in the High Court
of the East Central State of Nigeria, Umuahia, *Umuahia Ibeku Butchers' Union
v. Umuahia Ibeku Butchers' Union*, no. HU/13/73, September 28, 1973.

death, sending a stern message that property disputes in the war's aftermath had to be resolved through law, not violence.[50] Yet making claims through official channels – to property or anything else – proved very difficult for those on the war's losing side.

The Legal Problems of Reconciliation

Reconciliation raised difficult legal questions. What was to be done with decisions made by Biafran courts, and how should Nigerian administrators treat documents issued by Biafran agencies? Officially, Biafra was simply excised from the legal record. With the exception of some civil documents like birth certificates, legal documents issued there were declared void. Appeals filed on decisions originating in its courts were rejected out of hand. When an appellant tried to bring a case decided in a Biafran court before the Supreme Court of Nigeria in 1974, the court ruled that it had "no jurisdiction to entertain Appeal originating from a territory not in Nigeria, vis – the 'High Court of Biafra.'"[51] With this decision, Biafra was quietly elided from precedent. Erasing it from politics and memory would prove more difficult.

What, for example, was to be done with the assets of Biafran institutions? A few days before the final surrender, several employees of Biafra's Central Bank looted what remained of its holdings, amounting to £177,000 in foreign and Nigerian currency. When they were caught, the question of what to do with the money became a matter of law. Their lawyer argued that, since the "Central Bank of Biafra" had never existed, they had committed no crime. They were initially convicted of conspiracy and theft for stealing from the Central Bank of Nigeria, which the court of original jurisdiction considered the predecessor to the Central Bank of Biafra; but their conviction was overturned by a higher court after a debate over where the currency had come from. It transpired that the particular currency that the men stole had been obtained by the Biafran state over the course of the war, and it had therefore never technically been the property of the Central Bank of

---

[50] ESHC uncatalogued collection, in the High Court of the East Central State of Nigeria, Onitsha, no. O/10c/71, *The State v. Ezekiel Okoye*, November 8, 1971.
[51] SC.154/1973, *Okwuosa v. Okwuosa*, February 21, 1974. See also NNAE BCA 1/1/23, Chief Registrar's Office, High Court, Enugu to the Registrar, High Court Registry, Enugu, Charge no. E/106c/66, *A. Okoli and three others v. The State*, April 4, 1970.

Nigeria. To say that it *had*, the high court ruled, would amount to recognizing the Central Bank of Biafra as a real institution, one that had vested the funds on behalf of the Central Bank of Nigeria for the duration of the war. The problem with this logic, ruled Justice Agbakoba, was that "there never was a bank of biafra. Since the bank of biafra is not a legal institution or corporation it is not a person legally capable of owning property." Moreover, the Nigerian Central Bank could not seize the money because "the acts of the bank of biafra are tainted with illegality which can never be ratified by the Central Bank [of Nigeria]." The men were acquitted. What became of the currency is not clear, but the case suggested how Biafra's official nonexistence could be difficult to square with the practical demands of reconciliation.[52]

The war haunted many cases, and acts of violence that had happened in the heat of battle made for especially difficult legal problems. In July 1969, a lieutenant in the Biafran Army named Pius Nwaoga had been ordered by his superiors to find and kill a fellow officer and childhood friend named Robert Ngwu. Ngwu had allegedly committed treason by embezzling money from the army, and Ojukwu decided to have him killed extrajudicially rather than try to bring him before a tribunal. Nwaoga and two Biafran lieutenants traveled to Ngwu's hiding place in Ibagwu Nike – a village that Biafra claimed but was at that time nominally controlled by Nigeria – and executed him. They fled the village, and Nwaoga was captured by Nigerian soldiers patrolling a nearby checkpoint. Nwaoga was then charged with murder in a Nigerian court. The judge found him guilty of murdering Robert Ngwu, citing an English case to establish that a soldier is only "bound to obey lawful orders and is not responsible if he obeys an order not strictly lawful." The high court judge found that, since the "order to eliminate the deceased was given by an officer of an illegal regime [Biafra], his orders therefore are necessarily unlawful and obedience to them involves a violation of the law and the defence of superior orders is untenable." In other words, while Nwaoga saw himself as a Biafran soldier carrying out orders on Biafran soil, in the eyes of the Nigerian court he was a Nigerian civilian who had killed another civilian in Nigerian territory.

---

[52] The decision not to capitalize "Biafra" was intentional. East Central State Law Reports, *The State v. Jerry C. Emezie and five others*, 1970 and 1971.

The war ended while Nwaoga was in prison, and his case came before the Nigerian Supreme Court on appeal in 1972. Nwaoga's defense remained that "he had to obey the orders of his superior officers." The appeal raised the question of who counts as a soldier in a civil war. Concurring with the lower ruling, Chief Justice Adetokunbo Ademola elaborated why Nwaoga was not entitled to the defense he was simply following orders. First of all, the killing took place in a village that was, as the court saw it, in Nigerian territory. Theoretically, of course, *all* of Biafra was Nigerian territory but Ibagwu Nike was especially so because it was under the guns of the Nigerian Army at the time of Nwaoga's actions. Moreover, since the appellant was not wearing a uniform at the time of the killing, he could not be considered to be acting as a soldier and was therefore "liable for punishment, just like any civilian would be, whether or not he is acting under Orders." Citing foreign precedent (a sabotage case from the Russo-Japanese War), the court upheld the appellant's conviction and characterized his actions as a "deliberate and intentional killing of an unarmed person living peacefully inside the Federal territory." It was therefore "a crime against humanity, and even if committed during a civil war is in violation of the domestic law of the country, and must be punished."[53] Nwaoga was hanged.

A 1973 case before a Nigerian high court raised a related question. If, in the midst of the war, a Biafran officer court-martialed and then shot a Biafran infantryman for raping a civilian, was that execution to be considered an act of murder or an exercise of the officer's prerogative to maintain discipline in his unit? The Nwaoga case from the year before had made it easy to make criminal charges like this stick, especially since Nigeria did not accept that what had happened between 1967 and 1970 was a war with another sovereign state.[54] By ignoring extenuating circumstances like the state of warfare, Nigerian judges could plausibly rule that the ordinary tasks of soldiering constituted acts of "murder" or "theft" (or, for those giving the orders, provocations thereof). A Nigerian high court ruled in this case that the execution could be considered murder, since the Biafran Army was an illegal militia and therefore could not exercise the sovereign right to take a life. The Supreme Court of Nigeria

---

[53] Supreme Court of Nigeria Law Reports 345/1970, *Pius Nwaoga v. The State*, March 1972.

[54] *The Renaissance*, December 10, 1973.

overturned this decision on appeal the following year, citing the impracticality of investigating every wartime execution by Biafra and its army, of which there were probably hundreds. It did not, however, unambiguously rule that the execution was *not* murder, leaving unsettled how martial acts of violence were to be considered before the law.[55]

Nigerian judges were troubled by one kind of case in particular. Killings had happened during the war that appeared to be neither murders in a criminological sense nor combat deaths but arbitrary enactments of the ability to kill – a Nigerian soldier who strangled his bunkmate, for example, or a Biafran who killed a boy unprovoked at a checkpoint. When these acts came to trial after the war, courts did not know what to make of them, especially if the judge had not experienced the fighting himself. Killings for the sake of killing, or acts that showed "blood lust" by soldiers, as one lawyer called it, jammed the analytical tools that judges used to understand violence.[56] The absence of motive and intent confounded them, and these cases ended inconclusively, in mistrials or hasty dismissals. Law was not a salve for what had taken place in Biafra. This was never more obvious than in trying to understand deaths that had happened for no reason – or at least, no reason comprehensible in a society at peace.

What to do with Nigerian officers who had fought in the Biafran Army was another problem. Even telling who had served was difficult. By the end of the war, there were no uniforms or military identification documents being issued, and high rates of participation in unofficial paramilitaries made the distinction between soldier and civilian almost irrelevant. Nigerian officers who had fought on the Biafran side were brought before boards of inquiry to determine whether to reintegrate them into the Nigerian Army. The boards were advisory rather than punitive, and the total number of men tried did not exceed 200. Most of the officers who were investigated were reabsorbed, sometimes at a lower rank. The handful who were detained were nominally punished for their participation during the January 1966 coup rather than for defecting to the Biafran side.[57] Most Biafran soldiers were treated, in effect, as civilians – never formally punished but left to fend for themselves.

---

[55] Later, in the context of the Niger Delta crisis and today in the north, these questions would arise again.

[56] Interview with anonymous informant, Aba, February 2015.

[57] Olukunle Ojeleye, *The Politics of Post-War Demobilisation and Reintegration in Nigeria* (Aldershot: Ashgate, 2010): pp.114–115; Ogbemudia, *Years of Challenge*, pp. 115–118.

The imprisonment of two Nigerian officers for "sadistic" acts committed during the war was intended to show that those who had overstepped their authority would be held accountable. A lawyer succinctly summed up the eastern public's response to this effort: "Only two?"[58] Wartime atrocities were addressed through commissions of inquiry within the military, quietly, leaving no public trace. These inquiries did not satisfy those who wanted some form of justice – if anything, they confirmed that Nigeria had little interest in investigating its own army; but hardly anyone expressed this openly. This may have been because people feared speaking up against the military government. To some degree, however, it was probably motivated by a different fear – the fear that dissecting what had happened between 1967 and 1970 would turn up not only Nigerian misdeeds, but Biafran ones.

Political Reintegration

Postwar politics were marked by whiplash, as soldiers whose political experience was limited to commanding their units haltingly learned how to administer a peacetime society. There were tensions between the federal government and the twelve state governments and a great deal of bitterness over the unequal distribution of revenues and resources. A legal scholar expressed concern about the growth of nativism, which was on the rise everywhere but especially in the east:

Ill-feeling is of such a degree that one would not be surprised if it is reflected in decisions, in both civil and criminal matters, of some State Courts in cases involving natives of those other States. Ill-will apart, State attachment, State prejudices, State jealousies and interests might sometimes obstruct or control the regular administration of justice in cases where one party is a local citizen and the other a native of another State.[59]

These problems had been present before the war, but its outcome created new and deeper cleavages between the units of Nigeria's complicated federal structure.[60]

[58] Interview with Mike Onwuzunike, Enugu, September 14, 2014.
[59] Gaius Ezejiofor, "Nigerian Judicial Structure and Distribution of Judicial Competence," *The Nigerian Bar Journal (Annual Journal of the Nigeria Bar Association)* vol. 10 (1972): p. 78.
[60] They would become even more immutable as the three states carved out of Biafra splintered further. A 1977 British intelligence report noted how firm political and regional identities became in the former Biafra: "In the old Eastern

The East Central State was the only state with a civilian administrator, Ukpabi Asika, deridingly called "the pigeon among the eagles"
for this reason.[61] Asika was an Igbo loyalist who had spent the war
teaching political science at the University of Ibadan. He was an erudite
politician who published lengthy exegeses on Igbo history and
European philosophy in the newspaper, and he was almost universally
disliked.[62] A former Biafran official recalled that "we had a type of
'Cold War' relationship with the Government of the East Central State,
under Administrator Ukpabi Asika. There was no love lost between
him and the Igbo people, yet he was there as the agent of the victorious
government, still regarded as an alien one."[63]

Tensions were sharp between the states that made up the former
Biafra. The Eastern Region had been divided into three states at the
beginning of the war to meet the demands of eastern minority groups,
but Biafra's secession prevented the state governments from being set
up until after the war was over. From distributing oil revenues down to
divvying up the office furniture in the former statehouse in Enugu, the
state governments proved unwilling to work together. The military
governors in the Rivers State and South-Eastern State were especially
wary of the East Central State trying to exert control over them.[64] In

Region the minority tribes of Rivers and Cross River States still guard their
separate identity jealously; and in the Ibo heartland of Imo and Anambra States
tribalism takes the form of preoccupation with internal reconstruction and
a professed disinterest in what happens elsewhere, particularly in Lagos."
NAUK FCO 65/1920, J.R. Johnson, British High Commission, Lagos to Foreign
and Commonwealth Office, February 8, 1977. For a novelistic treatment of the
politics around state creation, see T. M. Aluko, *A State of Our Own* (Ibadan:
Heinemann, 1986).

[61] The other governors in the eastern states were all military officers, including
Colonel John Esuene in the South-Eastern State, Lieutenant Commander Alfred
Diette-Spiff in Rivers State and Colonel Sam Ogbemudia in the Mid-West State.
For most of the period of military rule Nigerian state governors were officially
called "military governors" or "administrators" in the rare cases where civilians
held office. Interview with Dr. Jacob Ibik, SAN, Enugu, September 26, 2014.

[62] Interview with Dr. Jacob Ibik, SAN, Enugu, September 26, 2014.

[63] Godwin Alaoma Onyegbula, *The Memoirs of the Nigerian-Biafran Bureaucrat:
An Account of Life in Biafra and Within Nigeria* (Ibadan: Spectrum, 2005): pp.
196–199.

[64] As a result of this hostility toward the East Central State, government agencies,
parastatals, and other services that had previously served the entire eastern
region from Enugu were replicated in Calabar and Port Harcourt. Services were
duplicated in highly inefficient ways for reasons of regional pride, in the interest
of controlling resources, and to create jobs for state "indigenes." Each state had

August 1970, the Rivers governor gave a heated speech in which he pledged to resist Igbo domination of the federal institutions – a problem that was fictional but rhetorically potent. He also made a claim to a larger share of the profits from the oil parastatals, on the grounds that his state was where the bulk of the extraction took place and where its worst externalities were felt.[65]

Igbos felt that Nigeria's plans to rebuild infrastructure in the former Biafra were designed to punish them. Among other grievances, there was the decision that the coal industry, formerly at the center of Enugu's economic life, would be moved to the north and the locomotives that Biafra had seized from the Nigerian Railway Corporation at the start of the war would be transferred to Lagos.[66] The decision to postpone rebuilding the bridge over the Niger River – the main artery between east and west – was also seen as punitive. Few former Biafrans were represented in the federal bureaucracy, especially at its higher levels. Minister of Health Josiah Okezie was the only member of the postwar Federal Executive Council who had been a Biafran, and he constantly reminded people that he had never been a true believer in the Biafran cause.[67] Gowon cited his presence as proof that Nigeria welcomed Igbos in its highest ranks, but not many were convinced.

What to do with Biafra's former head of state was an important piece in the reconciliation puzzle. The publisher Arthur Nwankwo recalled that "the fashionable logic was that Ojukwu misled the Igbos into secession. This expedient, but untruthful verdict served a useful purpose, because the absent Ojukwu provided a scapegoat to vent all frustrations of the war on and made reintegration with the erstwhile 'enemy' easy."[68] Ojukwu spent the 1970s in Ivory Coast, where he kept a low political profile. His exile was comfortable, spent mostly watching television and walking the

to have its own university, for example, leading to the creation of the University of Calabar in 1973 and the University of Port Harcourt in 1975.

[65] SOAS Nigerian Civil War Collections MS 321463 Box 13, *Biafra News*, September 18, 1970.
[66] NAUK FCO 38/297, H.H. Stewart, British High Commission, Lagos to Commonwealth Office, April 17, 1968.
[67] SOAS Nigerian Civil War Collections MS 321463 Box 1, *The Flamingo* vol. 9, no. 11 (1970): p. 6.
[68] Arthur A. Nwankwo, *Thoughts on Nigeria* (Enugu: Fourth Dimension, 1986): p. 140. A similar sentiment can be found in a pamphlet Azikiwe wrote after defecting to the Nigerian side: Nnamdi Azikiwe, *Origins of the Nigerian Civil War* (Lagos: Government Printer, 1969).

Figure 4.3 Wooden planks placed over the Niger Bridge, 1971 (A. Abbas/ Magnum Photos)

perimeter of the spacious compound loaned to him by Félix Houphouët-Boigny.[69] He did, however, want to have a role in the reintegration process. In his first postwar interview, he told a journalist that "I think the shock of the defeat is beginning to pass, and I owe it to them, I owe it to my people, both inside and outside, to give them certain directions." Ultimately, he argued:

It's in the court of the Nigerians, it depends on how they play the ball back. If they play it in a friendly way then there would be no need for resistance. If of course, they play it back viciously then I am sure that our people will consider again whether this forced unity is worthwhile ... we must learn to be patient.[70]

Few people in postwar Nigeria were interested in Ojukwu's thoughts on reconciliation. To Nigeria he was a war criminal, and to his former

[69] Houphouët-Boigny did not want Ojukwu's stay in Ivory Coast to be permanent, and he tried to arrange for him to settle in Portugal. José Manuel Duarte de Jesus, *A guerra secreta de Salazar em África* (Lisbon: Publicações Dom Quixote, 2012): p. 187.
[70] SOAS Nigerian Civil War Collections MS 321463 Box 1, *The Flamingo* vol. 9, no. 12 (1970): p. 20.

comrades his eleventh hour escape was a cowardly betrayal – suicide would have been the more honorable exit. Gowon made a brief effort to extradite Ojukwu to Nigeria, but he gave up for fear that a public trial might sour the reconciliation process. The United Kingdom cooperated with Nigeria to prevent Ojukwu and his entourage from settling there, where there was a fear that the Biafran government might try to regroup.[71] Ojukwu would eventually return to Nigeria in 1982 after being pardoned by President Shehu Shagari. He remade himself as a powerful businessman, politician, and traditional ruler.[72]

For ordinary civilians, "reconciling" with the Nigerian government required no special action. Nigerian soldiers and administrators sometimes demanded that civilians pledge their loyalty by greeting them with the slogan "One Nigeria!," but reintegration entailed no formal action or ritual.[73] The Nigerian government had never recognized Biafra's separate existence, so, from a bureaucratic perspective, there was no need to ratify that Biafrans were now Nigerians again.[74] There were, however, certain actions that compelled Biafrans to pledge their loyalty to Nigeria. In the early 1970s, they returned home, reclaimed their property, and went about the painstaking process of replacing identity documents that had been lost or destroyed. Doing so involved filing an affidavit at a magistrate's court and making an oath of allegiance to the Federal Military Government of Nigeria.[75] Couples who had married in Biafra had to file affidavits to have their marriages

---

[71] NAUK FCO 65/1198, A. H. Wyatt, British High Commission, Lagos to Foreign and Commonwealth Office, November 16, 1972.

[72] In the 1980s the anthropologist Misty Bastian would note the bitterness that some people in the former Biafra felt toward Ojukwu after the war: "Ojukwu himself drives the Onitsha-Enugu expressway today in a Mercedes, ignoring the pathetic display of wheelchaired, veteran beggars who sit alongside. Much of the selfishness displayed during the war escaped punishment." Misty Bastian, "The World as Marketplace: Historical, Cosmological, and Popular Constructions of the Onitsha Market System," (Doctoral dissertation, University of Chicago, 1992).

[73] Alfred Obiora Uzokwe, *Surviving in Biafra: The Story of the Nigerian Civil War: Over Two Million Died* (self-published, 2003): p. 145.

[74] The most relevant case is summarized in the following terms: "during the civil war the Ibos have always been regarded as Nigerians and treated as such, as they have never been excluded from the Nigerian society." See Mowoe V. Agboha (1968) MNALR 352, *Nigerian Law Through The Cases* vol. 24 (1998): p. 5E.20.

[75] See, for example, NNAE ENJUST 33/1/67, "Statutory Declaration of Age," June 4, 1970.

legally recognized.[76] Sorting out property claims – large and small – entailed a similar process. Clara Akwarandu returned home in 1970 to find a neighbor brazenly wearing her clothes around town. She filed a claim to get them back, and, in so doing, she gave a lengthy account of where she had been and what she had done during the war.[77] Thousands of these small reckonings took place in the years immediately after the war – but its survivors would have to wait much longer for a formal coming-to-terms with the events of 1967–1970.

The Criminalization of the State

The fact that the policemen and soldiers tasked with controlling crime were also sometimes its culprits made Nigeria feel like a vast protection racket.[78] The war had unleashed something latent in the military government, and, to those who lived under its thumb, day-to-day administration was hard to distinguish from crime. Nigerians complained that the order of things had been upended – soldiers and the police engaged in crime, while ordinary people took law enforcement into their own hands. As the musician Fela Kuti lamented,

The newspapers are crying "armed robbers, thieves," so the public think they have to take care of themselves. Any thief they think they see they lynch, they kill by themselves. This is wrong. It's very un-African. Africans don't behave like that. This is the kind of criminal behavior, the criminal atmosphere, our government has put in the country.[79]

To many Nigerians in the 1970s (including those less radical than Fela Kuti), the crime that pervaded the corridors of state was tied to the crime that took place in the streets. This was the case first, and most dramatically, in the region where the war had been fought. In the public

[76] NNAE ENJUST 33/1/67, "Affidavits of Marriage," 1970.
[77] NNAE ENJUST 33/1/69, "Affidavit of Mrs. Clara Adarina Akwarandu," February 19, 1970.
[78] On the state as racketeer, see Charles Tilly, "War Making and State Making as Organized Crime," in Peter Evans, Dietrich Rueschemeyer, and Theda Skocpol, eds., *Bringing the State Back In* (Cambridge: Cambridge University Press, 1985): pp. 169–187. Though the maxim that best describes postwar Nigeria is Hannah Arendt's – "whatever political organization men may have achieved has its origins in crime." Hannah Arendt, *On Revolution* (New York: Penguin, 1990): p. 20.
[79] *Fela Kuti: Music is the Weapon* (video recording, Los Angeles: Geffen Records, 2004).

imagination, the disorder of the East Central State was never purely the work of "criminals" but a coproduction between those who made the law – soldiers, the police, and the judiciary – and those who broke it.

Venality was everywhere, and those in power seemed increasingly tolerant of it. In 1973, for example, the Mid-Western State responded to a wave of embezzlements not with a crackdown but with a defeatist attempt to minimize their losses. In the past, the Ministry of Local Government had energetically pursued acts of fraud or theft. "Experience has, however, shown that such immediate report to the Police has often led to rather protracted criminal proceedings, which more often than not, has resulted in the acquittal/conviction of the culprit without his really making good the loss sustained by the Council." Hoping to recoup more of these losses, the ministry directed civil servants who discovered thefts to give the suspected embezzler a three-week grace period to return the money voluntarily before taking action.[80] This was a markedly permissive attitude toward theft from the state, and, to its critics, it looked like impunity. To its defenders, it was a pragmatic necessity. Taking a hard line against embezzlement would mean firing so many civil servants that the state bureaucracy would grind to a halt.[81]

Yet bureaucrats who skimmed funds from public accounts were not the greatest of easterners' worries. Agents of the Nigerian state also engaged in criminal violence, and some of the most feared figures of the occupation were civilian policemen. After surrender, Gowon promised that the East Central State would be policed by its own locally commissioned force rather than the military.[82] He hoped that this would reassure Igbos that Nigeria's intentions were good and make for a more convivial relationship between civilians and the state.[83] Local administration worked differently in practice; the East Central State was a conquered territory, and the police treated it as such. Policemen

---

[80] HIA, Nigerian Subject Collection XX787, Box 6, "Midwestern State of Nigeria, Local Government Circulars, 1973, no. 22."

[81] Three years later this dilemma would be reenacted at the federal level, as Murtala Mohammed's purge of the civil service ensnared so many corrupt officials that some ministries simply stopped functioning.

[82] The federal government also reassured Igbos by pointing to the fact that the Nigerian Army counted Igbos among its ranks. NAUK FCO 65/213, Sir L. Glass to Foreign and Commonwealth Office, January 15, 1970.

[83] NAUK FCO 65/213, Sir L. Glass to Foreign and Commonwealth Office, January 15, 1970.

often overstepped their authority. Empowered by a growing mandate to maintain public order, many took the opportunity to requisition materials and intimidate people. A few even saw a posting to the deprived East Central State as an opportunity, going out of their way to secure transfers from other, ostensibly more desirable posts.

One such unscrupulous policeman was the squadron leader of the Mobile Police Force in Aba, a Gabriel Ededey from Warri. In June 1970, Ededey staged a week-long binge of arrests, thefts, and beatings on the pretense that someone had stolen money from the local woman he had just married.[84] His actions were an act of collective punishment and a well-organized criminal shakedown of a large segment of the town – all under the sign of enforcing law and order. During the rampage, Ededey and his men confiscated every valuable they could find, including cars, radios, appliances, tires, jewelry, and dry goods. Anyone who stood in his way was beaten and publicly humiliated. Many of the incidents during that week suggested that the crackdown was a punishment for Aba having been one of Biafra's strongholds – though greed surely motivated it too.

Following the theft of his wife's money, Ededey was, as the judgment related, "thrown into an outburst of temperament and he resolved there and then that he must recover the stolen amount by all means. He got the mobile police out on parade fully armed, some with pistols, some with sub-machine guns, and others with Mark 4 rifles and some with horse whips or kobokos [rawhide whips]." Loading into a convoy with flags flying and sirens blaring, the policemen went to the main market, where Ededey

instructed that the policemen should beat up the people around, arrest them, seize their goods and carry both men and goods into the Police lorry. [...] The relatives of Ededey's wife who were in that neighbourhood jubilated and sang songs in praise of the Mobile Police. The Police lorry went on four trips to the station with loads of goods and those arrested. The operation continued until the market was bare and no more people could be seen except unwary passerby who were then terrorised and rough handled.

The frenzy lasted all night, ending with Ededey "requisitioning" everything from the market and stockpiling the goods in the police

---

[84] ESHC uncatalogued collection, in the High Court of the East Central State of Nigeria, Aba, no. A/8c/71, *The State v. Gabriel Ededey and Frank Odita*, March 31, 1971.

warehouse. When that filled up, the loot was brought to the squadron leader's house. When Ededey was challenged by a fellow policeman, Ededey ordered the man to "arrest himself" and deposit his car at the station. This was repeated several days in a row in various parts of Aba. Market women were severely beaten, and many valuables disappeared in the melee. To those who testified against him, Ededey was clearly targeting Igbos. Toward the end of his reign of terror, Ededey took his officers and took over a petrol station. The manager of the station, Timothy Onuoha, testified that

I attempted to run away and another of them held me back, tore my singlet and then used a piece of wire to flog me and I bled. [. . .] He then looked round and said "Ibo man, you own these vehicles," and I said that they were not mine but belong to my customers. He went to one of the vehicles, drew out the driver and beat him.

When the owner of the petrol station went to the police station to file a complaint, the officers on duty "declined to record the complaint and gave as their reason that the 1st accused [Ededey] would beat up whoever made any such entry." Over the following days, the goods were sold onto the black market by the officer in charge of the storeroom.

This kind of reprisal happened all over the East Central State in the months after surrender. Ededey crossed the wrong person, however, and it was for that reason that he ended up in court. Some of Ededey's victims complained about him to a federal official, a Muslim northerner who was passing through Aba. The official summoned Ededey to his hotel, where he accused him of creating "fear and consternation and a feeling of absolute insecurity in the township." Ededey retorted that he "did not want to see any Resident or D.O. and remarked that these Ibos who had only just come out of the bush were very ungrateful in that they had stolen his wife's money which he said he must do everything possible to recover adding that the purpose of the operation was to see that his wife's stolen money was recovered." "Aba was too rough," Ededey explained, and he was "out to teach the people of Aba a bit of lesson so that they could desist from evil." The official responded that "not everybody in Aba is a thief." Ededey lost his temper and ordered his men to arrest the "meddling" northerner. Realizing that arresting a federal official would be a step too far, they refused.

The northerner was incensed at how he had been treated, and he took up the issue with the state Ministry of Justice. Several months later, the state prosecutor filed charges against Ededey and his accomplices. The investigation revealed that there were many grievances against the Aba police – they had been "molesting the inhabitants of Aba and had been raiding, robbing and pillaging" since the moment they arrived in the fallen city. Ededey and his main accomplice were charged with nine counts of robbery and three counts of assault and found guilty of most of them. In addition to being dismissed from the police force, Ededey was given a prison term and publicly reprimanded. The high court ruling characterized him as "a tin god and a bully and terror." The decision was a warning to other officials to behave well – or at least not to be too brazen in their misconduct in the former Biafra: "the operations had no lawful basis and was not within the purview of the officers' lawful duties; it was savage to the extreme and was nothing but a naked show of power and an abuse of his authority." On appeal, the Federal Supreme Court of Nigeria concurred with that assessment.[85]

Ededey's case illustrates how crime and the Nigerian occupation could overlap. It also suggests that the principle of "no victor, no vanquished" did not always guide Nigeria's actions in the former Biafran territories – especially at the lower levels of administration. The court ruled that Ededey and his main accomplice were proverbial bad apples, whose actions did not represent the Nigeria Police Force at large; but Justice Chuba Ikpeazu was disturbed that the rank-and-file officers had followed Ededey's orders even when they had become blatantly illegal. To him, this pointed to a moral flaw in the unit that could not be ascribed solely to their corrupt leader. Ededey's victims seem to have been satisfied by how the case turned out, but this did not mean that officials who abused their power were always – or even usually – made to answer for their actions. The trial would never have happened had the powerful northerner not taken an interest.

The police were unpopular well before the war, and the Nigerian Police Force was arguably repressive by design – its colonial genealogy and its close relationship to power had made it that way.[86] Yet, like other dynamics described in this book, the excesses of policing were

---

[85] Although they did quash one of the charges of theft. Supreme Court of Nigeria Law Reports 85/1971, *Gabriel Ededey v. The State*, January 21, 1972.

[86] Samuel Fury Childs Daly, "From Crime to Coercion: Policing Dissent in Abeokuta, Nigeria, 1900–1940," *Journal of Imperial and Commonwealth*

exacerbated by the war. Not all abuses were spectacular events like Ededey's spree of arrests. The proliferation of roadside checkpoints, where shakedowns and harassment became routine, made many Nigerians see the police as "armed robbers in uniform," as a lawyer recalled.[87] The fact that there were more checkpoints in the East Central State than anywhere else in Nigeria gave the impression that there was a conspiracy to confine easterners to their home villages. As had been the case in Biafra, passes were required for travel within the East Central State, and Igbos who wished to resettle elsewhere in Nigeria were often asked by local governments to produce documents attesting to their loyalty.[88] This illegal (but officially tolerated) practice served as the pretext for shakedowns, scams, and corruption. Igbos argued that harassment by local officials was just another form of crime perpetrated against them. They were not alone in this feeling – humiliation was something that all Nigerians experienced under military rule. Yet Igbos believed, with some justification, that they were singled out more frequently than others.[89]

Men in uniform involved themselves in everyday quarrels, aggravating disagreements more often than they diffused them. When they felt that their authority was disrespected, they responded with force.[90] The face of state authority was not always a soldier or a policeman, however, and mistrust also marked interactions with

---

History vol. 47, no. 1 (2019). Generally, see Tekena N. Tamuno, *The Police in Modern Nigeria, 1861–1965: Origins, Development and Role* (Ibadan: Ibadan University Press, 1970); Kemi Rotimi, *The Police in a Federal State: The Nigerian Experience* (Ibadan: College Press, 2001); Cyprian O. Okonkwo, *The Police and the Public in Nigeria* (London: Sweet and Maxwell, 1966); David M. Anderson and David Killingray, eds., *Policing the Empire: Government, Authority and Control, 1830–1940* (Manchester: Manchester University Press, 1991).

[87] Interview with Kola Babalola, SAN, Port Harcourt, March 5, 2015.

[88] Paul Obi-Ani, *Post-Civil War Political and Economic Reconstruction of Igboland, 1970–1983* (Nsukka: Great AP Express Publishers, 2009): p. 26. The quasi-legal demand for "certificates of indigeneity" remains a problem in Nigeria today – and one that leads to a substantial amount of forgery. See Laurent Fourchard, "Bureaucrats and Indigenes: Producing and Bypassing Certificates of Origin in Nigeria," *Africa* vol. 85, no. 1 (2015): pp. 37–58.

[89] Interview with Kola Babalola, SAN, Port Harcourt, March 5, 2015.

[90] Such was the case when a wealthy trader from the delta ordered his servant to slap an "insolent" soldier, who retaliated by beating the servant to death. ESHC uncatalogued collection, in the High Court of the East Central State of Nigeria, Aba, no. A/12CA/73, *The State v. S.I. Guinness*, May 13, 1974.

civilian bureaucrats.[91] One casualty of this tension was a tax collector named Emeka Njoku, who was killed by a mob while making his rounds in a village near Abakaliki in 1971.[92] Resentment toward a distant central government was not new in the postwar period, and the idea that that the state did little besides collecting taxes and making arrests had a long colonial pedigree; but the recent, bitter experience of the war made for explosive encounters between easterners and the Nigerian government's representatives (even those, like the tax collector, who not long ago had been Biafrans themselves).

Conclusion

The most popular song of 1970 in the East Central State was Eddie Okwedy's "Happy Survival," a high-life dirge for Biafra that encouraged people to get on with their lives and leave matters of justice to God. Few people were happy, but having survived the war was cause for exhausted relief – even though it was cut with melancholy. In the years that followed Biafra's defeat, relief turned to bitterness over how reconstruction and rehabilitation proceeded. The security situation, already bad at the end of the war, deteriorated. Like wartime Biafra, the postwar East Central State seemed like a place of unabated lawlessness to those who lived there. Violent armed robberies became common, and acts of fraud featured prominently in postwar courts.[93] Crime was widely seen as a direct result of the war: "the young people involved went to war, came back and found that there was nothing else they could do," as an Onitsha lawyer recalled.[94] It was driven by poverty, dysfunction within the criminal justice system, and the erosion of informal guarantors of security. Things that people had done without a second thought before the war – drinking in bars, driving around

---

[91] This dynamic was not limited to the East Central State. The best-known example of it is the Agbekoya Uprising, a nearly contemporary outburst of civil unrest arising from taxation policies in southwestern Nigeria. See Tunde Adeniran, "The Dynamics of Peasant Revolt: A Conceptual Analysis of the *Agbekoya Parapo* Uprising in the Western State of Nigeria," *Journal of Black Studies* vol. 4 no. 4 (June 1974).

[92] Supreme Court of Nigeria Law Reports 92/75, *Michael Odigiji and six others v. The State*, June 1976.

[93] Chike Ofodile, *The Mettlesome Man: Hon. Justice Akunwafor Chuba Ikpeazu Through the Cases* (Self-published, [2000]): pp. 268–272.

[94] Interview with Chidube Ezebilo, SAN, Onitsha, March 12, 2015.

at night, chatting with strangers – came to be seen as dangerous.[95] In the 1970s, few people felt they could completely trust their friends, neighbors, village associations, and others whom they might have leaned on in difficult times. Even fewer felt they could count on the state.

Yet this was also a time of possibility, even if most of the opportunities on offer in decimated eastern Nigeria were on the wrong side of the law. As a chief in Awka recalled, young people were determined to find ways of thriving: "They became hardened and ready to withstand the vicissitudes of life. They moved out to the world empty handed with a firm determination to nail and destroy poverty."[96] People jockeyed for position in the new landscape, making their fortunes or remaking their lives, sometimes at the expense of others. The final chapters will consider why the forms of crime present at the war's end persisted in the 1970s and beyond.

---

[95] Interview with Jerome H.C. Okolo, SAN, Enugu, September 17, 2014.
[96] Chief Sir Abolle Okey Okoyeagu, *Igbo Resurgence* (Awka: Demercury Bright Printing and Publishing, [2002]): p. 93.

5 | A Long Heated Moment: Violent Crime in the Postwar East Central State

In my understanding acts of violence are committed when a man is denied the opportunity of being educated, of getting a job, of feeding himself and his family properly, of getting medical attention cheaply, quickly and promptly. We often do not realize that it is the society, the type of economic and hence the political system which we are operating in our country that brutalizes the individual, rapes his manhood. We often do not realise that when such men of poor and limited opportunities react, they are only in a certain measure, answering violence with violence.

Festus Iyayi, *Violence*[1]

In September 1970, Samuel Nwarungwa killed his neighbor for no apparent reason. In a lucid moment, he realized what he had done, walked several miles to the nearest police station, and turned himself in. The criminal case that followed turned on whether he could claim an insanity defense.[2] This was straightforward as a legal question, but it was poignant as an illustration of the world the war had made. Nwarungwa was schizophrenic, but at the time of Biafra's secession he had been holding down a job as a porter at the university in Nsukka. After Nsukka fell to Nigeria, he lived as a refugee in a hamlet outside of Aba. There, for the duration of the war, his insanity went unnoticed. His outbursts, in which he would walk around the village brandishing a machete and talking to himself, were considered strange but not unduly threatening by his neighbors, who did not know of his diagnosis. In a context where violence had become normal, one more man making threats did not raise much alarm. He even served in the local civil defense corps, where he gained a reputation for bravery and thoroughness in conscription campaigns. When the war ended and Nwarungwa

---

[1] Festus Iyayi, *Violence* (Lagos: Longman Nigeria, 2004 [first published 1979]): p. 105.

[2] For a general discussion of insanity cases in Biafra, see Ekong Sampson, *Evergreen Memories of Sir Louis Mbanefo* (Lagos: Lomanc, 2002): pp. 113–117.

continued to menace people, his neighbors began to suspect that he had
not just imbibed the martial spirit of the times but was mentally ill. A few
months later, he killed one of them with a machete. Showing mercy, the
judge acquitted him of manslaughter and sentenced him to treatment in
a federal asylum.[3] In the context of Biafra's independence struggle, it had
become hard to see the difference between martial valor and forms of
violence that would be considered insane in peacetime. Both sides
trained men to be fearless and impetuous; "you have to behave like
a small imbecile in some cases," recalled a Nigerian commander in
Oron. "A normal person this time, a little crazy that time for you to
move forward. You cannot behave like a gentleman."[4] When the war
was over, sorting out "mental infirmity" from good soldiering was not
easy. Samuel Nwarungwa's temporarily unnoticed condition was
a symptom of a larger abatement of norms in wartime Biafra – one
that carried over into reintegrated Nigeria.

   After the Republic of Biafra's defeat, violent crime spread, as Tekena
Tamuno described, "like cancer."[5] Hundreds of armed robbery cases
were heard in the East Central State's courts and tribunals in the 1970s.
Many of these crimes fit a pattern: They were usually conducted late at
night, by units of between five and fifteen men armed with military-
grade firearms. In most cases, they were former soldiers, from both the
Biafran and Nigerian armies (though rarely did veterans of the two
armies act together). A handful included young women in their ranks,
which judges found strange and disturbing – women were not thought
to be capable of this type of crime.[6] Most were home invasions, though
government offices, warehouses, and shops were also robbed. In his
testimony, a railway stationmaster described a representative example:

---

[3] ESHC uncatalogued collection, in the High Court of the East Central State of
     Nigeria, Aba, no. A/30c/72, *The State v. Samuel Nwarungwa*, November 4,
     1972.
[4] "Lieutenant Colonel M. Abdu (Rtd.)," in H. B. Momoh, ed., *The Nigerian Civil
     War, 1967–1970: History and Reminiscences* (Ibadan: Sam Bookman, 2000): p.
     211.
[5] Tekena Tamuno, "Trends in Policy: The Police and Prisons," in Tekena Tamuno,
     ed., *Nigeria Since Independence: The First Twenty-Five Years*, Vol. 4 (Ibadan:
     Heinemann, 1989).
[6] In the 1990s, a similar disbelief surrounded women's involvement in cultism.
     C. Chukuezi, "Change in Pattern of Female Crime in Owerri, Nigeria
     1980–2000," *Current Research Journal of Social Sciences* vol. 1, no. 2 (2009):
     pp. 9–13.

It is his evidence that he was awakened from his slumber at about 2 a.m. on the 11th of December 1971, in his house by the noise of people shouting outside "This is mobile; we are in town; open." He said before he god [got] up from bed those who were shouting were already at the verandah of his house and were thumping heavily at his door and demanding that he should open the door. When he dared to ask who the intruders were he was ordered to shut up and open the door. He sensed danger and tried an escape through the back door when he was prevented by a gun shot in that direction. He then opened the front door. He had a lighted lantern in the parlour of his house. As he opened the door he saw the accused by the light from the lantern pointing a gun at him and querying if he the witness was the person wasting their time. The accused, witness said, then ordered him to lie prone on the floor. As the witness obeyed the order of the accused, other persons with accused surged into witness's house armed with guns, clubs and pieces of iron.

The thief, who was known to the stationmaster, beat him senseless and left with virtually the entire contents of his house and the adjoining railway office.[7] Thousands of crimes like this took place in the early 1970s, conveying the ambiance of the battlefield into postwar towns and cities.[8] As a columnist wrote in *The Renaissance* in 1973, "crime in Nigeria is spreading to areas once viewed as secure. That is the growing cancer of civilization. There used to be a time when criminals were locked up behind bars and the people felt secure in the streets. But today, the people are locked up in their homes and the criminals are happy in the streets."[9] Indeed, streets and neighborhoods were redesigned in light of this new situation, as walls, gates, and barbed wire unfurled across the urban landscape in the 1970s.[10]

The sensibilities of war – the easy recourse to violence, the reflex to conceal – did not end when the shooting stopped in January 1970. Some Biafrans found that the skills that they had developed to survive the war could be useful in surviving the peace. A few prospered by them. As one

[7] ESHC uncatalogued collection, in the High Court of the East Central State of Nigeria, Aba, no. A/2c/72, *The State v. Festus Alozie*, February 23, 1972.

[8] This was not lost on foreign observers watching Nigeria. A South African intelligence report noted in late 1970 that "delinquency is reaching an alarming level, especially in the southern states where armed robbery is increasing rapidly." SADF CSI GP 15, Box 26, "Nigeria: Elements of the Situation," [1970].

[9] *The Renaissance* [Enugu], July 30, 1973, p. 3

[10] Tejumola Olaniyan, "African Urban Garrison Architecture: Property, Armed Robbery, Para-Capitalism," in Tejumola Olaniyan, ed. *State and Culture in Postcolonial Africa: Enchantings* (Bloomington: Indiana University Press, 2017): p. 294.

prominent lawyer recalled from his opulent chambers in Enugu, armed robbers "learned a trade during the war and they could not stop it. The law only could catch up with some of them. Some people still trade on what they learned during the war." After a moment of reflection, he added, "in a way, we all do," and hastily changed the subject.[11] Crime's most alarming trait was its broadness. It seemed to touch all areas of life, to permeate all areas of government, and to be perpetrated by an ever-widening group of people. Forms of violence that had commingled during the war – criminal and martial, personal and political, state and private – could not be easily disentangled in its aftermath. In the years following Biafra's defeat, as an Umuahia lawyer lamented, "injustice became part of our blood."[12]

The notion that martial violence might alchemically transform into crime is not unique to the Nigerian Civil War, but nor is this a feature of every conflict. The habits of battle are sublimated into crime after some wars but not others, and not every postwar society looks the same. Some of Nigeria's closest analogues are outside the continent, among them the United States after its civil war. In Missouri and Arkansas, the practice of rural guerilla warfare known as "bushwhacking" transformed into armed banditry by criminal gangs – groups of men that had operated as irregular military units allied to the Confederacy during the war. They spread into the American west and into regions that had been far from the lines of battle.[13] The history of crime in southeastern Europe following the Yugoslav Wars, too, follows a similar pattern to what I describe here.[14] In Africa, the most obvious points of comparison would seem to be other civil wars.[15] A rash of

---

[11] Interview with anonymous informant, Enugu, October 2014. A similar sentiment is expressed in Tekena N. Tamuno, *Peace and Violence in Nigeria: Conflict Resolution in Society and the State* (Ibadan: Panel on Nigeria Since Independence History Project, 1991): p. 366.

[12] Interview with A. M. O. Onukaogu, Umuahia, March 9, 2015.

[13] See Thomas Goodrich, *Black Flag: Guerrilla Warfare on the Western Border, 1861–1865* (Bloomington: Indiana University Press, 1995); on forms of corruption that followed a similar pattern, see Eric Foner, *Reconstruction: America's Unfinished Revolution: 1863–1877* (New York: History Book Club, 2005): pp. 365–369.

[14] See Peter Andreas, *Blue Helmets and Black Markets: The Business of Survival in the Siege of Sarajevo* (Ithaca, NY: Cornell University Press, 2008).

[15] The comparison that Biafran partisans made most frequently was to Bangladesh. The secession of East Pakistan took place in 1971 in circumstances very similar to Biafra's, but the results of that war were very different –

fratricidal conflicts followed Biafra – an incomplete list includes Liberia, Sierra Leone, the Democratic Republic of the Congo, Somalia, Sudan, the Central African Republic, and Libya. These wars blurred lines and upended lives too, but they did not produce the long-lasting alloy of deceit and violence that Biafra did.[16]

This chapter and Chapter 6 ask a question about continuity: Why did forms of survivalism that emerged on the front lines persist after the fighting was over? In other words, what prevented Nigeria from returning to normal? Whatever definition of "normal" judges and members of the public had in mind (and there were several), it was slow to return in the 1970s. To understand why, I tighten the focus from the former Biafra in general to the postwar East Central State. This was the place where the fighting had been the most destructive, and the pockets of Biafra that held out longest were located there. The reasons why the behaviors of war persisted there included ongoing conditions of postwar scarcity as outlined in Chapter 4, the availability of firearms, the tenacious problem of unemployment, and the unfortunate fact that demobilization and reintegration coincided with the 1973 oil boom.

Where one stands shapes where one places the fulcrum of historical change. Standing in the Biafran archive leads me to place it there, but this is not to blame one side for everything that happened in this period. Others have, including most directly Usman Faruk, who writes that Biafra's secession was "the real genesis of the current nation-wide problems of insecurity, armed robberies, vandalism, criminal hostage taking and cheating by deceit, otherwise known as four-one-nine (419)."[17] I reject Faruk's unequivocal statement of blame, but I admit that placing the war at the center of Nigeria's late twentieth-century history of crime ensnares this work in a problem of scale; it takes one region of a heterogeneous and fractured country and uses what happened there to explain events in places far removed from it in

---

Bangladesh succeeded in obtaining international recognition and ultimately won its war.

[16] That said, many of these wars are not over. Perhaps their effects will come to look more like Biafra's in the long view. Comparatively, see William Reno, "Crime Versus War," in Hew Strachan and Sibylle Scheipers, eds., *The Changing Character of War* (Oxford: Oxford University Press, 2011): pp. 220–240.

[17] Usman Faruk, *The Victors and the Vanquished of the Nigerian Civil War, 1967–1970: Triumph of Truth and Valour over Greed and Ambition* (Zaria: Ahmadu Bello University Press, 2011): p. 153.

geography and character. Nonetheless, the fact is that Nigeria came to look more like the East Central State in the 1970s than the other way around. Reintegration allowed the customs of war to metastasize rather than bringing them to an end.

The East Central State was not a metonym for Nigeria as a whole, but events there shaped its larger history. Nigerian society had been reorganized to fight a war, and the martial spirit had taken hold everywhere – not just in Biafra. Places that had never been touched by the fighting would come to feel its effects. Nigerian soldiers were demobilized with nothing but the clothes on their backs and a sense of entitlement born of victory. Former Biafrans returned home with a set of illicit wartime skills and a determination to rebuild their lives. Both of these combinations were toxic. Life after the war, as a former Biafran officer recalled, became "a similitude of the Hobbesian state of nature – nasty, short and brutish" – first in the east and shortly thereafter in Nigeria at large.[18]

The crime that flourished along the war front had not been isolated to a particular class, community, or "type." Crime, both in Biafra and in the postwar East Central State, cut across social and economic categories, affecting people from all walks of life.[19] One could look for a "criminal profile" here in vain. There was no singular notion of how crime worked, and no "underclass" to which its perpetrators added up. Judges often displayed their prejudices in their decisions – witness Chuba Ikpeazu's excoriation of the "primitive illiterate peasants of this country whose passions are more readily aroused than those of a civilised and enlightened class" in a 1971 murder case.[20] Yet the situation shook their convictions about what types of people were disposed toward crime. The people hauled before criminal courts in postwar Nigeria came from places high and low and from all ethnicities and backgrounds. There were petty thieves with university degrees, market women who carried out sophisticated confidence scams, and

---

[18] Achike Udenwa, *Nigeria/Biafra Civil War: My Experience* (Ibadan: Spectrum, 2011): p. 184.

[19] Later crime waves, such as the spate of kidnappings in the south-south region from the 1990s until the 2010s, tended to disproportionately affect the well-off. This was not the case during and immediately after the war, when the targets of crime crossed the social spectrum.

[20] ESHC uncatalogued collection, in the High Court of the East Central State of Nigeria, Owerri, *The State v. Innocent Uzokwe*, HOW/23c/71, November 10, 1971.

elite military officers who raped or stole. The cross-cutting quality of crime alarmed Nigerian judges and administrators, whose assumptions about what kinds of people broke the law were shaken. No one was above suspicion; former Biafrans were suspect simply by virtue of having managed to stay alive.

As in the previous chapters, the legal records used here are partial and scattered. Procedure was irregular, and little was done to redraw the boundary between civilian and military jurisdiction. But even if it was chaotic, law was vital; it structured commerce and public life after the war, and the courts played a role in the region's reconstruction. The most important of them was the high court of the East Central State, which also has the best-preserved records. With branches in every major town, this was the highest judicial authority in the state. Below the high courts lay the magistrate's courts and a handful of customary authorities, although few of their records have been preserved. Sitting parallel to the civilian courts were tribunals, which included both military tribunals and commissions convened to address specific problems. The chapter begins with a description of conditions in the East Central State at the end of the fighting, showing how poverty, unemployment, and a boom in oil production conspired to create an environment where crime was necessary to succeed. The later part of the chapter looks inward on domestic life in the former Biafra, considering how strained family dynamics shaped crime and were in turn shaped by it. Like many wars, the Nigerian Civil War rerouted ideas about gender and restructured how men and women interacted.[21]

The Fate of Biafra's Firearms

Against the backdrop of three convicts being tied to barrels on a dusty street in Umuahia, a British television report painted a picture of the stern legal order there: "Ex-Biafran soldiers, jobless and hungry, are

---

[21]   The study of gender and warfare is not, however, only about how the division of labor changes when men are away at the front. Here, the description of violence as lived experience is indebted to literature from gender studies (and feminist scholarship more broadly) on the affective dimensions of violence, for which military history lacks a language despite its centrality in warfare. See Veena Das, *Life and Words: Violence and the Descent into the Ordinary* (Berkeley: University of California Press, 2006); Sayak Valencia, *Gore Capitalism* (South Pasadena: Semiotext(e), 2018); Judith Butler, *Precarious Life: The Powers of Mourning and Violence* (London: Verso, 2006).

thought to be responsible for the spate of armed robberies. A vast crowd watches as the Nigerian army carries out the sentence. These public executions, there's been a half dozen so far, show the Nigerian army at its toughest, in fact the Ibos are living under a military occupation."[22] The East Central State's Commissioner of Police objected to this grim characterization, insisting in late 1970 that "armed robbery and burglary had declined very sharply." He pointed out that since the promulgation of the Robbery and Firearms Special Provisions Decree – a hard-line measure that made armed robbery a capital offense with no possibility of appeal – criminals knew that they were "operating on a very risky basis. Many have therefore given up."[23] Oral accounts and legal records reveal this to have been wishful thinking on the commissioner's part. The connection between the war and armed robbery was widely remarked on. "Since the end of the Nigerian civil war in 1970," went a common criminology textbook, "armed robbery in the country has become a source of worry to both the rich and the poor, the privileged and commoners alike."[24] Armed crime was nothing new in Nigeria, but its scale and character – the propensity of thieves to kill their victims, and the fact that it was carried out with military surplus – made it different from what had come before.

There were many famous criminals in postcolonial Nigeria, most notably men like Ishola Oyenusi and Lawrence Anini. Oyenusi's violent robberies made him a household name until his execution on Lagos's Bar Beach in 1971, where he laughed and taunted the crowd as he faced the firing squad. Anini's criminal alias, "The Law," evoked a connection between crime and the state that was lost on no one at the time.[25] Their depravity sold newspapers, and they had an aura of dark

---

[22] SOAS Nigerian Civil War Collections MS 321463 Box 13, Transcript of Independent Television News program, News at Ten, September 1, 1970.
[23] SOAS Nigerian Civil War Collections MS 321463 Box 13, *Biafra News*, October 30, 1970.
[24] C. U. Ugwuoke, *Criminology: Explaining Crime in the Nigerian Context* (Nsukka: Great AP Express, 2010): p. 193.
[25] Ben Okezie, *Dark Clouds: Confessions of Notorious Armed Robbers in Nigeria* (Lagos: Brane Communications Nigeria Limited, 2002): p. 191. On Anini, see Otwin Marenin, "The Anini Saga: Armed Robbery and the Reproduction of Ideology in Nigeria," *Journal of Modern African Studies* vol. 25, no. 2 (June, 1987): pp. 259–281; Lai Olurode, *The Story of Anini: Society, Police and Crime in Nigeria* (Lagos: Rebonik Publications, 2008).

heroism even though they were widely feared. Yet crime was a more ordinary phenomenon than these famous bandits suggest. As an editorialist wrote in a Port Harcourt newspaper, "the robbers live amongst members of the public, eat and drink in the same beer parlours with them, travel in the same bus with them and even sometimes share their loot in the same house where they live."[26] Crime, it seemed, was everywhere one looked.

When asked what they recalled about the years after the war, the first thing many people mentioned was robbery, followed by acts of "requisitioning" by Nigerian soldiers. These could be difficult to tell apart. Paul Obi-Ani called the first year after Biafra's defeat a "reign of terror," in which Nigerian soldiers "commandeered livestock, looted private and public property, raped women and teenage girls, forcefully married others and murdered anybody who challenged their highhandedness. Such senseless brutality had never been witnessed by the Igbo in their homeland. Even the colonial conquest at the beginning of the 20th century was far less brutal and cruel."[27] Not all observers described the situation in such strong terms, but theft and violence by soldiers were indeed common experiences. A farmer in Ogoja remembered looting as "a kind of joint venture between Nigerian soldiers and civilians of Northern origin."[28] Many such stories came to light in court.

The postwar East Central State bristled with guns. As had been the case in Biafra, the availability of firearms was one of the factors driving crime. The arms that circulated there included weapons from both the Nigerian and Biafran sides. An intelligence source told the British High Commissioner that "it is a very common practice for soldiers to take or send home weapons, ammunition, and assorted items of equipment as souvenirs, and indeed [the source] himself had received several weapons sent to him in Lagos as gifts from Nigerians he had known."[29] Rudimentary locally made firearms, the production of which had expanded greatly in Biafra, continued to be illicitly produced in the East Central State.[30] The Nigerian Army had liquidated what it could

[26] *Nigerian Tide* [Port Harcourt], January 29, 1972, p. 4
[27] Paul Obi-Ani, *Post-Civil War Political and Economic Reconstruction of Igboland, 1970–1983* (Nsukka: Great AP Express Publishers, 2009): p. 26.
[28] Axel Harneit-Sievers, Jones O. Ahazuem, and Sydney Emezue, eds., *A Social History of the Nigerian Civil War* (Enugu: Jemezie Associates, 1997): p. 153.
[29] NAUK FCO 38/285, "Conversation with WO II James," December 22, 1967.
[30] This "artisanal" firearm manufacturing would continue in Awka and elsewhere into the 1990s. Okezie, *Dark Clouds*, p. 187.

find of Biafra's arsenals and set up roadblocks throughout the east to seize guns from ex-soldiers and civilians, but collecting firearms from people who wanted to hide them proved difficult.[31]

Firearms from the war, of both Biafran and Nigerian issue, turned up as evidence in criminal courts for decades after the war. Conventional wisdom held that any weapon encrusted with red, silty dirt had likely come from the former Biafra, where ex-combatants had buried their weapons in the thousands in "unmarked jungle spots."[32] Not all of them came from Biafra, however. Nigerian veterans also found ways to keep the weapons they had been issued, and entire truck-loads of arms disappeared in the immediate aftermath of the war. Some were sold by the Nigerian officers tasked with disposing of them.[33] Kola Babalola recalled that

There was no commerce as such in Rivers State after the war. As a result of the war there was armed robbery. A lot of those boys came about weapons illegally. A soldier would be issued a weapon, go and hide the rifle, and collect it after the war. There was no work at all for the boys, and so many of them used those weapons to feed themselves.[34]

Few ex-soldiers likely kept their weapons for the purpose of staging robberies – a general sense of insecurity explains that decision better; but robberies were where they ended up.

In the east, former Biafrans explained crime as the work of poorly trained Nigerian conscripts – a mass of "erstwhile vagabonds, motor-park touts, pickpockets and other budding criminals," as one criminologist called them. His claim that Nigerian soldiers' sole intention was to "[make] their own fortunes though looting in the war-zones" was an exaggeration;[35] but judges fully appreciated that soldiers could be

---

[31] The Federal Military Government had reason to fear that these guns might be used not only in crimes in the East Central State, but for political purposes. There was an acute concern that demobilized Nigerian soldiers might bring their guns to other parts of Nigeria experiencing political discord, especially the Tiv region of the middle belt. NAUK FCO 38/287, Col. R. E. Scott, British High Commission, Lagos to Col. P. H. Moir, Ministry of Defence, June 15, 1968; Interview with Emeka Ofodile, SAN, Onitsha, March 16, 2015.

[32] *The Renaissance* [Enugu], May 21, 1972, p. 4. Interview with Mike Onwuzunike, Enugu, September 14, 2014.

[33] SADF CSI GP 15, Box 26, "Nigeria: Elements of the Situation" [1970].

[34] Interview with Kola Babalola, SAN, Port Harcourt, March 5, 2015.

[35] Sina Idowu, *Armed Robbery in Nigeria* (Lagos: Jacob and Johnson Books, 1980): p. 12.

violent and larcenous. Many of those charged with property crimes in the East Central State were noncommissioned officers, stationed far from home amid people they viewed (truthfully or not) as hostile.[36] Different Nigerian authorities blamed one another for the problem of disorder. When a group of soldiers in Onitsha commandeered a car owned by an Igbo employee of Shell in 1971, the case against them revealed how little faith courts had in the Nigerian Army. The judge ruled that, "considering all the circumstances, the presence of the soldiers, the time of the offence soon after the civil war when soldiers were not very polite and the notorious fact that soldiers were then removing peoples cars and forcing anybody close by to help load those cars into their lorries," all gave credence to the case against the accused.[37] The court found the soldiers guilty of theft, precipitating a tussle with the military authorities over their incarceration. The Nigerian Army won, and rather than serving a sentence they were returned to their unit.[38]

Nigerian soldiers were not the only perpetrators of crime and violence, however. Armed robbery by civilians also became common in the occupied areas of the east, reaching crisis levels by the end of 1970.[39] "After a most bloody, most macabre, fratricidal bloodbath for nearly three years," wrote a Port Harcourt editorialist, "[we] needed no ghost from the grave to warn us against a predictable increase in crime."[40] Tekena Tamuno recalled that, in a situation of profound shortage, armed robbery became "one of Nigeria's freest markets for people with guts or lack of scruple."[41] Some of these crimes were brazen, like a coordinated robbery of an entire hospital and its bedridden patients in Owerri.[42] A Nigerian civil servant accurately predicted that, in the years following the end of the war, "there would be a very

[36] *Nigerian Tide* [Port Harcourt], April 1, 1972, p. 3.
[37] ESHC uncatalogued collection, in the High Court of the East Central State of Nigeria, Onitsha, no. O/25c/71, *The State v. Clarence Mbagwu and three others*, November 1, 1971.
[38] The army did not always defend its own, however. Senior officers appreciated the need, as one told a foreign intelligence officer, "for a purge to rid the army of criminal elements that took refuge [in the army] during the war. Riches illegally acquired by soldiers are being quietly investigated." SADF CSI GP 15, Box 26, intelligence report, "New Aircraft, Conditions in the Army," July 22, 1970.
[39] Interview with Ejike O. Ume, SAN, Onitsha, March 12, 2015.
[40] *Nigerian Tide* [Port Harcourt], April 29, 1972, p. 13.
[41] Tamuno, *Peace and Violence in Nigeria*, p. 84.
[42] NAUK FCO 65/213, "Evacuation Plan," June 20, 1970.

serious problem with armed stragglers of the rebel troops indulging in general banditry trying to obtain whatever they could."[43] That former soldiers might turn their weapons against civilians was not surprising, but no one expected that so many civilians would rob one another. Far from constituting a "class" of the sort that judges and the police usually grouped criminals into, the people who wielded guns in postwar Nigeria included women, the highly educated, the elderly, and others not conventionally seen as disposed toward violence. "The society is teeming with thieves," wrote Emmanuel Obiechina. "Big thieves, small thieves, professional thieves and amateurs, young and inexperienced thieves in high places who make away with staggering sums of public money, and lowly, cynical ones who will cut a widow's throat to snatch away her handbag."[44]

Nigeria's first response was to ban the possession of firearms outright, which proved impossible to enforce. Illegally carrying handguns became common for rich and poor alike, and prominent people urged the state to allow the possession of firearms for self-defense. One editorialist in the East Central State's main newspaper opined that the state and federal governments were misguided in banning personal firearms during a crime wave, especially since the ban was only enforced in the east:

Armed robbers in this part of the country have grown intolerable in their display of "courage" and bravado. [. . .] All sorts of excuses have been given to justify the prolongation of the ban on the possession of fire arms by respectable citizens in this part of the federation. Before the war, respectable citizens in all parts of the federation – bishops, civil servants, well-known businessmen – were given permits to bear small arms. It was never a free-for-all affair and so never constituted any danger to the constituted authority.[45]

Judges were often sympathetic to wealthy people who armed themselves – perhaps because, as high-ranking public servants, they themselves were at risk of robbery and kidnapping. The people who illegally carried guns for self-defense were often inexperienced in handling them. There was a rash of accidental shootings in the early 1970s, such as when a Warri

---

[43] NAUK FCO 65/213, B. P. Austin to John Wilson, January 16, 1970. B. P. Austin to John Wilson, January 16, 1970.

[44] Emmanuel N. Obiechina, *Functional Ideology for African States* (Lagos: Chisado Enterprises, 1978): p. 28.

[45] *The Renaissance* [Enugu], January 8, 1974.

businessman trading in Aba unintentionally shot a young boy with his handgun. He was acquitted on appeal, but the court expressed concern at how easy it had been for him to obtain a pistol.[46]

Even when they were not being used for robbery or harassment, leftover guns had a destabilizing effect in the East Central State. In one case, a young veteran of the Biafran Army brought his revolver to the wake of a girl who had died a few days after the war's end. After getting drunk, he began shooting his gun into the air. This was an old funerary tradition (albeit one more commonly performed at the burials of men), but given the circumstances his actions made everyone nervous. Knowing that he was supposed to have surrendered his gun, and fearing that the shooting would attract the attention of the police, the girl's father warned him that she "was too young for guns to be fired at her funeral ceremony" and that this "pagan" rite was unwelcome at his Christian daughter's wake. The young man ignored the father, and he continued to drink and fire off rounds. Sure enough, later that evening he accidentally shot another mourner. He was found guilty of manslaughter.[47]

The military government's priority was to create public order, even if it meant trampling over principles that judges cherished. Emblematic was the decision to create tribunals specifically for armed robbery.[48] The Robbery and Firearms (Special Provisions) Act of 1970 made armed robbery a capital offense, punishable by public execution by firing squad – a "sordid spectacle" that led some judges and administrators to express moral reservations.[49] Others welcomed the move to public executions. An Enugu editorialist asked "why the heck a priest is assigned to step forward and bless the red-eyed brute" before being

---

[46] ESHC uncatalogued collection, in the High Court of the East Central State of Nigeria, Aba, no. A/12CA/73, *The State v. S.I. Guinness*, May 13, 1974.

[47] ESHC uncatalogued collection, in the High Court of the East Central State, Owerri, no. HOW/5c/1970, *The State v. Onochie Howard*, December 15, 1970.

[48] This approach to crime was not unique to Nigeria. Two years later, Uganda under Idi Amin would enact a similar measure in the form of the Robbery Suspects Decree. Alicia C. Decker, *In Idi Amin's Shadow: Women, Gender, and Militarism in Uganda* (Athens: Ohio University Press, 2014): p. 52.

[49] On the tribunal and the various acts that followed it, see Theresa Oby Ileghune, *Nigerian Law and Criminology of Robbery* (Lagos: Malthouse, 1998). The many decrees and state tribunals set up to combat armed robbery in this period can be found in A. P. A. Ogefere, *Nigerian Law Through the Cases: Vol. 24, Legal History* (Benin City: Uri Publishing, 1988): pp. 104–106.

shot, "an action which is aimed to rush the dead thief to God's Kingdom, thereby stirring some envy among the living who were supposed to be deterred!"[50] In 1972, magistrates were given jurisdiction over armed robbery, empowering courts at the lowest level of the legal system to impose death sentences with no possibility of appeal. Jurisdictional confusion deepened: "I do not know why this case was not handled by the Armed Robbery Tribunal," Justice Oputa remarked in an armed robbery case brought before him in the high court, "but whatever the reason is I have to pass such a sentence that will serve to deter others from imitating the example of the accused persons." Oputa consigned the robbery's ringleader to death – a sentence to match those handed down by the tribunal.[51]

Like most crackdowns, the establishment of the Armed Robbery Tribunal had political valences. A Port Harcourt lawyer recalled a case in which people in Iwofe tried to displace a foreign oil company that had set up on their land by threatening its employees with a gun leftover from the war. Knowing that armed robbery had become a capital offense, the police pursued a charge of it against the villagers. Under pressure from the company, seven of them were found guilty (even though no attempt at robbery had been made) and sentenced to death. The lawyer who represented the villagers remembered the case as a great miscarriage of justice, and it was at this point that he began to question the impartiality of the legal system.[52] Due process was being sacrificed with nothing to show for it; no matter how many people were publicly executed, the East Central State continued to spiral into chaos.

From some angles, the suppression of armed robbery looked like retribution masquerading as a law and order initiative. Many of the armed robbers executed in the East Central State were ex-combatants, sentenced through hasty and irregular procedures, leading the London-based *Biafra News* – still carrying the torch in the early 1970s – to call the crackdown a "purge" of the rebel army's young veterans. The publication quoted some of the defenses these men made:

---

[50] *The Renaissance* [Enugu], "Armed Robbers for Heaven?" September 26, 1972, p. 11.

[51] ESHC uncatalogued collection, in the High Court of the East Central State of Nigeria, Onitsha, no. O/42c/71, *The State v. Ogechi Dim and four others*, December 7, 1971.

[52] He recalled the case as having taken place in 1973 in Port Harcourt. Since it took place before a "one off" tribunal convened for the occasion, I can find no extant record of it. Interview with Kola Babalola, SAN, Port Harcourt, March 5, 2015.

Madubukwu for instance said: "Allow me say something. But I no thief."
Onyekwere said: "Nothing was found on me. People don't want to bring out
their guns. I have done nothing ... " Fineface said: "I was moving on the
road. People got me, said I thief something. Nothing was found on me.
I know a lot of people who keep arms. But now I am dying – an innocent
man. I have done nothing Heaven and earth know."[53]

It was not unreasonable to conclude that these executions were reprisals against Biafrans. This was not the whole story, however;
hundreds of veterans of the Nigerian Army were also executed for
armed robbery on slim evidence. Biafran veterans and sympathizers
had much to fear from Nigeria's military government, but so did
everyone else.

Poverty in the East Central State

Other factors besides the availability of firearms drove the incidence of
crime. Poverty was closely linked to both property crime and violence.
The immediate danger of starvation had ended with Biafra's defeat, as
relief supplies were rushed into the area around Orlu. The horrifying
cases of kwashiorkor that had become synonymous with Biafra came
to an end, but more banal problems continued. The sympathy that
journalists and aid workers had evinced for Biafra had already begun to
dissipate. "Biafrans do not easily fit any stereotype of martyrdom,"
wrote Renata Adler shortly before the final surrender. "It takes a high
tolerance for the sheer, bitterly comic ugliness of human suffering to
care much for these survivors out of Bertolt Brecht."[54] The East Central
State's economy stagnated. The brief cash influx that oil would bring
was barely felt there, and the east experienced the 1970s as a period of
unremitting economic decline.[55] Millions of impoverished people traversed the region, often on foot, to claim what was left of their homes.

The Nigerian government took responsibility for the humanitarian
situation in the East Central State. The International Committee of the
Red Cross and other humanitarian organizations wrapped up their

---

[53] SOAS Nigerian Civil War Collections MS 321463 Box 13, *Biafra News*,
October 2, 1970.
[54] Renata Adler, "Letter From Biafra," *The New Yorker*, October 4, 1969, p. 47.
[55] Nigeria shared this experience with most of the rest of the continent. See
John Iliffe, *The African Poor: A History* (Cambridge: Cambridge University
Press, 1989): pp. 240–244.

operations, the military junta having made it clear to them that their presence in reunited Nigeria would no longer be begrudgingly tolerated as it had been during the war.[56] Biafra's sympathizers immediately claimed that Nigeria's treatment of the defeated civilian population would be punitive – or at the very least engineered to make conditions worse in the East Central State than elsewhere in Nigeria. The federal government promised that the distribution of relief was not biased against the Igbo-majority region and that, in fact, it received a disproportionately large percentage of aid; 40 percent was remitted to the East Central State, compared to 30 percent for the South-Eastern State, 20 percent for Rivers, and 10 percent for the Mid-West.[57]

A rehabilitation commission was established in each state, the first task of which was to resettle the civilians living in small "refugee" camps all over the east. In the East Central State, the camps were humanitarian installations, where administrators and propagandists distributed food and tried to convince Igbos that Nigeria's intentions were peaceable. The camps were more like a form of protective custody in the South-Eastern State and Rivers State, where Igbo civilians feared reprisals by their neighbors. Although they were dirty, overcrowded, and sometimes dangerous places, few people in the camps went hungry.[58] A French journalist who had been sympathetic to the Biafran cause wrote that "it is difficult to appreciate exactly the food situation in former Biafra, because reports, and there are large numbers of them, are contradictory. It seems, however, almost certain that the

---

[56] The Nigerian government was determined that the relief and rehabilitation of the former Biafran territories must not be undertaken by foreign aid organizations or governments. The federal government declared that no aid would be accepted from the countries and organizations that had supported Biafra, including France, Portugal, Rhodesia, and South Africa, and also Caritas, Canair Relief, Joint Church Aid, the Nordic Red Cross, and the French Red Cross. Any foreign aid workers who had worked in Biafra would not be allowed to enter Nigeria. NAUK PREM 13/3376, Sir L. Glass to Foreign and Commonwealth Office, January 15, 1970. See also Arua Oko Omaka, "Victor's Justice: Atrocities in Postwar Nigeria," *Medicine, Conflict and Survival* vol. 32, no. 3 (2016): pp. 228–246.

[57] From the moment the war ended, former Biafrans claimed that this money was being misused and misdirected. SOAS I. A. Walsworth-Bell Papers MS 380827/5, collection of press clippings, 1970.

[58] R. B. Alade, *The Broken Bridge: Reflections and Experiences of a Medical Doctor During the Nigerian Civil War* (Ibadan: The Caxton Press, 1975): p. 135.

famine which decimated civilian populations in the short-lived Biafran republic can only be a dreadful memory."[59]

Nonetheless the situation was dire, especially in the war-devastated triangle between Orlu, Umuahia, and Owerri. The Nigerian aid distributed there ensured that refugees could do little more than stay alive. This material deprivation was exacerbated by the fact that practically everyone not in a camp was on the move. In a fictionalized account, S. Okechukwu Mezu described the situation at the end of the war:

> There was not enough food to go round and not enough beds to rest tired heads. Some of the refugees did not know where they were. They just followed the crowd as it moved out of besieged Owerri. They stopped when the movement stopped. Others stopped when darkness fell or when they tired of running. Even families could not take in all their distant relations, cousins, great-grandchildren, all kinds of in-laws and friends-in-law. Some families were separated into three or four groups. The man went to a refugee camp. The children stayed perhaps with the relations of the mother. The mother went to another family. Sometimes the grown-up children roamed from camp to camp, from house to house, waiting for darkness to fall.[60]

Counting the refugees with any degree of confidence was impossible. An oil worker estimated that the line of people leaving Owerri was 250,000 people long in January 1970. He further reported that "there was a serious situation of banditry developing with troops from the rebel and Federal Armies in undisciplined bands. This was particularly bad along either bank of the River Niger but covered the whole area."[61] On both sides, soldiers who had not been formally demobilized but knew that the war was over scrambled to claim what they could from civilians, sometimes setting up roadblocks to seize the personal effects of refugees. In a few cases, small-scale mutinies by restive Nigerian conscripts attended the news of Biafra's surrender.[62]

Nearly everyone had been reduced to penury, and the Nigerian government's financial policies seemed to contradict its larger promises

---

[59] SOAS I. A. Walsworth-Bell Papers MS 380827/5, Translated article from *Le Monde*, November 25, 1970.

[60] S. Okechukwu Mezu, *Behind the Rising Sun* (London: Heinemann, 1971): p. 222.

[61] NAUK FCO 65/213, "Internal Situation," January 26, 1970.

[62] SADF CSI GP 15, Box 26, intelligence report, "New Aircraft, Conditions in the Army," July 22, 1970.

of reconciliation. Early in the war, Nigeria had introduced new currency notes in order to make Nigerian pounds circulating in Biafra
useless for purchasing arms abroad. Biafrans who held their savings in
cash were left penniless.[63] After surrender, punitive banking regulations targeted those who had kept their money in banks. In 1970,
Nigeria seized the contents of all bank accounts in the East Central
State that had been used at any point during the war. In return, Nigeria
made a token payment of twenty pounds to every person affected by the
war for "rehabilitation," which for most was less than the amount that
they had held in their prewar accounts. Millions of people lost their
savings, which the Nigerian government justified by arguing that easterners ought to pay for reconstruction themselves.[64] People of all
classes and backgrounds were made paupers. Cyprian Ekwensi, the
internationally acclaimed novelist and former director of Biafra's propaganda agency, subsisted by collecting used bottles. He was hardly
unique in his humiliation.[65] As a university graduate who supported
her family by hawking groundnuts in the early 1970s recalled, "it had
been a war of survival, and then we had to survive after the war."[66]

Contracts that had not been fully executed in Biafra were declared
void, and agreements denominated in Biafran currency were deemed
unenforceable under Nigerian law. This caused major problems for
businesspeople in the East Central State, who could not collect debts
owed to them or substantiate claims to property that they had purchased in Biafra.[67] The postwar courts generally did not recognize
financial transactions that had taken place there, throwing the region's
mercantile economy into flux.[68] The many commercial disputes that

---

[63] E. I. Nwogugu, "Aspects of the Effects of the Nigerian Civil War on Commercial
     Transactions," *Nigerian Bar Journal* vol 14, no. 2 (1977): p. 138.
[64] Interview with Chief A. N. Kanu, Umuahia, March 9, 2015. The fall from
     affluence to poverty is a theme of many memoirs. See, for example, Nnamdi
     P. Agbakoba, *Terrors of War* (Lagos: Cat-War Publishers, 2004).
[65] Ekwensi shortly decamped to the more comfortable environs of the University of
     Iowa, where he completed the manuscript for his fictionalized account of
     postwar life, *Survive the Peace* (London: Heinemann, 1976).
[66] Interview with Mary Okehe, Lagos, July 17, 2013.
[67] Foreign banks that had operated in the former Biafra were highly critical of the
     postwar banking regulations. *West Africa*, February 21, 1970, p. 201.
[68] Interview with Jerome H.C. Okolo, SAN, Enugu, September 17, 2014. On the
     implications of the war for areas of commercial law, including contracts and
     insurance, see D. I. O. Ewelukwa, "The Abandoned Property Laws," *Nigerian
     Bar Journal* vol. 14 (1977); Awa U. Kalu, "Secession of Eastern Nigeria," in

followed made a bad economic situation worse, and it was made harder by the fact that people could not seek remedies through the law – at least if they were disputing a Biafran contract.

The imposition of strict import controls to protect domestic manufacturing added to the perception that there was a conspiracy against Igbos. National-level protectionist measures disproportionately affected the mercantile economy of the east, where the trade in manufactured goods was largely the domain of Igbos. Bans on the importation of stockfish and secondhand clothes (to protect fisheries in the Delta and cloth production in the north), both key goods in trade and lifestyle in Igbo communities, were widely seen as a kind of collective punishment.[69] Protests elsewhere in Nigeria convinced the federal government to lift the trade restrictions, but by that point many merchants had already moved into new markets.[70] The import bans pushed eastern businesspeople into the importation of goods that were still legal – including cars, electronics, household appliances, and cheap manufactured items from places like Taiwan, where Igbo traders began to beat a path between Africa and Asia that would become much wider in the decades to come.

The flow of commerce found its way around whatever restrictions Nigeria imposed, and a black market flourished.[71] Anything could be

Epiphany Azinge and Adejoke O. Adediran, ed., *Nigeria: A Century of Constitutional Evolution, 1914–2014* (Lagos: Nigerian Institute of Advanced Legal Studies, 2013); A. G. Karibi-Whyte, "Private contractual obligations and the Nigerian Civil War," *Nigerian Law Journal* vol. 8 (1974).

[69] These customs regulations were passed as part of the federal budget in 1971, drafted by Finance Commissioner Obafemi Awolowo. In the east, Awolowo was remembered as an architect of Nigeria's wartime starvation policy. On Awolowo's politics see Insa Nolte, *Obafemi Awolowo and the Making of Remo: The Local Politics of a Nigerian Nationalist* (Trenton: Africa World Press, 2010).

[70] *The Renaissance* [Enugu], January 20, 1974; NAUK FCO 65/1195, A. P. F. Bache, British High Commission, Lagos to Foreign and Commonwealth Office, April 8, 1972.

[71] Black marketeering also emerged through the apparently disorganized manner in which humanitarian aid was distributed by the Nigerian government. A sociologist from the University of Ibadan who visited an occupied part of the East Central State just before the war ended found that "the present practice of doling out food almost indiscriminately to large numbers of people, many of whom no longer need additional support will only kill the people's initiative and defeat the purpose of the relief exercise. It is depressing, but not surprising that stock-fish, and other relief items have found their way into many of the local markets, and are being offered for sale." NAUK FCO 65/213, "Nutrition and

obtained for a price – even human blood, which "mercenary blood donors" sold outside of the University of Nigeria Teaching Hospital in Enugu by the pint.[72] Eastern Nigeria's porous border with Cameroon and its busy ports were ideal for illegal (and quasi-legal) commerce. Used appliances were in high demand, as was canned food. One former lawyer admitted that he made ends meet by smuggling dried fish, even though he risked being disbarred. "There were decrees saying you could not import this and that," which few people took very seriously. "Smuggling really took off because people preferred foreign-made goods."[73] The traffic in illegal imports was common to the point of being unofficially tolerated, and it carried almost no public stigma. Igbos saw the new trade regulations as biased against them, so violating them did not attract much opprobrium.

Given the general deprivation, commercial and social transactions in the East Central State carried high stakes. Quarrels that would have been peaceably resolved in normal circumstances became violent and sometimes mortal. Markets, empty of goods and crammed with people trying to sell whatever they could, were especially charged places. At Nkwerre Market in 1971, two women who had stalls beside one another had an altercation after one asked the other to shift her wares over a few inches. She refused, and in the fight that followed she hit her neighbor in the head with a chair, giving her an injury that killed her the following day. "The offence is a serious one and the accused's act was savage to the extreme," the judge remarked, stunned that such a small matter had escalated without anyone intervening. "I am sure she has no qualms of moral compunction for what she did. The attack was unprovoked. A deterrent sentence is in my view desirable for the justice of the case."[74] This was not normal behavior, and judges were appalled by the things that people did to one another as the dust of the war settled. In Abakaliki, an upstanding schoolteacher brandished a gun at his crippled neighbor in a dispute over a piece of horsemeat, leading the judge to remark that "the entire place has been driven mad

Disease Patterns in a War Affected Area of Eastern Nigeria," J. B. Familusi, Institute of Child Health, University of Ibadan, 1969.

[72] *The Renaissance* [Enugu], July 29, 1973, p. 1.

[73] Interview with anonymous informant, Enugu, March 2015. NAUK FCO 65/ 2092, Foreign and Commonwealth Office to British High Commission, Lagos, March 31, 1978.

[74] ESHC uncatalogued collection, in the High Court of the East Central State of Nigeria, Owerri, *The State v. Evelin Mbaeli*, November 17, 1971.

and has gone low."[75] Ordinary people survived by extraordinary and sometimes illegal means.

Demobilization, Unemployment, and Oil

The lack of economic opportunity was the most trenchant problem in the former Biafra, where one foreign observer noted that "the most embittered are the unemployed," a group numbering in the millions and including men and women of all ages.[76] It was made worse by the poorly planned demobilization of the two armies. Demobilization did not directly cause crime, but it created problems that many individual soldiers solved by breaking the law. The confluence of unemployment with the availability of arms was at the root of insecurity in the East Central State. "After the war so many people were left without jobs and so many arms were not relinquished to the government. So it was very unsafe for innocent citizens," recalled Michael Ajogwu.[77] As a British diplomatic tour found in 1972, in Aba, Onitsha, and elsewhere,

An inevitable result of the lack of adequate employment opportunities is an increase in robbery, theft and extortion. A fertile field for the latter activity is in the motor parks made available in the various towns for the coaches, mini-buses and lorries that ply between them. There have been a number of violent clashes at these parks between rival gangs of touts, whose income depends on the number of passengers they can persuade, or force, into a vehicle and the commission they can demand for each one. I was told in Enugu that these touts now had a nation-wide organisation and that this constituted a serious threat to law and order in the towns.[78]

Politicians and administrators had long recognized the destabilizing potential of mass youth unemployment, but this had been more a fear than a reality until the war.[79] The problem was most acute in the East Central State. A British intelligence report estimated that 800,000

[75] ESHC uncatalogued collection, in the High Court of the East Central State of Nigeria, Abakaliki, no. AB/86c/71, *The State v. Nwigboji Afiaukwaoke*, January 17, 1972.
[76] SADF CSI GP 15, Box 26, "Nigeria – Political Situation," October 1970.
[77] Interview with Michael Ajogwu, SAN, Enugu, March 19, 2015.
[78] NAUK FCO 65/1195, "Tour Report: East, Central, Rivers and South-Eastern States," November 4–27, 1972.
[79] NAUK FCO 186/14, Minute by the Deputy High Commissioner for the United Kingdom, Enugu, "Politics and the Young," April 26, 1963.

people were unemployed there, which only accounted for those who
had worked in the formal sector at some point and was therefore likely
much higher. Most had no immediate prospects for employment. Some
33,000 of them were permanently disabled, and the sight of amputee
Biafran veterans begging in markets or alongside roads would be
common in the eastern states well into the 1990s.[80]

Demobilization was not just a problem for the former Biafra. The
Nigerian armed forces delayed demobilization as long as they could,
and civilian administrators argued that troops should be used for
reconstruction projects. They hoped this would hold off the problem
of unemployment (and, consequently, crime) that would result from
hastily dissolving the standing army in a time of economic stagnation.
They were particularly worried about western Nigeria, where several
hundred thousand migrants who had been expelled from Ghana the
previous year had already flooded the labor market.[81] Yet demobilization could not be delayed forever. Conscripts were eager to return
home, and men saw being transferred from combat to reconstruction
projects – essentially, manual labor in uniform – as dishonorable. The
failure to discharge federal troops systematically led many recruits to
simply walk away from their camps when the war was over. Several
hundred thousand federal soldiers returned home in 1970, with few
provisions made for their welfare and no clear path back to civilian life.
Biafran veterans found their way home as well, though even more
haphazardly – the Nigerian government did not class them as soldiers
but as "rebels" to whom no special assistance was owed. The Biafran
Army, one woman recalled in her memoirs, "evaporated, leaving only
items of uniform, pay books, guns and other 'incriminating
evidence.'"[82] The Nigerian government hoped that all of these men

---

[80] Obi-Ani, *Post-Civil War Political and Economic Reconstruction of Igboland*,
     p. 27. In 1975, disabled Biafran veterans begging in Enugu and elsewhere were
     brought to a former leper colony along the Oji River, where a camp was set up
     for them by the Asika government. The camp still exists, funded mostly by pro-
     Biafra organizations and local politicians.
[81] This set off a series of reciprocal deportations between the two countries that
     lasted until the 1980s. See Johnson Olaosebikan Aremu and Adeyinka
     Theresa Ajayi, "Expulsion of Nigerian Immigrant Community from Ghana in
     1969: Causes and Impact," *Developing Country Studies* vol. 4, no. 10 (2014):
     pp. 176–186.
[82] Leslie Jean Ofoegbu, *Blow the Fire* (Enugu: Tana Press, 1985): p. 152.

would find work on farms or perhaps in industry.[83] They did not, and the reason why had to do with oil.

Oil extraction by foreign companies resumed after declining (though never fully stopping) during the war. In the context of the 1973 OPEC oil embargo, oil suddenly became the center of Nigeria's political and economic life. The "oil boom" made Nigeria a middle-income country practically overnight (at least on paper), but it also disrupted national politics at a moment when the country had just come back from the brink. Oil brought ostentatious wealth to a region very close to the former war zone, and it channeled money (and the political power that came with it) toward the small group of well-connected people who controlled the spigot. To use a common metaphor of the time, oil made the national "pie" sweeter, and the fight over who would get the largest piece became sharper. The wealth that oil generated did little to improve the lives of ordinary people in the early 1970s, and to many it seemed to exacerbate the problem of crime. The oil industry become the site of mass, institutionalized theft. This took the form of "bunkering" – the offshore misappropriation of crude oil on an industrial scale, sometimes in collusion with company and state officials – along with more quotidian acts of siphoning and corruption in the "downstream" refining sector.[84]

Counterintuitively, oil exacerbated the problem of unemployment in the east. It precipitated a turn away from agriculture, which employed millions, toward extraction, which employed very few (many of them foreigners). Oil brought a sudden influx of foreign exchange into

[83] Others suggested job training programs for former soldiers, but they did not materialize. G. O. Olusanya, "Resettling the Soldiers," *West Africa*, February 7, 1970, p. 157. Another plan to "give the army something to do" was allegedly to annex the islands of São Tomé and Príncipe, still under Portuguese control, to "get even with Portugal for supporting Biafra." This also did not come to pass. SADF CSI GP 15, Box 26, Military, Air, and Naval Attache, South African Embassy, Lisbon to Director of Military Intelligence, Pretoria, January 27, 1970.

[84] See Elizabeth Gelber, "Black Oil Business: Rogue Pipelines, Hydrocarbon Dealers, and the 'Economics' of Oil Theft," in Hannah Appel, Arthur Mason, and Michael Watts, eds., *Subterranean Estates: Life Worlds of Oil and Gas* (Ithaca, NY: Cornell University Press, 2015); Michael Watts, "Sweet and Sour," in Michael Watts, ed., *Curse of the Black Gold: 50 Years of Oil in the Niger Delta* (New York: Powerhouse Books, 2008): p. 44. For a comparative account of oil and its relationship to crime, see Fernando Coronil, *The Magical State: Nature, Money, and Modernity in Venezuela* (Chicago: University of Chicago Press, 1997).

Nigeria, leading to the appreciation of Nigeria's new currency, the naira, and making its other exports less price-competitive internationally. Cocoa and palm production, and the nascent manufacturing sector, were crippled.[85] In other circumstances, the legions of demobilized young men might have done wage labor on farms or supported themselves by selling products that they grew on their own land. Instead, they found themselves unemployed – unable to return to the withered agricultural sector and even less likely to find jobs in the skeletal workforce of the oil industry. Crime sparked in places like Port Harcourt, where "we find opulent, naira-millionaires rubbing buttocks with famished paupers without so much as a *kobo* to their account," as an embittered drafter of the Ahiara Declaration observed in the 1970s. "We inhabit a topsy-turvy world in which the hedonistic rich are dying from over-eating and over-drinking and too much blood while the poor just fades away."[86] As money pooled in Port Harcourt and Lagos, norms of what constituted legitimate wealth, and how it should be distributed, became unsettled.[87] Oil wealth made an attractive target for property crime, and the widespread perception that it was ill-gotten gave a moral gloss to acts of theft committed by ex-soldiers, who cast themselves as Robin Hood figures when called to account for their actions.[88]

[85] Economists call this phenomenon "Dutch disease" after a similar case where the discovery of natural gas in the Netherlands precipitated a decline in the manufacturing sector in the 1950s. See Ezekiel Ayodele Walker, "Structural Change, the Oil Boom and the Cocoa Economy of Southwestern Nigeria, 1973–1980s," *The Journal of Modern African Studies* vol. 38, no.1 (March 2000): pp. 71–87; Michael Watts, ed., *State, Oil, and Agriculture in Nigeria* (Berkeley: University of California Press, 1987); Ann Genova and Toyin Falola, "Oil in Nigeria: A Bibliographical Reconnaissance," *History in Africa* vol. 30 (2003): pp. 133–156.

[86] Obiechina, *Functional Ideology for African States*, p. 12.

[87] See Andrew Apter, *The Pan-African Nation: Oil and the Spectacle of Culture in Nigeria* (Chicago: University of Chicago Press, 2005): p. 36. How oil changed ideas about wealth, religious observance, and "modernity" in general became the subject of much ethnographic work. See Karin Barber, "Popular Reactions to the Petro Naira," *The Journal of Modern African Studies* vol. 20, no. 3 (1982): pp. 431–450; Michael Watts, "The Shock of Modernity: Petroleum, Protest, and Fast Capitalism in an Industrializing Society," in Allan Pred and Michael Watts, eds., *Reworking Modernity: Capitalisms and Symbolic Discontent* (New Brunswick, NJ: Rutgers University Press, 1992).

[88] See, for example, Imo State High Court, uncatalogued collection, in the High Court of the East Central State of Nigeria, Owerri, *The State v. Chibuzo Nwokedi*, September 3, 1974.

Goods and money poured into the East Central State in 1970, creating highly visible wealth disparities. Nigerian soldiers brought currency with them, and the leaders of the occupying Third Marine Commando did extensive business in the conquered territories, much to the consternation of their superiors in Lagos.[89] Traders from the north and west arrived in the East Central State with long-unavailable goods in tow, but the only people who could afford them were soldiers and a tiny civilian elite. Nigerian public servants, including the judges who decided the cases cited here, were among the few prosperous people in a place still reeling from starvation. Their affluence caused resentment, as did the apparent ease with which they returned to the Nigerian civil service. Resentment spurred robberies. The most common targets were civilian officials, the wives of Nigerian soldiers (though rarely soldiers themselves), and the "carpetbagging" traders who came to take advantage of reconstruction. No one dared rob a judge, but Igbos who worked for the Nigerian government were whispered to be sell-outs, and there was not much ignominy attached to robbing or scamming them.[90]

Unemployed young people were surrounded by the Mercedes-Benzes and color televisions that the oil boom had brought to Nigeria, but they had no way of taking part in this rush of consumerism through legitimate work. Popular wisdom held that this explained the boom in robbery; but the temptations of conspicuous consumption alone were not enough to account for the swell of crime in the 1970s.[91] As this book has shown, armed robbery, deception, and other forms of malfeasance often explained by oil had already emerged before the oil boom of 1973. Moreover, the luxury goods that oil could buy were not the main things being stolen; food, clothing, and other humble necessities were the more common objects of armed robbery. As had been the case during the war, criminals' pleas were pitiable statements of desperation. Defendants claimed that they stole in order to pay for their children's schooling – a particularly painful deprivation for people who had long prized formal education.[92] Others explained that

---

[89] Benjamin Adekunle, *The Nigeria Biafra War Letters: A Soldier's Story* (Atlanta: Phoenix, 2004): p. 204.

[90] Interview with Mary Okehe, Lagos, July 17, 2013.

[91] For an analysis of how the "wanton display of wealth" influenced crime, see Idowu, *Armed Robbery in Nigeria*, pp. 14–19.

[92] Sending children to school before the war had usually not been a problem – education had been plentiful and valued in southeastern Nigeria, where village associations and informal family structures ensured that schooling was

they could not pay for hospital bills or medicine or support sons who had been crippled in battle. Women facing prostitution charges testified that they were the sole providers in their families, their husbands physically disabled or unable to find work. As residents of the East Central State – who themselves lived in the war's ruins, albeit in better circumstances than most – judges were inclined to believe these stories, even if their credulity did not always lead them to mercy.

Social Crisis and Violence in the Family

The war's shortages and displacements had forced people into new familial relationships, which often boiled over into crime. Many acts of violence took place in households that had been shaped by the war – or in some cases formed by it. Tempers flared in close living arrangements, and families split apart over disputes arising from scarcity.[93] In one case, a nine-year-old girl was charged with manslaughter when she threw a knife during a shouting match between her parents, accidentally killing another child. The girl lived in a crowded and deprived compound near Aba, where her family had returned from a refugee camp. She was acquitted on a technicality.[94] Many in the former Biafra understood themselves to be living in a time of moral decline. "Whatever was the cultural bedrock of the Ibo man," wrote an angry pamphleteer in Onitsha, "[it has] been corroded by forces beyond his control."[95] In a 1971 case, a woman filed a criminal complaint against her unemployed son after he beat her for having uprooted the marijuana plants he grew to dull the pain of a lost limb. The judge

accessible to most of those who wanted it. After the war, with many schools destroyed and nearly everyone penniless, school fees became a large burden. Interview with Jerome H. C. Okolo, SAN, Enugu, September 17, 2014. See also Augustine O. Okore, "The Value of Children Among Ibo Households in Nigeria: A Study of Arochukwu Division and Urban Umuahia in Imo State" (Doctoral dissertation, Australian National University, 1977): p. 344.

[93] Beyond the legal record, a discussion of this tension can be found in the memoirs of R. B. Alade, *The Broken Bridge*, p. 60.

[94] ESHC uncatalogued collection, in the High Court of the East Central State of Nigeria, Aba, no. A/1C/1970, *The State v. Monday Nwugo*, November 24, 1970. See also ESHC uncatalogued collection, in the High Court of the East Central State of Nigeria, Aba, no. A/20.c/73, *The State v. John Chikezie and Nwakwu Erondu*, May 1, 1974.

[95] Sam Ifeka, *Looking at Ourselves (A Post-Biafra Social Analysis)* (Onitsha, Herald Books, n.d.): p. 7.

excoriated the young veteran of the Biafran Army and mourned "the hallowed tradition of the Ibos, of youngsters respecting their elders," which the war had destroyed. "The accused must see himself for what he is – an outcast to decent and responsible living, a disgrace to himself and society."[96] This and many similar cases show that it was hard for men to transition into other forms of work, sociality, or family life.[97] The war had reordered people's priorities and ethics, and the legal system struggled to deal with the social problems that resulted. Judges were caught between the letter of the law and the reality that concepts like motive and intent meant something different in a society coming back from the brink of disaster.

This was especially apparent in criminal cases that turned on the meaning of "provocation," of which there were many. Provocation is a defense that can be mounted in a murder trial, where the defendant claims that a killing was committed "in the heat of the moment" and "before passion had cooled." If successful, it results in the lesser charge of manslaughter. The fact that many murder charges were reduced to manslaughter in postwar courts – far more than usual, and often on grounds that would not usually be recognized as provocation – shows that judges were aware of how difficult conditions had become in the East Central State.[98] Turning a legal term of art into a general lament, judges described life in the former war zone as one long "heated moment." This was how a judge understood a 1971 case in which a man killed his junior wife

[96] ESHC uncatalogued collection, in the High Court of the East Central State of Nigeria, Umuahia, *The State v. Arthur Ugwueje*, December 13, 1971.

[97] Comparatively, consider Danny Hoffman's description of young ex-combatants transitioning to other forms of dangerous labor in mines or mercenary bands. Danny Hoffman, *War Machines: Young Men and Violence in Sierra Leone and Liberia* (Durham, NC: Duke University Press, 2011).

[98] The historicity of provocation has recently become a topic of interest in legal historical scholarship more generally. See Krista Kesselring, "No Greater Provocation? Adultery and the Mitigation of Murder in English Law," *Law and History Review* vol. 34, no. 1 (2016): pp. 199–225; Elizabeth Papp Kamali, "Felonia felonice facta: Felony and Intentionality in Medieval England," *Journal of Criminal Law and Philosophy* vol. 9 (2015): pp. 397–421. In Africanist scholarship, see Stacey Hynd, "Murder and Mercy: Capital Punishment in Colonial Kenya, ca. 1909–1956," *International Journal of African Historical Studies* vol. 45, no. 1 (2012): pp. 81–101; Katherine Luongo, "Domestic Dramas and Occult Acts: Witchcraft and Violence in the Arena of the Intimate," in Emily Burrill, Richard Roberts, and Elizabeth Thornberry, eds., *Domestic Violence and the Law in Colonial and Postcolonial Africa* (Athens: Ohio University Press, 2010).

when she revealed that she was pregnant with the child of a Nigerian soldier. The court found him guilty of manslaughter rather than murder, even though the crime took place "dispassionately," ruling that the act of infidelity with the former enemy was enough to constitute provocation. It was sufficient to note that the general atmosphere of the occupied village was "heated," even though the man had killed his wife in full presence of mind.[99] Yet these cases were troubling even if provocation offered a tool to understand them. "The offence of killing people on slight provocation by the peasants around here is so rampant," remarked an Owerri judge in a case where a farmer decapitated his wife following a dispute over some cassava stems. "In my brief stay here several such cases of this nature have come before me and I must be failing in my duty if I do not impose a deterrent penalty."[100] The man was executed.

The war's fallout affected women most harshly, and it is not insignificant that the two cases discussed here involved femicide. Domestic and sexual dynamics shaped how crime unfolded in the 1970s in many different ways. The generation of men impoverished by the war found it difficult to raise the money to marry, which led some of them to steal what they could not earn through work. Sexual relationships between Igbo women and Nigerian soldiers were often the sites of discord – though others created lasting bonds. Relationships between soldiers and local women were flashpoints for larger conflicts between occupying troops and the communities that hosted them. Nigerian army camps became semi-permanent villages in the early 1970s, and local women took up residence with soldiers in or around their barracks.[101] Even if they married, their relationships were seen as akin to prostitution.[102] When children resulted, both mother and child faced social exclusion.[103] As a judge remarked,

---

[99]   ESHC uncatalogued collection, in the High Court of the East Central State of Nigeria, Aba, no. A/19c/72, *The State v. Godswill Ufomba*, November 9, 1972.

[100] ESHC uncatalogued collection, in the High Court of the East Central State of Nigeria, Owerri, *The State v. Innocent Uzokwe*, HOW/23c/71, November 10, 1971.

[101] A discussion of this phenomenon can be found in the following case: ESHC uncatalogued collection, in the High Court of the East Central State of Nigeria, Aba, no. A/4c/70, *The State v. Francis Odijie and Marcus Alimi*, November 20, 1970.

[102] Harneit-Sievers, Ahazuem, and Emezue, *A Social History of the Nigerian Civil War*, p. 205.

[103] Reflecting a widespread sentiment, a pastor in Asaba stated that women who had been raped by Nigerian soldiers "brought forth bastards to the land . . .

Children with Nigerian soldiers as their fathers were not very popular with the local natives in this area, more so if their mothers are unmarried [...] Perhaps the local parents care little or nothing about their daughters living with Nigerian soldiers so long as they bring home some money for them. But it is a different matter if and when they also bring back children from the Nigerian soldiers.[104]

Young women bore the brunt of the occupation – both as victims of sexual violence and as targets of contempt by their own communities.

Anxiety about weakened family structures often took the form of concern about women's behavior. A female editorialist in a Port Harcourt newspaper opined that the war had slackened women's morals: "The ill-winds of the war blew into their brains a complete new code of behavior – a sinister code. They may like to have 'good time' with the affluent married men but are not prepared to come into any home as second wives. What they want is a coup d'état."[105] Ukpabi Asika described how gender figured in the process of reintegration:

In this terrible and harrowing situation the choice before a man seems to be either to go mad or to become a vegetable. It is not surprising therefore that many of our leading women spend each waking day from one drunken stupor to another; that many of our honest young men are today hooked on "wee-wee" [cannabis], or alcoholism and nihilism. It is especially sad this drunkenness among our women. But it is not surprising. For it is our women who have always been the last anchor and conscience of our Ibo people.[106]

Asika and others within the federal government believed that the success of reintegration depended on women. They would be the ones to lead their families back to their villages, care for the sick and

a generation of people who are not really Asaba ... it is a very ugly social abnormality." S. Elizabeth Bird and Fraser M. Ottanelli, *The Asaba Massacre: Trauma, Memory, and the Nigerian Civil War* (Cambridge: Cambridge University Press, 2017): p. 197.

[104] ESHC uncatalogued collection, in the High Court of the East Central State of Nigeria, Okigwe, no. HO/360/18, *The State v. Basemath Ukazu*, May 31, 1973.

[105] Kate George, "Has the War Changed Our Women?" *Nigerian Tide* [Port Harcourt], March 11, 1972, p. 14. The author may have actually been a male journalist, as was often the case with pseudonymous editorials. See Stephanie Newell, *The Power to Name: A History of Anonymity in Colonial West Africa* (Athens: Ohio University Press, 2013): pp. 159–169.

[106] NAUK FCO 65/213, "Asika Appeals for a New Era," November 11, 1968.

wounded, and set the tone for how Nigerians and ex-Biafrans interacted in the reoccupied territories. When conditions did not improve,
women would also be the first ones to be blamed.[107]

The fact that Nigerian soldiers often had intimate relationships with
local women, and sometimes married them, did not preclude them
from feeling fear or contempt for one another. One northern
Nigerian soldier stationed near Aba mentioned in court that he brought
his gun with him when he went to visit the parents of the Igbo woman
he intended to marry. When asked why he felt he had to be armed for
that visit, he responded that "it was necessary as the villagers were
cannibals. He added that [he] was entitled to carry his gun anywhere he
wanted [as he] is the head of his own unit."[108] This did not make for the
best start to a marriage, and she left him before it could be solemnized.
Some of these relationships were stronger than the forces working
against them, enduring despite politics and the disapproval of their
families. But most did not. Divorce was rife in the early 1970s, which
an official in the East Central State Ministry of Social Welfare put down
to the hastiness of wartime marriages, which fell apart when "the
brides discovered that their husbands' status ceased to be what it was
during the war."[109] Some relationships ended in disaster. In a 1971
case from Owerri, a Nigerian officer fatally assaulted his local girl-
friend, who was pregnant. She had refused to have sex with him again
until he agreed to undergo the traditional marriage ceremony of her
community, which sparked an argument that ended in him beating her
to death in front of their landlady. The judge found it especially
disturbing because the accused officer was "not a primitive peasant
but a literate and disciplined Army Corporal," who ought to have
known better.[110] He was hanged.

---

[107] Comparatively, see Thavolia Glymph, *The Women's Fight: The Civil War's
Battles for Home, Freedom, and Nation* (Chapel Hill: University of North
Carolina Press, 2020); Stephanie McCurry, *Women's War: Fighting and
Surviving the American Civil War* (Cambridge, MA: Harvard University Press,
2019): pp. 124–127.

[108] ESHC uncatalogued collection, in the High Court of the East Central State of
Nigeria, Aba, no. A/4c/70, *The State v. Francis Odijie and Oseni Alimi*,
November 20, 1970.

[109] *The Renaissance* [Enugu], August 12, 1973, p. 16.

[110] ESHC uncatalogued collection, in the High Court of the East Central State of
Nigeria, Owerri, no. [illegible], *The State v.* [illegible] *Ojo*, December 8, 1971.

A murder case from Urualla illustrates the kinds of decisions women were faced with.[111] A few months after Biafra's surrender, Basemath Ukazu began living with a Nigerian soldier "of Hausa extraction" in his barracks outside of her village. She became pregnant and gave birth to a son. Ukazu's family was furious that she had a child with a Nigerian soldier, but they hoped that matrimony might salvage the situation. He refused to marry her. Two weeks after the child was born, Ukazu took him to his father's barracks and tried to drown him in a latrine. A soldier discovered the child the next day and took him to a hospital, where he died waiting for medical care from nurses who refused to treat him unless they were paid in advance. Their actions became the subject of a separate case.

In court, Ukazu testified that her uncle had threatened to kill her unless she got rid of the child and that her entire village had "[made] mockery of her for getting her baby from an Hausa soldier[,] a thing apparently loathed by the local natives." The judge warned that "young women like the accused who choose to embark on reckless living must be prepared to face the consequences of their actions." Yet the blame did not lie with Ukazu alone. "In the normal circumstances this court would have no difficulty in condemning the accused to death," he ruled, but "the balance of the mind of the accused was disturbed by reason of her not having fully recovered from the effect of her giving birth to a child coupled also with the reaction to this persecution and taunt from her co-villagers for having her baby from a non-Ibo man." Judges were horrified by cases like this, but they also recognized that they did not take place in a vacuum. Allowances had to be made for the conditions of the times. Ukazu was found guilty of murder, but she was given a light prison sentence.

Old arguments put on the back burner during the fighting simmered again, and wartime betrayals came to light. Crime and the settling of domestic or sexual disputes sometimes overlapped. In April 1972, a group of Biafran veterans staged a series of armed home invasions in Aba. Their targets were all people who they felt had wronged them during the war. One victim had slept with one of their wives while he

---

[111] ESHC uncatalogued collection, in the High Court of the East Central State of Nigeria, Okigwe, no. HO/360/18, *The State v. Basemath Ukazu*, May 31, 1973.

Figure 5.1 A village near Aba poses for a group photograph, 1971 (A. Abbas/Magnum Photos)

was away at the front, and another had threatened to kill one of their mothers when she asked him for help. Their state-appointed lawyer, a young woman who had spent the war studying in England, argued that, despite their guilt, "bygones should be let alone." The judge agreed with her, and the two men who could be identified were given a token prison sentence.[112] They were lucky – had their case come before the Armed Robbery Tribunal, they would probably have been executed.

Families were reunited after the war, and these meetings were not always happy. A man killed his wife "with hot temper" when they were reunited in 1972, each believing the other to have died in Biafra. She had absconded to the federal side with their savings, thinking that her husband would be killed by the advancing Nigerian troops. He was not, and when they met again in Umuahia he murdered her for having abandoned him. The judge resignedly sentenced him to death.[113] Gatherings to mark the end of the war became venues for accusations, fights, and reckonings. There were enough parties that ended in bloodshed that the problem received official judicial notice.[114] In April 1970, a clerk named Eyo Okpo returned home to Oron after a long separation from his family during the war. His return was "a matter of rejoicing by his relatives and friends. There was plenty to drink, the appellant himself providing some of the drinks. There was general merriment including singing and dancing in which the appellant also played a prominent part." In the midst of the party, Okpo took the opportunity to kill his brother by striking him from behind with a machete. In his trial, he claimed that he had been moved by a spirit, testifying that "the reason why I cut [my brother] is because he bewitched me that I should not see any fortune in my life."[115] It was not strange that a defendant would use enchantment

---

[112] ESHC uncatalogued collection, in the High Court of the East Central State of Nigeria, Aba, no. A/20.c/73, *The State v. John Chikezie and Nwakwu Erondu*, May 1, 1974.

[113] ESHC uncatalogued collection, in the High Court of the East Central State of Nigeria, Umuahia, *The State v. Nnokwam Akwali*, July 26, 1973.

[114] See, for example, Supreme Court of Nigeria Law Reports 276/1971, *Ominyi Ogeikpa v. The State*, February 1972, Supreme Court of Nigeria Law Reports 220/1971, *Ayogu Ugwu and Onu Ugwuanyi v. The State*, January 1972.

[115] Supreme Court of Nigeria Law Reports 196/1971, *Eyo Okpo v. The State*, February 1972.

to explain his behavior – this had long figured in criminal courts, and as a defense it was sometimes successful.[116] Here, the judge did not believe that Okpo had really been possessed; but judges knew that the war had spoiled fortunes and futures and created an army's worth of ghosts. Metaphorically speaking, they haunted the courtroom regularly.

Conclusion

The final scene of Cyprien Ekwensi's novel *Survive the Peace* is a burial in a shattered Igbo village. It is interrupted by an armed robbery. "War has changed everything!" laments an old woman. "The young men want to become rich before morning, without working. There are still many guns, hidden away ... many are in evil hands ... Our lives are worth nothing, nothing!"[117] What Ekwensi and others found most disturbing about postwar life was the breakdown of everyday morality. Survival continued to be the order of the day, but, after defeat, the galvanizing experience of a shared cause was gone. "At a time like this," recalled a nurse, "one finds out that people one expects to be kind will not be kind because they feel, well, this is war and everybody is levelled. We are all Igbo, we are all the same; why should anybody go to help anybody else?"[118] Cases from the 1970s gave many variations on the theme of self-preservation. "Nobody from the neighbouring compounds responded to their alarm because they were scared away by the gun shots," testified a witness to an armed robbery, in language so common that

[116] On the invocation of the supernatural in explaining crime in Africa, see, among many, W. Clifford, *An Introduction to African Criminology* (Nairobi: Oxford University Press, 1974): pp. 22–34; Stephen Ellis and Gerrie Ter Haar, *Worlds of Power: Political Thought and Political Practice in Africa* (New York: Oxford University Press, 2004): pp. 149–154. The presence of spirits, bewitchment, and other forms of the "un-real" in Nigerian jurisprudence is not the residue of a particularly "African" legal imagination. On figurative and "real" spirits in other legal traditions, see Colin Dayan, *The Law is a White Dog: How Legal Rituals Make and Unmake Persons* (Princeton: Princeton University Press, 2011); Natasha Wheatley, "Spectral Legal Personality in Interwar International Law: On New Ways of Not Being a State," *Law and History Review* vol. 35, no. 3 (2017): pp. 753–787.
[117] Cyprien Ekwensi, *Survive the Peace* (Ibadan: Heinemann, 1976): p. 173.
[118] Alex O. Animalu, *Life and Thoughts of Professor Kenneth O. Dike* (Enugu: Ucheakonam Foundation, 1997): p. 158.

it became a sort of boilerplate.[119] The self-defense instinct made people turn inward, away from the Nigerian public, and toward the more primordial space of the family, the street, or the village.[120] "After the war," Jerome Okolo recalled, "no one wanted to be a martyr."[121]

The difficult years that followed the war offer lessons not only for Nigeria but for the study of crime and law generally. Popular criminology posits that there is a sliding scale between freedom and security – that the more democratic a system is, and the more liberties it allows, the less secure daily life will be. Street crime and violence appear as the price a society pays for freedom.[122] In this way of thinking, the one virtue of living under an authoritarian regime is that one does not have to worry much about being mugged, scammed, or assaulted. Nigeria's postwar experience disproves this truism. In the 1970s, Nigeria was ruled by military regimes that gave few freedoms and had no pretense of democracy – and yet it was also rife with violence, deception, and corruption.

[119] ESHC uncatalogued collection, in the High Court of the East Central State of Nigeria, Aba, no. A/20.c/73, *The State v. John Chikezie and Nwakwu Erondu*, May 1, 1974.
[120] The divide between national and "primordial" ethnic politics was theorized by one of the most important scholars of this period, Peter P. Ekeh, "Colonialism and the Two Publics in Africa: A Theoretical Statement," *Comparative Studies in Society and History* vol. 17, no. 1 (1975): pp. 91–112.
[121] Interview with Jerome H. C. Okolo, SAN, Enugu, September 17, 2014.
[122] See, for example, Tom Gash, *Criminal: The Truth About Why People Do Bad Things* (London: Allen Lane, 2016): pp. 30–39.

6 | No Longer at Ease: Fraud and Deception in Postwar Nigeria

In the early 2000s, a Lagos journalist described the archetypal 419 scammer as "a *go-go* man":

He is always on the move. He is a party man, a high society man, present at any important social gathering. In the various government ministries, parastatals, in central banks, in commercial and merchant banks, in major multinationals, in oil companies, among security forces, churches and mosques, he has insiders that are his paid informants and procurers of sensitive documents, official stamps and seals.[1]

Thirty years earlier, the average practitioner of 419 would have looked very different from this high-flying cosmopolite. He would be poor, with some education but little way of putting it to use. He would likely be involved in fraud not to get rich but to get by – to feed himself, or provide for his family, or maybe to find a way out of a wartime entanglement. He would not be a suave con man with a "bevy of beautiful ladies whom he uses as private operatives"[2] but rather a student displaced many times over, a low-level clerk without a job, or a former soldier who had been decommissioned with nothing but the clothes on his back. This person might be a woman. In the early 1970s, she would also likely be a former citizen of the Republic of Biafra. An earlier tract on 419 argued that its practitioners were in a "quest for survival," which also captures the postwar spirit: "Like the greedy gatherer, the one who engages in gather-gather business pounces on riches, property, titles, honours, glories and the like with a ferocity associated with a wounded lion."[3] It was woundedness and desperation, not *savoir faire*, that characterized the first generation of people doing what came to be called "419."

---

[1] B. C. Okagbare, *The Twilight of Nigerian "419" Fraudsters* (Lagos: Mbeyi and Associates, 2003): p. xiii.

[2] Ibid., p. xi.

[3] Chuu Anoliefo, *419 & the Rest of Us: Our Quest for Survival* (Lagos: Delence Publishing Company, 1992): p. 1

218

Armed conflict warps the standards of what behaviors are normal or permissible, both in law and in private life. It also teaches skills, and the Nigerian Civil War taught people how deception could serve their personal survival. It made mendacity a part of everyday life, and in this way the war paved the way for 419. Chapter 5 described the postwar expansion of armed robbery and violent crime. This chapter tells a similar story about the growth of fraud and other forms of dishonesty. The practice of 419 would not reach its apogee until later – popular memory usually recalls the 1980s and 1990s as the time when it became a major concern – but its outline had been drawn earlier. Fraud was a more nebulous type of crime than armed robbery. Since it took many forms, it is more difficult to trace it through the legal record. Moreover, it was usually adjudicated by low-level magistrates' courts, the records of which seldom survive. For this reason, this chapter is more interpretive than the ones that precede it. I identify echoes of the war in postwar stories about deception – places where 419's wires crossed with Biafra's – but my sources do not allow me to link the two with the same degree of confidence that I can with armed violence. Nonetheless, postwar cases show how 419 and its cognates fed on the recent experience of the war.

The relationship between the war and 419 is visible in traces in the legal record, and in life stories. Some of the people who made 419 an international phenomenon in the 1990s had been adolescents during the war. A paradigmatic case is the con artist-turned-pastor Obiora Chukudebelu. His path was similar to that of other early 419ers: a wartime youth, an impoverished adolescence in postwar Enugu, an unsuccessful stint as a college student at the University of Lagos, where he began his first postal scams, to lucrative work as a smuggler in the north and later in Ghana and Ivory Coast, where he began to use fax machines and word processors in his increasingly elaborate 419 schemes. After being born again in the 1990s, he repented and wrote a full (though not very contrite) account of his activities.[4] Like Arnold Akpan, his life story links 419 to the war.

There was something distinct about the crime that Chukudebelu and others like him practiced. To be sure, deception was not a new

---

[4] Obiora Chukudebelu, *Restitution: The Thrilling Testimony of a 419 Fraudster Who Repented* (Lagos: self-published, 1999). A similar memoir linking the war and crime is Iyke Uzorma, *Uzorma Warfare Treatise: Occult Grand Master Now in Christ* (Benin City: Osasu Publications, 1994): p. 92.

phenomenon, and Nigeria had experienced panics about crime before, most notably during the Great Depression;[5] but "crime waves" had been situational and temporary, usually arising in response to periods of scarcity. They did not permeate the political system, nor did they capture the public imagination in the way that 419 and its correlates would later.[6] Nigeria's similarity to other former British colonies underscores the importance of the civil war in its history. If colonialism explained crime's long embrace of Nigeria, it would stand to reason that other former colonies – Ghana, for example, which shares Nigeria's colonial structure and much of its postcolonial history – would share its experience of crime. Something else is required to understand why crime thrived in Nigeria but not in the places most structurally similar to it.[7] This final chapter shows how 419 was part of the Nigerian Civil War's long tail and how it became, as Daniel Jordan Smith writes, "a way of life."[8] The war did not cause 419 precisely, but it created the conditions where it could take root.

Crime took a particular shape in Biafra and the postwar east. Yet the aim of this argument emphatically is not to assign blame to those who had lived in Biafra – much less to point a finger at Igbos. Others do; accounts of Igbo involvement in crime abound, and some refer to "Igbo 419" as if those terms go together.[9] The journalist Misha Glenny has called Igbos "among the most phlegmatic and inventive" of the world's criminals, describing how Igbo traders are "infected by the corruption of the Nigerian state." He tells the story of Nigerian crime as one of contamination; "soon the Yoruba, the Hausa, and dozens more of Nigeria's ethnic groups took up the example of the Igbo," he writes, "and began indulging in one of the

[5] See Steven Pierce, *Moral Economies of Corruption: State Formation and Political Culture in Nigeria* (Durham, NC: Duke University Press, 2016); Moses Ochonu, *Colonial Meltdown: Northern Nigeria in the Great Depression* (Athens: Ohio University Press, 2009): pp. 71–99.
[6] An exception would be the string of murders in colonial-era Annang staged to appear as if they had been committed by leopards; but, while these famous killings were discussed widely, they did not embrace the whole of Nigeria in the way that 419 would. See David Pratten, *The Man-Leopard Murders: History and Society in Colonial Nigeria* (Edinburgh: Edinburgh University Press, 2007).
[7] Most Ghanaians would not relish the comparison. Nigeria's neighbors behold it with a mixture of fear, awe, and disdain.
[8] Daniel Jordan Smith, *A Culture of Corruption: Everyday Deception and Popular Discontent in Nigeria* (Princeton: Princeton University Press, 2008): p. 226.
[9] See, for example, Abubakar Momoh, "Youth Culture and Area Boys in Lagos," in Attahiru Jega, ed., *Identity Transformation and Identity Politics Under Structural Adjustment in Nigeria* (Uppsala: Nordiska Afrikainstitutet, 2000): p. 195.

most mischievous examples of crime in history."[10] Glenny, like many chroniclers of crime, relates 419's colorful stories without much sense of what might drive them, other than greed. I also use a contagion metaphor to understand crime, but I argue that its etiology was not a person, a gang, or an ethnic group. Rather, like the literal diseases of battle – typhoid, cholera – crime spread because the structural conditions of warfare allowed it to.

Deception, Subterfuge, and "419" after the War

In the 1980s, Ojukwu would angrily write that Nigerians are "tyrannized by the pseudo – nothing looks like it truly is. Our leaders are pseudo-leaders; our intellectuals, pseudo-intellectuals; our professionals are pseudo-professionals, whilst our occupations are pseudo-occupations. [...] It is this unreality that breeds a general alienation from the true and from truth."[11] Ojukwu meant this characteristically sweeping statement as an indictment of Nigeria's political class, which he was desperate to reenter even as he disdained it; but his words captured a larger truth. In the decades after the war, it could be difficult to tell the difference between the real and the "pseudo." Biafra's brief existence had given cover for many forms of untruth, and fraud continued to boom after its defeat. A description of what one needed to engage in 419 could double as a picture of the Biafran state's elaborate performance of legitimacy:

To succeed, he needs a chain of fake things. He needs fake passports, fake dresses, fake complimentary cards, fake names, in fact fake everything. His most primary concern is, therefore, to make the fake look as much as possible like the real. The OBTs [Obtain-By-Tricks] are therefore masters of the art of deception. They act, the camouflage, they pretend; so unless one is careful enough, one may not be able to distinguish the weed from the wheat.[12]

The surfeit of fakes and doubles would make Nigeria into a kind of house of mirrors by the 1990s – a place where hazards were everywhere and mistrust was the norm. In short, it continued to feel like wartime.

---

[10] Misha Glenny, *McMafia: A Journey Through the Global Criminal Underworld* (New York: Knopf, 2008): p. 177.

[11] Chukwuemeka Odumegwu Ojukwu, *Because I am Involved* (Ibadan: Spectrum Books, 2011 [originally published 1989]): pp. xii–xiii.

[12] Anoliefo, *419 & the Rest of Us*, p. 21.

The people who had managed to make money during the war were those who had found ways of bending uncertainty to their advantage. To prosper in this environment, one needed not only standard business skills – a sense of local tastes, knowledge of trade routes, access to credit – but partners who could be trusted not to abscond into the chaotic maw of the East Central State with goods or money. Trust had been hard to come by in Biafra, but partnerships born during the war had been forged in fire; if a partner could be relied upon at the front, he could be trusted anywhere. Postwar commerce, both legitimate and "criminal," had to be discreet so as not to attract the attention of the police, tax collectors, or acquisitive neighbors. Those who had developed networks cloaked in secrecy were the people who were best positioned to succeed or at least to get by.[13] The same skills that had made a woman successful in *ahia attack*, for instance, might make her a successful smuggler. Money could be made by fencing stolen goods, circumventing customs regulations, and trading on the black market. Others prospered through fraud. Just like during the war, fraud was a means for people with smarts and savvy (but not the jobs that required them) to survive in a setting where opportunities were slim. It became, as a popular pamphlet writer argued, a problem of "idle minds," who "design all kinds of satanic deception to make money and reap where they did not sow."[14] It was at this point that "419" first entered the public parlance as code for deceit.[15]

Fraud did not stand alone as a criminal practice, and it was tightly intertwined with other forms of misconduct. Armed robbery and "pen robbery" were linked forms of "moral degradation," argued a Nigerian businessman, who devoted most of his memoir to describing the various schemes he had fallen for.[16] Armed robbery required various forms of

---

[13] Sina Idowu, *Armed Robbery in Nigeria* (Lagos: Jacob and Johnson Books, 1980): p. 14.

[14] Tunde Akingbade, *Historical Studies on Global Scam and Nigeria's 419 – How to Overcome Fraudsters and Con* (Lagos: Climate International, 2007): p. 20.

[15] The earliest usage that I have seen of "419" as a general noun, rather than a technical term for the section of the criminal code, is in a circular on the problem of missing identity documents in the reappointment of Igbo employees to the Lagos State government after the war. LASRAB CSG 2.43, "Re-Absorption of Public Officials," April 4, 1971. The term is commonly thought of as being of more recent origin. A reference work on Nigerian English defines but does not provide a history of the term. Herbert Igboanusi, *A Dictionary of Nigerian English Usage* (Ibadan: Enicrownfit Publishers, 2002): p. 117.

[16] M. O. Gafari, *In Niamey Without Visa: A Case Study in Political Decay* (Ijebu-Ode: Adebola Gafari Enterprises, 1994): p. 68.

money laundering, which the burgeoning 419 sector could supply, and a cottage industry emerged to supply forged receipts and deeds to middlemen selling stolen property.[17] A textbook for police cadets noted that

The *modus operandi* of armed robbers immediately after the civil war, particularly in the former East Central State, was to write letters demanding that a potential victim deposit a specified sum of money at a pre-arranged spot, under cover of darkness, on a specific date and time. Such letters were usually followed with threats of death to the intended victims and their family, should they fail to comply or if they played "pranks" by informing the police.[18]

Likewise, scams required "muscle" in the form of armed men as part of their theatrics (and sometimes to make sure that the scammed parties followed through on the bogus agreements they had entered into). They involved elaborate impersonations, usually of government officials, though in some cases it was bureaucrats themselves doing the mimicry. In her memoirs, a Lagos magistrate described a case from the mid-1970s in which a police superintendent hired fake policemen, fake moneylenders, and a magician to stage an elaborate con involving an implausible new way to transform naira into American dollars.[19] The more complicated 419 scams could collapse into all-out armed robbery, especially if they stumbled at the crucial final stages of a con.

As Tekena Tamuno wrote, violent crime was related to a litany of other illegal behaviors, "from fraud, piracy, narcotics, gun-running to miscellaneous forms of corruption."[20] In the popular imagination, armed robbery grew to fill the void in the formal economy that 419 and corruption had created. As the protagonist of a pulpy crime novel put it, "the armed robber is out in the street stealing and killing because the pen robbers have made the system not accommodate him."[21] Some

---

[17] A description of this industry can be found in a case about the robbery and sale of a bus owned by a Port Harcourt oil company in 1970. ESHC uncatalogued collection, in the High Court of the East Central State of Nigeria, Aba, no. A/ 330/71, *The State v. Bartholomew Eseugo, Hyacinth Nwige, and Sylvanus Onuoha*, July 11, 1972. See also Tekena N. Tamuno, *Peace and Violence in Nigeria: Conflict Resolution in Society and the State* (Ibadan: Panel on Nigeria Since Independence History Project, 1991): pp. 84–85.

[18] E. U. M. Igbo, *Introduction to Criminology* (Nsukka: University of Nigeria Press, 2007): p. 168.

[19] Dulcie Adunola Oguntoye, *Your Estranged Faces* (self-published, 2008): p. 144.

[20] Tamuno, *Peace and Violence in Nigeria*, pp. 84–85.

[21] Clifford Abonyi, *Squad 419* (Nsukka: Fulladu Publishing Company, 1995): p. 20.

argued that illicit wealth that appeared to be from 419 was often actually from other, more sinister sources. "It seems more likely," wrote Emmanuel Igbo, "that many [419ers] may have actually made their money through trafficking in hard drugs abroad or via 'ritual murders' at home."[22] In its popular sense, 419 was a category that could expand to accommodate almost any type of misconduct.

Fraud, forgery, and counterfeiting cases became a fixture of Nigerian law reports in the 1970s. More elaborate with every passing month, these cases reveal how it became a national problem that took place at many different levels of society. Crimes like currency counterfeiting became rife. As a judge noted in a 1971 case, counterfeiting was "an offence in which repetition is quite easy by those who are adept in the illegal trade; it is an offence in which obliteration of evidence is again quite easy."[23] The shrewdness of these scams can be seen in the case against James Igwe, a currency counterfeiter who returned to Ibadan from the former Biafra in early 1970, where he set up a press producing low-denomination notes. When caught and prosecuted, he mounted the defense that, because the notes he was found with did not contain the phrase "payable to bearer on demand," they were not forged "currency" because, by definition, "currency" required such a promissory statement. He was acquitted by a high court, which the Federal Court of Appeal upheld.[24] Igwe was lucky that his forgery case was not tried until 1981, during the brief period of civilian rule under President Shehu Shagari. Had he been tried at the time of his arrest, during military administration, he would have almost certainly been executed. A 1973 decree had made currency counterfeiting a capital offense – and it had no loopholes around phrasing.

Courts in the postwar east were flummoxed by the proliferation of false identities, which forged identity documents from the war enabled. Imposture sometimes reached farcical proportions, as when a grifter assumed the identity of an Enugu journalist and went around the city collecting information for his "column," to be used in future cons.[25]

---

[22] How wealth is derived from ritual killings, which were indeed regularly reported in Nigeria in the 1980s and 1990s, is not elaborated. E. U. M. Igbo, *Introduction to Criminology* (Nsukka: University of Nigeria Press, 2007): p. 165.

[23] ESHC uncatalogued collection, High Court of the East Central State, *Commissioner of Police v. James Usong*, September 8, 1971.

[24] Nigerian Criminal Reports, Federal Court of Appeal, *Federal Republic v. Igwe*, March 6, 1981.

[25] *The Renaissance* [Enugu], July 10, 1973, p. 16.

Hundreds of thousands of people had lost their papers, and the fact that many government registries had been destroyed meant that sorting out who was who was no easy matter. In a few cases, courts admitted that they simply had no way of knowing who stood before them. This was the situation of a convicted forger in Aba, who used multiple identities and a deft ability to mimic handwriting to steal money from several banks in 1971.[26] The man could produce no papers and testified that he had spent the war as a political prisoner in a Biafran jail, of which there were no records. He gave different accounts of his identity over the course of his trial, none of which could be corroborated. All that the court could be confident of was that the man before them in the dock was known by several Aba bank tellers as three different people, all of whom had tried to withdraw money from accounts that were not their own. His defense (rather unwisely) was to refuse to admit his true identity, and he was found guilty. He was sentenced as "Harrison Dan Jaja," one of his apparent aliases – but even in sentencing him the judge admitted that he did not really know who he was. It is hard to imagine this degree of ambiguity in normal circumstances, but the war's disruptions had made ciphers like Harrison Dan Jaja possible – undocumented people whose "true" identity was unclear and largely unknowable. Later, in Nigeria like everywhere else, biometrics would more firmly fix one body to one name; but, in this period, it was comparatively easy to be more than one person – for the body to be a *vehicle* for an identity, or a host for one, rather than a single, immutable unit. This flexibility was a tool of self-protection in wartime, and it remained useful after the war.

Fraud served many purposes. Deception worked like camouflage, and cultivating uncertainty about oneself was a way to hide from a postwar state that few people trusted. It could also be an avenue to start a new life or a way out of the poverty that crippled the region. Fake professional qualifications abounded, and newspapers reported frequently on the problem of forged General Certificate of Education credentials – the bearers of which always seemed to be Igbos.[27] Igbos were definitely not the only ones forging diplomas, but they were the ones singled out for it most often in the Nigerian press. Small fortunes

---

[26] ESHC uncatalogued collection, in the High Court of the East Central State, Aba, *The State v. Harrison Dan Jaja*, May 27, 1974.

[27] *Nigerian Tide* [Port Harcourt], October 14, 1972, p. 14; *The Renaissance* [Enugu], 9 January 1972, p. 16.

could be made through swindling. Commercial fraud took off, especially in the distribution of prescription drugs, and it began to reach into the pockets of foreign corporations.[28] In Aba, four "businessmen" were convicted of fraud for swindling an American company. In a con that prefigured 419's later international form, they used a dossier of forged letters and bank documents to obtain a large sum of money from the foreign dealer of livestock feed.[29] Con artists in Port Harcourt mimicked the freewheeling business practices of the oil industry, which often looked dubious even when they were legitimate. This was the tactic of a group of "smart guys" who presented themselves as agents of a shifty prospecting outfit and conned their "clients" out of money and equipment in 1972.[30] Fraud also took place in the course of reissuing identity documents, deeds, and other paperwork that had been lost during the war. Few such cases were investigated, but bureaucrats came to feel that they were being deceived by practically everyone who came to their offices.

Mistrust became endemic – and with good reason. Dangers lurked around every corner. In 1971, a preacher and self-proclaimed "prophet" named Maurice Nwogu defrauded Pleasure Mercy Ugwuzor of 500 pounds while she was staying in Aba to attend services at the Church of the Order of Cherubim and Seraphim, which offered healing services, miracles, and intercessions.[31] Nwogu gave her a protective elixir to guard her from armed robbers, after which she gave him her money for "safe keeping, she swore, because armed robbers threatened to visit her hotel and she knew that if they did they would remove [her] money." The commission of inquiry that investigated him concluded that he was "a confident trickster and a blackmailer," whose "spurious 'prophetic' activities had been the engine by which he perpetrated this fraud on people." Ugwuzor was then defrauded for a second time by a law agent, who promised that he could get her money back if she paid him a large fee upfront. Enough people were defrauded by this phony lawyer that a judicial commission of inquiry was convened to investigate him, which uncovered a string of acts of forgery, corruption, and theft. A prominent magistrate in Aba, Joseph Chukwuma Ononye, was

---

[28]   *Nigerian Tide* [Port Harcourt], August 5, 1972, p. 1.
[29]   *Nigerian Tide* [Port Harcourt], June 24, 1972, p. 1.
[30]   *Nigerian Tide* [Port Harcourt], June 24, 1972, p. 3.
[31]   *Report of the Honourable Mr Justice A.N. Aniagolu, Sole Commissioner, On the Conducts of Mr J.C. Ononye* (Enugu: Government Printer, 1973): p. 68.

also implicated. He was found to have accepted bribes from many parties – sometimes to ensure that a thief or confidence artist was exonerated and sometimes to ensure a guilty judgment against a rival. Even Ugwuzor, the putative victim of the case, turned out to have made her money by selling relief materials pilfered from the state government.[32] The corollary of the inquiry was that artifice had become an inescapable fact of life. "It is one of the lamentations of our society," remarked justice Aniagolu of one of the "charlatans" under investigation, "that such man should continue to carry on his deceitful trade and still walk the streets of our towns and villages, a free man." All of the parties involved had been Biafrans, and each of their deceptions flowed from the war in different ways.

The perception that fraud was an Igbo problem, which judges never said openly but the press often did, led to scapegoating. In 1976, charges were brought against Judith Agu, a "semi-literate market woman" who returned to the northern town of Sokoto after Biafra's defeat to resume her business supplying materials to an international construction company. Agu was accused of altering a check made out to her to inflate its amount. This relatively small-scale theft, which Agu claimed was a clerical error that she had not seen fit to correct, led to an investigation of the company's recordkeeping practices. It uncovered the embezzlement of a "colossal" sum of money, likely by the company's Dutch accountant and his Nigerian assistant. Judith Agu, along with the recipients of some sixty-nine other checks written by the accountant, was shown to be not a forger but rather an unwitting accessory to a money laundering scheme. The accountant faked a seizure and was medically evacuated to the Netherlands, leaving his subordinate to answer for their crimes in a Sokoto court. The high court found Agu guilty of fraud – the only person so found – but she was acquitted on appeal. The northern appeal judge did not make explicit mention of her ethnicity, but he alluded to the fact that she, an Igbo woman, rather than the culprits or any of the other accessories to the crime, had been made to answer for it: "It is a negation of justice and an abuse of criminal process to hand pick some of the culprits on criteria which cannot be justified by the facts of the case."[33]

[32] Interview with Anthony Mogboh, SAN, Enugu, October 2, 2014.

[33] Nigerian Criminal Reports, High Court of Sokoto State, *The State v. Agu*, July 27, 1981. [The original act was committed in 1976.]

"Nigeria na wa o": Anxiety and Broken Trust

The Pidgin expression "Nigeria na wa o" sums up the lasting influence of the Nigerian Civil War more succinctly and poetically than any court case. The phrase – effectively, "Nigeria is war" – serves as a catch-all expression of dismay for problems large and small. It is so much a part of everyday speech that the fact that it refers to a *literal* war has mostly been forgotten. "Nigeria is war" is not just a lament that modern life is a battlefield; it is a description of a long historical moment. The war-time problems of scarcity, violence, and danger endured after Biafra's defeat, and they became some of Nigeria's most defining features. They made everyone into survivalists, and Nigeria at large came to feel like it was still at war. "Beckon at anybody at Aba, Port Harcourt and some other big cities," recalled a frustrated pamphlet writer, "and he/she would just dismiss you."[34] Postwar Nigeria was a place where few people felt they could depend on one another or on the state.

The war had shattered relationships and broken trust, and the suspicion that former Biafrans felt toward one another sometimes reached pathological dimensions. In 1971, Herbert Aladum killed his wife Priscilla in a hotel room in Orlu and mutilated her body trying to find a two-way radio that he believed had been implanted inside her. In his garbled statements, he blamed his wife for "spoiling his fortunes," and made "incomprehensible allusions to some Overseas Organisations" – to wit, the imaginary "Executive Council of the Republic of Biafra in exile."[35] The records of Aladum's trial do not allow us to peer into his mind, but, in this case and others like it, judges argued that the source of mental disquiet was the recent trauma of the war. Aladum did not see the world clearly, but his allusions to sinister international plots and hidden technologies reflected the spirit of his times, albeit through a dark glass of insanity. The notion that there were enemies everywhere, that striking first was the best defense, and that prosperity required getting one's hands dirty – these were all things that sane people believed too. Very few acted on them in the way that Aladum did, but many subsisted through more prosaic forms of crime.

This crisis of trust manifested not only in the court and the family but in spiritual life. Biafrans had developed new devotional practices to

---

[34] Anoliefo, *419 & the Rest of Us*, p. 20.
[35] ESHC uncatalogued collection, in the High Court of the East Central State of Nigeria, Okigwe, *The State v. Herbert Aladum*, no. HO/30C/72, May 31, 1973.

deal with the situation they lived in, and some continued after the war ended.[36] Aba's administrator described how a "spurious" church called the Mercy of the Holy Nights became popular in Umuoba, one of many "mushrooming prayerhouses functioning like thriving business ventures in our area of authority."[37] The church offered healing services, divination to civilians, and tactical advice to soldiers – all at a price – with extensive theatrics and a veneer of Christian respectability. It was, in his description,

a highly organized, most intriguing place of nocturnal worship attracting an ample crowd of people said to be in distress. Its clientele – or, better still, its congregation – comprised men and women from all walks of life: senior as well as junior officers of the Biafran Armed Forces, plus a good number of the rank and file; doctors, lawyers, engineers, big-time contractors, barren women, high-ranking police officers and so on.

The Mercy of the Holy Nights remade itself as a millenarian prayer society after the war.

Many Catholics felt the church had betrayed them by not openly supporting Biafra, and the end of the war brought a surge of Pentecostalism as people sought new ways of understanding the dire world around them.[38] Others turned to traditional religion, and oracles and shrines prospered throughout the east. The sale of protective charms increased, and with it came a cluster of manslaughter charges when people invited their friends to test the efficacy of their new bulletproofing talismans by shooting at them.[39] In some places, the resurgence of traditional practices led to "violent community conflicts [...] involving masquerade communities and adherents of the Christian religion," or at least so one Catholic priest saw the matter.[40] As Tamuno

[36] C. O. Ogunkunle, "Prophet Ezekiel on False Prophets in the Context of Nigeria," in Rev. Prof. S. O. Abogunrin, ed., *Biblical Studies and Corruption in Africa* (Ibadan: Nigerian Association for Biblical Studies, 2007): pp. 158–174.
[37] Ben Gbulie, *The Fall of Biafra* (Enugu: Benlie Publishers, 1989): p. 109.
[38] See Olufemi Vaughan, *Religion and the Making of Nigeria* (Durham, NC: Duke University Press, 2016): p. 141. See also Ebenezer Obadare, *Pentecostal Republic: Religion and the Struggle for State Power in Nigeria* (London: Zed Books, 2018).
[39] Mentioned in East Central State Law Reports, *The State v. Ofoke Okezi*, 1972.
[40] Augustine O. Onyeneke, *The Dead Among the Living: Masquerades in Igbo Society* (Nimo: Holy Ghost Congregation, 1987): p. 10. The pattern of returning to "traditional" forms of religious practice emerged in some minority areas of the former Biafra as well, much to the chagrin of the clergy. Rev. Patrick

described, the crisis of faith also affected traditional religions: "the old gods and goddesses and other ancestral watchdogs could no longer be trusted."[41] Suspicion manifested in postwar life in many ways. Sometimes it took the form of witchcraft accusations, wherein selfishness and disregard for the plight of others attracted charges of occultism.[42] Witchcraft insinuated itself in relationships, and professional people – doctors and lawyers among them – consulted ritualists just like the "illiterate villagers" whom judges maintained did not know better.[43]

"Spiritual churches and faith healing temples of worship are sprouting," wrote an editorialist in the early 1970s. "Every third person belongs to the Aladura, Seraphim and Cherubim, or some Temple of The Holy Light or divine Shepherd. [...] Perhaps their days are numbered. Perhaps not! But there is no doubt that like what the Tijaniyya sect is to Islam, and the Lumpa is to Christianity in Zambia, spiritual churches and faith temples have come to stay."[44] Hucksters and false prophets prospered in war-shattered towns like Orlu and Owerri, where they found a large market of people seeking protection. "There's that prophet in tawdry colours and tatty drooping hairs," opined a popular columnist. "I've watched him umpteen times swallowing 'ogogoro,' diving into trance, seeing visions, communing with 'God,' burning incense and candles, whipping barren women with live pigeon, 'intervening' for long-time spinsters and lunatics, and above all, erecting colourful mansions for his poor, long-suffering self."[45] Scammers who offered miracles became a source of concern for the state government, and in 1971, a judicial commission of inquiry was

Akaninyene Basil Okure, *The Notion of Justice Among the Ibibio People* (Rome: Institutum Superius Theologiae Moralis, 1983): pp. 83–87.

[41] Tamuno, *Peace and Violence in Nigeria*, p. 84.

[42] See Misty L. Bastian, "'Bloodhounds Who Have No Friends': Witchcraft and Locality in the Nigerian Popular Press," in Jean Comaroff and John Comaroff, eds., *Modernity and Its Malcontents: Ritual and Power in Postcolonial Africa* (Chicago: University of Chicago Press, 1993): pp. 129–166. Comparatively see Peter Geschiere, *The Modernity of Witchcraft: Politics and the Occult in Postcolonial Africa* (Charlottesville: University of Virginia Press, 1997).

[43] *Report of the Honourable Mr Justice A.N. Aniagolu, Sole Commissioner, On the Conducts of Dr I.N.O. Asinobi, Dr E.N. Chidume and Mr F. Akujobi* (Enugu: Government Printer, 1973).

[44] *The Renaissance* [Enugu], January 9, 1972, p. 8.

[45] Ogogoro is a liquor made from raffia palm juice. *The Renaissance* [Enugu], January 16, 1972, p. 7.

established to investigate the sale of protective charms and elixirs that purported to guard their bearers from crime.[46] The East Central State would shut down many of these "churches," including the Mercy of the Holy Nights; but this did not address the underlying anxiety that drove people to them in the first place.

Anxiety about gender and generation also underpinned individual decisions to take up fraud. Most, though not all, 419ers were men. The war changed ideas about masculinity on both sides, and the experience of mass military service reordered ideas about what made a person a man. Historically, relatively few Igbo men had joined the military; the colonial preference for "martial races" meant that the eastern region had not been a place of heavy recruitment.[47] Although older conceptions of martial valor figured in vernacular understandings of Igbo masculinity, by the time of the war the most important ways men were measured against one another were, arguably, financial success and the accumulation of credentials. During the war, these measures quickly became militarized. When the war ended, a generation of young men found themselves stymied – uneasily demobilized into a civilian society that had no obvious outlet for their martial skills but unable to earn the money that they needed to come of age (and especially to marry). In this impoverished setting, crime – which combined martial skills with a commercial disposition – became an avenue not only to prosperity but to respectability. Men did not always succeed in transforming wealth obtained through crime into respectable fortunes, however, and flashy clothes and expensive cars tended to attract resentment rather than respect.[48] Given the general conditions of the East Central State, any outward display of wealth was suspect. Those

---

[46] *Report of the Honourable Mr Justice A.N. Aniagolu, Sole Commissioner, On the Conducts of Dr I.N.O. Asinobi, Dr E.N. Chidume and Mr F. Akujobi* (Enugu: Government Printer, 1973).

[47] See Moses Ochonu, *Colonialism By Proxy: Hausa Imperial Agents and Middle Belt Consciousness in Nigeria* (Bloomington: Indiana University Press, 2014): pp. 14–16; Ndubueze L. Mbah, *Emergent Masculinities: Gendered Power and Social Change in the Biafran Atlantic Age* (Athens: Ohio University Press, 2019): pp. 64–65.

[48] See, for example, Daniel Jordan Smith's description of a 419er with political ambitions who failed to convert his illicitly obtained wealth into the social relationships that he needed to win elections – and indeed to become a reputable man. Daniel Jordan Smith, *To Be a Man Is Not a One-Day Job: Masculinity, Money, and Intimacy in Nigeria* (Chicago: University of Chicago Press, 2017): pp. 158–161.

who seemed to be recovering from the war too easily or quickly attracted scrutiny. When a local school superintendent began to cast cement blocks for a new house in a village near Owerri in 1971, the behavior was so unusual that the local police investigated him. Sure enough, he had been embezzling money from the Ministry of Education.[49]

The Fortunes of War

Former Biafrans came to see commerce as one of the few avenues available to them in postwar Nigeria, and everyone was anxious to resume business.[50] "Trading was in the blood," recalled Rosina Umelo. "At a time when all legitimate opportunities for trading were at a standstill the chance of making money was just too much temptation for some."[51] Trade promised to restore fortunes depleted by the war and more generally to achieve "abundant life" – which increasingly meant not spiritual richness, as the biblical phrase promised, but material wealth. But there were not many legitimate ways to make money in these strained times, and the few on offer required chastening acts of conciliation or unsavory compromises. Many saw the appointment of the infamous Colonel Benjamin Adekunle as head of the Lagos port, for example, as an act of aggression by the federal government. It forced Igbo traders to conduct international commerce – the lifeblood of many eastern towns – through one of the people most closely associated with genocide.[52] Trade became more circuitous, and more surreptitious, to avoid passing under his watch.

Commerce was one of the most common sites of fraud. The twinned problems of black marketeering and graft meant that there was hardly any transaction conducted in the postwar east that did *not* in some way involve deceit in the eyes of the law. Moreover, there was an increasingly complex regime of customs regulations that easterners saw as stacked

---

[49]   ESHC uncatalogued collection, in the High Court of the East Central State of Nigeria, Aba, *The State v. Amos Atuomonyeogo*, July 4, 1974.

[50]   For a thorough description of this sentiment, see Chukwumezie V. Nnamdi, *Igbo: The People, Power and Politics* (Onitsha: Vytona Press, 2009): p. 103.

[51]   IWM 6687, Papers of Rosina Umelo, "Biafra, A World of Our Own," p. 203.

[52]   Similarly, General Murtala Muhammed, under whose command the killings at Asaba had taken place, would go on to become a popular head of state after overthrowing Gowon in 1975. Benjamin Adekunle, *The Nigeria Biafra War Letters: A Soldier's Story* (Atlanta: Phoenix, 2004).

against them. The result was that virtually every aspect of economic life could be considered criminal. Certain forms of fraud, deception, and armed violence that had become integral to wartime commerce continued to overlap with trade after the war came to an end.[53] Disputes over who was responsible for lost or damaged property, for example, often involved fraud. In Aba, a quarrel between a wealthy chief and the mechanic with whom he had left his Mercedes-Benz during the war turned into a charade. The car had been stolen during the Nigerian occupation, and both the chief and the mechanic produced letters purporting to be from one another taking responsibility for the car's protection. The judge expressed doubt that *either* letter was genuine – the wording of each was too on the nose, suggesting they had been forged after the fact. He eventually ruled in favor of the chief, however, falling back on the principle that as "bailee" the mechanic was obligated "to take reasonable care to protect the chattel" entrusted to him regardless of which (if either) of the letters was genuine.[54]

The State v. Ogechi Dim and four others, a case concerning the sale of stolen goods, illustrates how no transaction in postwar eastern Nigeria was untouched by crime and no commercial activity was entirely above the board. Testimony described an increasingly familiar series of events on a hot night in 1971:

It is not in dispute that those thieves were six in number; that there was shooting during the burglary; that the thieves came in an Army lorry; that one of the thieves was in Army Uniform; and that Innocent Orisakwe was assaulted and hit on the shoulders with an iron rod by one of the thieves. It is also uncontroverted that the thief in Army Uniform pointed a gun at Orisakwe and asked him to run for his life and that while running away Orisakwe was fired at but fortunately for him the bullet missed him and hit the coal tar road.[55]

---

[53] In this respect, a fruitful comparison can be made to Europe in the context of the Second World War. As Tony Judt wrote of Poland, "to live normally in occupied Europe meant breaking the law: in the first place the laws of the occupiers (curfews, travel regulations, race laws, etc.) but also conventional norms and laws as well." Tony Judt, *Postwar: A History of Europe Since 1945* (New York: Penguin, 2005): p. 37.

[54] ESHC uncatalogued collection, in the High Court of the East Central State of Nigeria, Aba, no. A/8/71, *Chief D. O. Ogugua and Angels Transport Ltd., Aba*, April 10, 1972.

[55] ESHC uncatalogued collection, in the High Court of the East Central State of Nigeria, Onitsha, no. O/42c/71, *The State v. Ogechi Dim and four others*, December 7, 1971.

The men proceeded to steal a few dozen tires owned by the Nigerian Army, a sewing machine, and other valuables from Orisakwe and two other shopkeepers on his street. They then sold the tires to merchants in Onitsha the following morning, who quickly sold them onwards at a large profit. The merchants, who knew that tires brought a very high price but had no way of obtaining a supply, appeared to have commissioned the robbery.

Justice Oputa's furious decision excoriated everyone involved, and he took the case as evidence that criminality had "infected" Onitsha root and branch.[56] Everyone, he argued, from the merchants who hired the thieves, to the people they hired to transport the tires, to the people who facilitated their sale, to the people who purchased them, was complicit in the theft – even if only the six armed robbers would be brought to trial. The decision implied that practically no transaction made in the rubble of the East Central State could be legitimate. The total collapse of legitimate commerce, the shortages of all essential goods, the lack of currency and other financial instruments, and the easy availability of firearms created a situation where buying virtually anything could make one complicit in theft. The fact that the middlemen had sold the tires in secret was proof to Oputa that they knew that there was wrongdoing involved.

As for the buyers, Oputa argued that in the present circumstances they should have known that finding tires for sale at any price was too good to be true. As he remarked of one of them, "he knew the 2nd accused well and ought then to have known his financial resources soon after a devastating civil war that left every one penniless [...] I reject in its entirety his evidence that he thought it was a genuine transaction and that he did not know the tyres were stolen." In a similar case over the theft and sale of a car, the judge criticized the people involved at every step of the way, arguing that the conditions after the war should have put everyone "on their guard" and that one would have to be delusional to believe that a car for sale in occupied Onitsha could be anything but ill-gotten.[57] The only way to remain on the right side of the

---

[56] Both judges and members of the public used the language of disease to describe crime in the 1970s. Later, the public language of crime would take a more martial tone, most famously with Muhammadu Buhari's "War On Indiscipline."

[57] ESHC uncatalogued collection, in the High Court of the East Central State of Nigeria, Onitsha, no. O/25c/71, *The State v. Clarence Mbagwu and three others*, November 1, 1971. See also ESHC uncatalogued collection, in the High Court of the East Central State of Nigeria, Aba, no. A/27c/72, *The State*

law, these decisions suggested, was to avoid commercial dealings, keep to yourself, and trust that the state would protect you. Except perhaps judges themselves, with their generous state salaries and security details, few people were in a position to remain above the fray like this.

Poverty, violence, and the constant reminders of the war's loss led some to abandon Nigeria altogether. Many Igbos, especially young people, felt that there was no future for them there despite the federal government's promises. A demographer who worked in the east in the early 1970s concluded that the experience of the war had strengthened Igbos' connections to their ancestral villages at the expense of their connections to the rest of Nigeria.[58] Yet, for those who had ambitions of wealth, staying in eastern villages was not much of an option. Some returned to the north, but others would "rather be struck dead here on the spot," as one Kaduna-born lawyer recalled, than return to live among the people who had run his family out of the city in 1966.[59] Unless one could finagle a position in the oil industry in the nearby Delta (where virulent anti-Igbo sentiment kept most away), or find some way to turn the disorder of the east into personal advantage (as both lawyers and thieves did, in their different ways), the path to material success probably led out of Nigeria.

The end of the war signaled the beginning of an exodus, as people scattered abroad to seek economic opportunity or to avoid the predations of the military regime at home. Migration was not new; Nigerian students, dockworkers, and professionals had long been present in the British Isles and the Caribbean. In Africa, the overland hajj had established communities of Nigerians across the Sahel, and enterprising traders (many of them Igbo) had roamed far and wide in the colonial period.[60] The archives of British consulates across French and Portuguese Africa are full of files about Nigerian British subjects who did business in places few other foreigners ventured. Like intrepid businesspeople anywhere, some succeeded while others lost everything.

---

v. Nwaosuagwu Ahiwe, Friday Nwosu and Ugboaja Ahiwe, November 30, 1972.

[58] Augustine O. Okore, "The Value of Children Among Ibo Households in Nigeria: A Study of Arochukwu Division and Urban Umuahia in Imo State" (Doctoral dissertation, Australian National University, 1977): p. 99.

[59] Interview with anonymous informant, Onitsha, August 2014.

[60] On the Nigerian diaspora in Africa, see C. Bawa Yamba, *Permanent Pilgrims: The Role of Pilgrimage in the Lives of West African Muslims in Sudan* (Edinburgh: Edinburgh University Press, 1995).

A few found themselves on the wrong side of the law, but that was not what they were known for. Of course, Nigeria's largest diaspora was a much older one, made up of the descendants of enslaved people brought to the western hemisphere from the territory that would one day be called "Nigeria"; but, after the war, a new diaspora emerged – one distinct from that of transatlantic slavery, or the British Empire, or the networks of study and commerce that Nigerians made over the course of the twentieth century.[61] This was the exodus of military rule.

The first wave of people who left in large numbers in the 1970s were Igbos, many of whom were young adults at the time the war ended.[62] Igbos still likely constitute the largest single group in Nigeria's vast and uncounted diaspora. In the past, the most beaten path had been to the United Kingdom. In the late twentieth century, the number of Nigerians moving to the United States increased exponentially, and destinations in the Middle East, Asia, and continental Europe became more common. Countries like Italy became home to large numbers of Nigerians, many of whom worked on the fringes of the formal economy. Both men and women left Nigeria in this period, although it was only women's emigration that was perceived as a problem at home. Elder men expressed concern that women who went abroad, especially those who went for purposes of trade rather than education, would turn to prostitution and other forms of crime. They also feared that the emigration of women would create a surplus of unmarried men at home in Nigeria – what an Enugu columnist called "maiden drain."[63]

A few of the circuits in Nigeria's global commercial network were criminal, and those who left found themselves tainted by association.[64] As one frustrated pamphleteer noted of his experiences traveling with a Nigerian passport, "the apothegm seems to be, 'take every Nigerian

---

[61] See Jayne O. Ifekwunigwe, *Scattered Belongings: Cultural Paradoxes of "Race," Nation and Gender* (New York: Routledge, 1999).

[62] For an opinionated description of how this diaspora emerged, see Gabriel Nwachukwu, *The Challenge of the Igbo Man* (Onitsha: Celex Prints, 1997). See also Maxwell Awana, "The Biafrans who won't come home," in Sally Dyson, ed., *Nigeria: The Birth of Africa's Greatest Country, From the Pages of Drum*, vol. 2 (Ibadan: Spectrum, 1998): pp. 237–238.

[63] *The Renaissance* [Enugu], March 19, 1972, p. 13.

[64] A depiction of this can be found in Segun Kuyinu's fictionalized account of fraud and the drug trade in 1980s London, *Andrew: "419" Galore* (Lagos: Aqua Books, 1992).

as a criminal until he proves that he/she is not.'"[65] Nigerians were intensely scrutinized, and they found themselves increasingly unwelcome in foreign ports. In some of the places where they settled, especially the United States, the growing perception that Nigeria was a bastion of crime dovetailed with parochial forms of anti-blackness.[66] The reputation was not helped by the fact that lawful trade usually took place through informal *hawala*-like arrangements instead of banks, lending support to the suspicion that there was always some criminal aspect to Nigerian business. In fact, there was nothing shady about the majority of their commerce – overwhelmingly more trade was licit than illicit – but this reputation quickly adhered to Nigerians and especially Igbos.

For those who stayed at home, the paths to prosperity were few, narrow, and dangerous. A picture of the opportunities on offer in postwar Nigeria can be found in the popular novels sold at markets and roadsides, among them Shakespeare C. N. Nwachukwu's *The Tragedy of Civilian Major* from 1972.[67] Nwachukwu tells the story of "Civilian Major," a young Igbo man who survives the war as a deserter through cunning and luck and then returns to Kano to open a market stall ("Survival Trading Company. Motto: No Condition is Permanent"). In a bar, he sees an old acquaintance from before the war, whom he overhears hatching a criminal scheme with some other men. Civilian Major offers his services, citing his wartime experience as proof of his criminal acumen: "*Eh* – me who don sleep for storm and thunder unafraid will find any work difficult? You know say I be soldier for Biafra?" After leading them through a series of schemes and robberies to teach them his ways, he sets off on his own, amassing a pile of cash, jewelry, and a car. He returns to his village in the east, where he is initially given a hero's welcome; but, after a series of drunken escapades that end in a local girl getting pregnant, he is fined and berated by the village elders. He tries to use his money to turn Nigerian soldiers and then the local police against the village elders,

---

[65] Anoliefo, *419 & the Rest of Us*, p. 24.

[66] See Onoso Imoagene, *Beyond Expectations: Second-Generation Nigerians in the United States and Britain* (Berkeley: University of California Press, 2017): pp. 13–14.

[67] Special Collections, University of Wisconsin-Madison [hereafter SCUW] CA 18275, no. 17, Shakespeare C. N. Nwachukwu, *The Tragedy of Civilian Major*, 1972.

leading to a court case, reproduced in full in the novel (which suggests that this is probably a real series of events). When the court rules against him, he commits suicide.

Popular works like *The Tragedy of Civilian Major* were important for their role in disseminating information about crime. After the war, the Onitsha printers who had long supplied Nigerian readers with pulp fiction and self-help guides turned their presses to the production of books and pamphlets describing crimes of passion and property in gruesome detail, often accompanied by advice about how to inure oneself from fraud or fortify a house against robbery. These guides served a dual purpose. In addition to suggesting how to avoid becoming a victim, they were also *how-to* guides for 419.[68] They provided a template for how to engage in fraud or how to avoid it, depending on one's predilection. Pamphlets that had been written before Biafra's secession could be put to these uses as well. Tracts like *How to Write Better Letters, Applications and Business Letters* could be used to craft a convincing scam, while *Money Hard to Get Because the World is Hard* and *Trust No-Body in Time Because Human Being is Trickish and Difficult* were useful guides to the treacherous postwar world.[69]

Fraud and the State

Certain political arrangements produce certain types of crime, and the same is true of the inverse. After the breakup of the Soviet Union, the "comrade criminals" who filled the void left by the Communist Party

[68]   The earliest such post-Biafra pamphlet that I have found is from about 1971: SCUW CA 18275 no. 10, Okenwa Olisah, *Money Palaver by Master of Life (Money Master)* (Onitsha: Chinyelu Printing Press, n.d.). The catalogue listing for this work estimates that it is from the 1960s, but the text itself indicates that it is from shortly after the end of the war. Later, books like the following served such a purpose explicitly: Anoliefo, *419 & the Rest of Us*; Uche I. Eke, *The 419 Fraud and Fraudsters: How to Avoid Their Deceptions and How to Make a Happy Investment* (Jos: Chekenet Technologies, 2009); P. A. Onyekosor, *Protect Yourself from Home-Based 419* (Lagos: Patson Commercial Ventures, 2005); Charles Tive, *419 Scam: Exploits of the Nigerian Con Man* (Lagos: Chicha Favours, 2002).

[69]   For these and many other Onitsha texts, see S. Okechukwu Mezu, ed., *Igbo Market Literature*, Vols. 1–5 (Buffalo: Black Academy Press, 1972). See generally Emmanuel Nwanonye Obiechina, *Literature for the Masses: An Analytical Study of Popular Pamphleteering in Nigeria* (Enugu: Nwankwo-Ifejika Publishers, 1971).

created syndicates mirroring the tightly organized, centrally controlled state that had just fallen.[70] In postwar Nigeria, the local practice of crime was chaotic and centerless, and it lived in the gray area between real and fake – much like Biafra had. The history of 419 in postwar Nigeria is not just the history of how people deceived one another but how crime shaped (and was shaped by) the Nigerian state. Crime in postwar Nigeria took certain cues from how the military government operated, and in turn the Nigerian state came to look more and more like a giant confidence scheme.

Arguably, Nigeria was built on fraud from the beginning. It had been colonized through sham treaties and force, and its leading public intellectuals (and even some of its founders) had long argued that pretense was the only thing holding the country together.[71] The Nigerian state's relationship with fraud and deceit is often glossed as "corruption." State corruption – including venality, nepotism, embezzlement, and the abuse of state authority – was definitionally distinct from 419, but the practices bore a resemblance to one another.[72] Some of the most important studies of contemporary Nigeria are about the points where corruption and fraud meet. Wale Adebanwi described 419 as a metonym for national politics; it is a form of "authority stealing" that happens in many different registers.[73] Andrew Apter gave a comprehensive account of the place of crime in politics under the Ibrahim Babangida regime, when "IBB = 419" became political shorthand for state corruption. In his view, the larger political malaise that overtook late twentieth-century Nigeria was a consequence of the oil boom (and the bust that followed it).[74] Browne Onuoha also

---

[70] Stephen Handelman, *Comrade Criminal: Russia's New Mafiya* (New Haven, CT: Yale University Press, 1995).

[71] Consider, for example, Obafemi Awolowo's famous 1947 statement that Nigeria was a "mere geographical expression." See Richard A. Joseph, *Democracy and Prebendal Politics in Nigeria* (Cambridge: Cambridge University Press, 1987): p. 184.

[72] There is a large social scientific literature on where corruption comes from. See, for example, Yvette M. M. Schoenmakers et. al., *Mountains of Gold: An Exploratory Research on 419 Fraud* (Amsterdam: SWP Publishers, 2009); Global Witness Report, "International Thief Thief: How British Banks are Complicit in Nigerian Corruption," 2010.

[73] Wale Adebanwi, *Authority Stealing: Anti-Corruption War and Democratic Politics in Post-Military Nigeria* (Durham, NC: Carolina Academic Press, 2012).

[74] Andrew Apter, *The Pan-African Nation: Oil and the Spectacle of Culture in Nigeria* (Chicago: University of Chicago Press, 2005).

elaborated the connection between oil, military politics, and the broader problem of indiscipline.[75] Steven Pierce's historical ethnography of corruption posited that, rather than mere "malpractice," corruption and critiques of it are inherent to the process of political change in Nigeria.[76] Pierce argued that 419 has greater historical depth and more complex moral valences than it has been given credit for; corruption was embedded in colonial administration since the beginning of indirect rule – or perhaps, as Steven Press suggests, since the colonial conquest, underpinned as it was by bogus contracts and agreements.[77] Daniel Jordan Smith has described how 419 and the war are connected in the politics of the present, interpreting Biafran nostalgia and fraud as related symptoms of a larger "culture of corruption."[78] In different ways, all show how fraud and the discourses of "corruption" bore into national politics and converged as 419. I argue that these long-present dynamics were accelerated by the unprecedented forms of danger and opportunity that emerged during the war and in its shadow.

In 1971, an editorialist in an Enugu newspaper asked, "What makes Nigerians frauds?" He concluded that the fault lay with the Nigerian state itself. Taking the example of obtaining a Nigerian passport, he described how "it is infinitely easier to get out of the Iron Curtain than to obtain a Nigerian passport no matter how much of a law-abiding citizen you are unless you know Peter who knows Paul who studied with James whose uncle is the business associate of John who incidentally heads one of the many passport rackets in the country."[79] The fact that there was no way to complete an ordinary task like obtaining a passport without some measure of chicanery made it seem as if the Nigerian state was a sham. This was not a new complaint, but the scale of official misconduct from the early 1970s to the end of military rule

---

[75] Browne Onuoha, "Publishing Postcolonial Africa: Nigeria and Ekeh's Two Publics a Generation After," *Social Dynamics* vol. 40, no. 2 (2014): pp. 322–337.

[76] Pierce, *Moral Economies of Corruption.*

[77] Steven Press, *Rogue Empires: Contracts and Conmen in Europe's Scramble for Africa* (Cambridge, MA: Harvard University Press, 2017).

[78] These scholars define "419" more broadly than the legalistic way courts construe it. As Smith contends, actions are labeled 419 when they violate "the expected morality of patrons" – when they lead to personal enrichment over that of the community or overstep the boundaries of "acceptable" corruption. Smith, *A Culture of Corruption*, pp. 222–223.

[79] *The Renaissance* [Enugu], September 5, 1971, p. 3.

became so extreme as to seem parodic.[80] For many years, it was virtually impossible to travel from one place to another, obtain a state service, start a business, or enter or leave the country without paying an illegal bribe, forging a document, or engaging in perjury. In a situation where nearly everyone was compelled to do these things, what ethical weight was attached to breaking the law? The answer, to many Nigerians, was very little.

Confidence artists presented themselves as corrupt government officials or claimed to operate under the aegis of obscure or nonexistent government agencies. One common scam in the 1980s involved the sale of unmarked "banknotes," which were allegedly at the final stage of production. Posing as corrupt officials of the Central Bank of Nigeria, scammers would stage demonstrations where they would "wash" real currency in a chemical solution – apparently the final stage of the printing process – and then sell boxes of blank paper to their victims, promising the slips of paper could be transformed into new naira notes through the same process.[81] All the buyer had to do to "finish" their printing was to soak them in a solution of mercury or another hard-to-obtain chemical – ideally one that might kill the victim before he realized that he was being conned. As knowledge about this scam caught on, the scammed became the scammers – a "victim" would knowingly allow himself to be "taken in" by a money washing scheme and then, at the last minute, turn around and claim to be an undercover policeman. He would then demand a "bribe" from the original scammers in return for letting them go. Both iterations of this scam started from the premise that the Nigerian government was corrupt, turning to their advantage the ethical vagueness that had come to be taken for granted during the war. Ambiguity about what constituted "the state" also helped scams succeed. The proliferation of parastatals, the indistinct line between public and private oil interests, and the convoluted structure of Nigerian federalism itself – all made it hard to tell who was part of the government and who was only pretending to be. The fact

---

[80] Corruption was a tragedy but that did not stop people from finding humor in Nigeria's predicament. Television shows like *Samanja* and *New Masquerade* turned state dysfunction into comedy with huge popular success, as did writers like Chinua Achebe in *The Trouble with Nigeria* (Oxford: Heinemann, 1984).

[81] A fictionalized account of this scam perpetrated by the not-coincidentally named "Emeka" can be found in a pamphlet by Chuu Anoliefo, *419 & the Rest of Us: Our Quest for Survival* (Lagos: Delence Publishing Company, 1992): pp. 26–30.

that anyone fell for the money washing scam may sound unlikely, relying as it did on a process bordering on magic; but desperation and avarice are powerful distorters of judgment, and both were widely felt in postwar Nigeria.

The scams that emerged in the war's aftermath fueled Nigeria's reputation for disorder, which in turn pushed out the limits of what kinds of corruption were imaginable.[82] At a time when Nigerian government officials were almost automatically presumed to be corrupt (by both Nigerians and foreigners), the idea that a Nigerian politician might be able to offer a lucrative and illicit deal was not implausible. Increasingly scandalous corruption in the Nigerian government made it seem like everything was up for grabs. When Muhammadu Buhari accused former minister Umaru Dikko of embezzling a vast sum of money in 1984, a flurry of scams invoking Dikko's name followed. The Nigerian government's famous attempt to "extradite" Dikko from London – by kidnapping him, drugging him, and transporting him back to Lagos in a crate, all done with the assistance of Israeli intelligence – lent credibility to the wildly inventive backstories that accompanied 419 schemes.[83] Fraud fed on the idea that society was chaotic, violent, disorderly, and corrupt, and real stories like Dikko's made even the most far-fetched schemes seem plausible. It also offered people a bargain; deception may be immoral, but the only way to avoid becoming a victim is to join in. "419 is just a game," went the chorus of a popular song. "You are the loser, I am the winner."[84]

---

[82] Some of those later frauds were enormous in scale. One of the largest banking scams in modern history was a 419 scheme, in which Emmanuel Nwude and five accomplices successfully defrauded Nelson Sakaguchi, the director of the Brazilian Banco Noroeste, of USD 242 million between 1995 and 1998 by convincing him to invest in an airport construction project that did not exist. This event was one of the driving forces behind the creation of Nigeria's Economic and Financial Crimes Commission in 2002. See unreported case, United Nations Office on Drugs and Crime, High Court of Lagos State, no. ID/ 92C/2004, *Federal Republic of Nigeria v. Chief Emmanuel Nwude and six others*, July 15, 2005.

[83] The plot was foiled when customs officials at Stansted Airport violated diplomatic protocol by opening the crate, leading to a spat between Britain and Nigeria. NAUK PREM 19/2368 [held by Cabinet Office], Umaru Dikko to Margaret Thatcher, July 20, 1984. See Pierce, *Moral Economies of Corruption*, pp. 136–142; Stephen Ellis, *This Present Darkness: A History of Nigerian Organised Crime* (Oxford: Oxford University Press, 2016): pp. 131–132.

[84] Nkem Owoh, "I Go Chop Your Dollar," 2005. The singer would later be arrested in Amsterdam for his involvement in a fraudulent lottery scheme.

Some 419 schemes alluded to Biafra or took place under its sign. An enterprising Nigerian student in Salzburg extorted people in the mid-1980s by presenting himself as a representative of the Biafran government – sometimes raising money for "aid," sometimes for a business opportunity, depending on who he was talking to.[85] The half-remembered Biafran cause, which had been popular in Austria like in most of Europe, was a handy cover for his ruse. Similarly, for decades people speculated about the fate of the reserves of the Enugu branch of the Central Bank of Nigeria. Most of the Nigerian currency there had gone to the purchase of weapons for Biafra, although a portion of it was taken to Lisbon and London, where it ended up in the hands of several shady "managers."[86] If any was left in Biafra, it had been rendered worthless after the Nigerian government's issuance of new notes in the middle of the war; but rumors circulated that foreign currency and bullion from the bank remained in the possession of Biafra's former administrators, which served as the grounds for at least one scam. An Onitsha lawyer recalled that his wife was approached in the early 1970s by a destitute former Biafran officer who asked for her help in transferring a large, probably fictitious sum of money looted from the bank out of the country.[87] This paralleled the form that international 419 scams would later take. Few of these actions were charged under section 419 of the criminal code. Yet, even if postwar "419" was only sometimes prosecuted as such, there were continuities between the scams that emerged immediately after the war and those that came later.

The growth of fraud was also linked to the problem of abandoned properties described in Chapter 5. Property disputes overlapped with official corruption, since court bailiffs were the ones who led squatters to abandoned properties, facilitated the production of fraudulent deeds and leases, and selectively enforced eviction orders given by magistrates – all for substantial fees.[88] In Port Harcourt, Calabar, and elsewhere, grifters used the ambiguity around who owned houses "abandoned" by Igbos to lay claim to them. Kola Babalola, a lawyer who began his practice in Port

[85] *Sunday Concord* [Lagos], April 14, 1985, p. 1.
[86] NAUK FCO 38/285, Sir David Hunt to Commonwealth Office, December 30, 1967.
[87] Interview with anonymous informant, Onitsha, March 2015.
[88] B. M. Wifa, *Towards a Just Society Through Just Laws (Selected Papers)* (Enugu: Fourth Dimension 2003): p. 73.

Harcourt in the early 1970s, recalled that people impersonated the war dead to lay claim to their houses. Giving the plausible story that they had lost their papers during the war, impersonators would present themselves to the abandoned property commissions set up in cities like Uyo and Calabar, list off the details of the house as remembered from visiting it as a friend, and file an affidavit of ownership.[89] Over time, real estate fraud became a national phenomenon, as schemes surrounding "abandoned" properties in Port Harcourt gave way to fraudulent sales of empty buildings elsewhere. A person posing as an agent or owner would offer a temporarily vacant building at a bargain price, along with the requisite (forged) paperwork, demand payment in cash, and then leave the duped "buyer" to sort out the matter when the real owner eventually returned. The fraudulent sale of buildings reached its high point in the 1980s, when property owners began painting the phrase "This House is Not For Sale – Beware of 419" across their façades to deter spurious real estate agents from "selling" them. Hundreds of thousands of buildings in Nigeria still carry this warning. As with other aspects of 419, the seed of real estate fraud lay in the war, when the absence of landlords in cities like Port Harcourt created an opening for double-dealing.

The fact that all of this was connected to the war was apparent to Nigerians at the time, but that connection was forgotten as 419 became more international. Hito Steyerl writes that 419 schemes "rewrite daily catastrophes as entrepreneurial plotlines. Shock capitalism and its consequences – wars over raw materials or privatization – are recast as interactive romance or adventure novels."[90] Indeed, 419 schemes feed on Nigeria's recent history, describing real political situations and citing actual people in order to "sell" the legitimacy of the opportunity on offer. If a suspicious target looks up one of the people mentioned in a 419 email, he will likely find that it is a real person, often a minor political figure or a family member of a disgraced head of state. The events of the Biafra War are too distant to serve as the grist for 419 schemes today, but in the 1970s and 1980s they were not. Fraud took place then, too, even if the forms it took were more rudimentary than the ones that Nigeria would become known for.

---

[89] Interview with Kola Babalola, SAN, Port Harcourt, March 5, 2015.
[90] Hito Steyerl *Duty Free Art: Art in the Age of Planetary Civil War* (London: Verso, 2017): p. 119.

Nigerian fraud would only come to the attention of the wider world later, but there were early hints that it might go global. Scammers turned the looseness of the international system to their advantage, finding a place for themselves in the slack of new institutions and technologies. Its future can be glimpsed in a 1973 case, in which employees of Nigeria Airways conned Abidjan-based Air Afrique out of a large sum of money. The technology underpinning the scam was not the Internet but the computerized accounting system of the International Air Transport Association.[91] At this time, however, 419 was a long way off from the digital form it takes today, and it was not only (or even primarily) an export. A far larger number of 419 scams were conducted by Nigerians against one another, as the cases described here demonstrate. To see 419 as a global Robin Hood scheme – as theft from the global north by a country hobbled by predation – is therefore not entirely accurate, even if there is a grain of truth there. The civil war does not explain everything about 419, nor about Nigeria in general. Nonetheless, if one is looking for an explanation for why Nigeria looks the way it does, Biafra is a good place to start.

Coda: Disorganized Crime

In 2015, in the middle of the research for this book, I was coming back from an interview in Port Harcourt at the end of a long day. Traffic came to a halt on an overpass and a few men crawled over a barrier and starting holding up the cars stalled ahead of me. Those of us further back in traffic quietly abandoned our vehicles and hustled down the freeway to safety in the street below. The same day, across town, a friend was accidentally caught up in the burial of a local bandit, and when we got back to our apartment that evening we were both somewhat rattled. This day made several things clear. It was a reminder that crime is not just a historical problem, but one that continues to animate daily life in Nigeria. More importantly, however, it was also a lesson about perception. In the moment, our harrowing experiences seemed like they were connected – different facets of a larger structure hidden beneath the city's surface. In fact, there was no such structure. The raucous burial and the freeway robbery were discrete events that

---

[91] Nigerian Criminal Reports, Federal Court of Appeal, *Emu and Adelumola v. The State*, June 12, 1980.

had nothing to do with one another. They simply seemed related because they had taken place on the same day, in the same city, to two people who knew each other. At the burial, my friend observed mourners wearing commemorative t-shirts that seemed to speak directly to criminologists: "RIP Peter O., a.k.a. The More You Look The Less You See."[92] I have come to think of this as a mantra for the study of crime. The more cases that one reads, and the more interviews one conducts, the harder it is to argue that crime is a conspiracy or a system. In Nigeria, and likely elsewhere, the criminal "syndicate" is a crutch that people use to understand social problems that are much more diffuse than that term implies.[93] Seeing clear structures, hierarchies, and chains of command in crime is a sign that the observer knows *less* about it, not more. In Nigeria, crime was a product of many people making small decisions about how to survive and prosper, not something planned by a godfather.

There was nothing very organized about Nigerian "organized crime" – *dis*organized crime might describe it better. It was placeless and diaphanous, and it was hard to see it in action, except perhaps in the internet cafés where its practitioners congregated in the days before mobile technology.[94] In most 419 scams, the relationship is between one confidence artist and one victim. 419 functions much like legitimate Nigerian commercial networks and sometimes it follows the same pathways. It consists of many independent actors who do not coordinate their activities except to the extent that they all follow money and opportunity – as businesspeople everywhere do. Of course, crime is a notoriously difficult thing to research, and it may simply be that its structures are too submerged to be visible. Scholars' inability to describe organized crime in Nigeria could be explained by the fact that criminal organizations do not expose their inner workings. This is not just a problem for historians and anthropologists. The Nigerian police, too, can offer only very general evidence about criminal

---

[92] Vivian Chenxue Lu, forthcoming.

[93] A similar argument about Mexico is developed in Oswaldo Zavala, *Los cárteles no existen: Narcotráfico y cultura en México* (Barcelona: Malpaso, 2018).

[94] Olawale Ismail argues that its center of gravity lies in the Oluwole district of Lagos Island. Ismail is entirely correct that 419 thrived there, but it was never limited to Oluwole or any other single location. See Olawale Ismail, "Deconstructing 'Oluwole': Political Economy at the Margins of the State," in Wale Adebanwi and Ebenezer Obadare, eds., *Encountering the Nigerian State* (Basingstoke: Palgrave, 2010): pp. 29–53.

organizations, which might be because they are good at hiding them-selves. But a more compelling explanation is that the very idea of a structured criminal "underworld" is a red herring.[95]

How, then, have these chimerical "mafias" become so much a part of popular accounts of Nigeria? Stories about syndicates are a function of rumors and reportage: Journalists and social scientists witness criminal activities that follow a pattern being done around the same time and place. They assume that the convergence of these practices means that they are being planned by a central figure. Hearsay fills in the rest of the details. A politician who owns the local internet café becomes the ringleader, a Chinese businessman sighted in the vicinity serves as evidence of a global conspiracy, and a flashy name is appended to the group ("Dreaded Friends of Friends," "The Kiss of Death").[96] A story coalesces about an inter-national criminal gang that is actually just a cluster of people, who may or may not know one another, engaged in overlapping forms of lawbreaking around the same time. The public – scholarly or lay, Nigerian or foreign – devours the colorful and dramatic stories that proliferate about them, and the allegedly "organized" nature of crime becomes a social fact. As one popular pastor writes matter-of-factly, "mafioso and secret cult cabals rule Nigeria and everyone knows their activities even a six year old child." When pressed to describe how this conspiracy actually works, he alludes vaguely to corruption as if that explains it all: "Militocracy is Demo-crazy, and all their agents are 419ers."[97]

This is not to say that all organized crime is a mirage. The closest thing that Nigeria has ever had to a mafia are the student societies known as "cults." Cults are secret clubs that started on university campuses, on the Anglo-American model of fraternities.[98] The first of these, the National Association of Seadogs (also known as the Pyrates Confraternity), was founded in 1952 at University College, Ibadan, with Wole Soyinka as

---

[95] Or, if it does exist, it is so tightly bound to the state that there is not much difference between them. See Stephen Ellis and Mark Shaw, "Does Organized Crime Exist in Africa?" *African Affairs* vol. 114, no. 457 (2015): pp. 505–529.

[96] Ellis, *This Present Darkness*, p. 231.

[97] Hugo Africa, *The Man Who Forgave God – Faces of 419 Scam* (Johannesburg: Isumele Publishing, 2011): p. 17.

[98] Nduka Okafor, *One and a Half Centuries of the University in Nigeria, 1868–2011: A Historical Account* (Enugu: Progress Publishing, 2011): pp. 177–201.

one of its original members.[99] For the next twenty-five years, student confraternities multiplied, split into factions, and dabbled in politics. As the formal economy contracted in the 1980s, university graduates found that the well-paid positions that had awaited their predecessors were no longer available to them. In this era of diminishing expectations, cults became more than undergraduate societies – they reinvented themselves as oil-stealing conglomerates, kidnapping cartels, or violent shadow administrations of the university campuses where they were based.[100] Cultism fed into other criminal activities, including both armed robbery and 419.[101] The journalist Ben Okezie interviewed a number of young men who had this experience. One "Buccaneer" at Yaba College of Technology resorted to armed robbery when a complex 419 scheme that he had staged fell apart, illustrating how 419, armed robbery, and cultism could overlap.[102] Yet cults only became associated with fraud in the 1980s, after the practices discussed here had become a feature of Nigerian life. As elite societies, their membership and reach remained narrow even at their peak in the 1990s.[103] Their members describe them as disciplined hierarchies, but the loose way they operate suggests there might be less there than meets the eye.[104] As with other criminal organizations, when one scratches beneath the surface, even apparently well-organized groups often prove to share little more than an aesthetic.[105]

[99] See Misty L. Bastian, "Vulture Men, Campus Cultists and Teenaged Witches: Modern Magics in Nigerian Popular Media," in Henrietta L. Moore and Todd Sanders, eds., *Magical Interpretations, Material Realities: Modernity, Witchcraft and the Occult in Postcolonial Africa* (London: Routledge, 2001): pp. 76–81.

[100] On this transition, see Ellis, *This Present Darkness*, pp. 106–114, 191–198.

[101] Emperor Kpangban, "The Menace of Secret Cults in Higher Educational Institutions in Nigeria," *Journal of Social Sciences* vol. 17, no. 2 (2008): pp. 139–148.

[102] Ben Okezie, *Dark Clouds: Confessions of Notorious Armed Robbers in Nigeria* (Lagos: Brane Communications Nigeria Limited, 2002): p. 125.

[103] Their representation in popular culture exploded, however, especially through films like the 1992 Nollywood classic *Living in Bondage* (and hundreds of imitators). Films that connected crime to the occult were especially popular.

[104] For a journalistic description of a contemporary cult, see Sean Williams, "The Black Axe: How a Pan-African Freedom Movement Lost its Way," *Harpers*, September 2019.

[105] A fascinating account of this aesthetic can be found in David Pratten's discussion of *agaba* groups in the late 1990s, "The 'Rugged Life': Youth and Violence in Southern Nigeria," in Pal Ahluwalia, Louise Bethlehem, and Ruth Ginio, eds., *Violence and Non-Violence in Africa* (London: Routledge, 2007): p. 93.

Syndicates have never had a monopoly on crime, and the notion that they do is a fiction that states and police tell themselves. It is a comforting fiction; if criminal cells all add up to a single organism, all that has to be done to kill it is to cut off its head. A description that comes closer to the truth, but is much harder to grapple with using the tools of social science, is that crime is a *tactic* that many people turned to around the same time – independently and largely of their own volition. Because of this history, 419 does not have the tight, state-like management that one might expect from a form of crime that seems so orchestrated. It was not the doing of a sinister conspiracy within the Nigerian government, even though invoking crime to explain the Nigerian state became a trope of both scholarship and everyday discourse. Nor was it the doing of a professional class of criminals in the style of Cosa Nostra or the Sinaloa Cartel. In most cases, there were no "godfathers" of 419, nor were there formal "guilds."[106] Perhaps the better analogue to the 419er is not the American mafioso but one closer to home – the trickster of West African folklore, who prospers by guile, often at the margins of morality. That archetype has taken on new meaning in the precarious times of the West African present.[107]

Crime was not an Igbo problem, nor can its origins be traced to Igbos. Those who engaged in 419 learned from one another and occasionally worked together in the postwar east; but the idea that there was some single entity pulling the strings, Igbo or otherwise, was a myth. As a popular writer noted after the war, "it may have been convenient in our daily lives to say, for example, that such and such an action is 'typical of' Ibibios, Efiks, and so on, and so forth; but all the same it is dangerous to regard it as a self-evident truth, and consequently to base our

---

[106] Jean-François Bayart notes that 419 schemes are "said to be run" by members of such guilds, though what such a guild might look like is left to the imagination. Jean-François Bayart, "The Social Capital of the Felonious State, or the Ruses of Political Intelligence," in Jean-François Bayart, Stephen Ellis, and Béatrice Hibou, eds., *The Criminalization of the State in Africa* (Oxford: James Currey, 1999): p. 40. B. C. Okagbare notes that 419 is run by "gangs," describes their hierarchies generally, and then goes on to describe dozens of 419 schemes in which no such gangs appear. Okagbare, *The Twilight of Nigerian "419" Fraudsters*, pp. 3–8. See also Human Rights Watch, "Criminal Politics: Violence, 'Godfathers' and Corruption in Nigeria," 2007.

[107] See Charles Piot with Kodjo Nicolas Batema, *The Fixer: Visa Lottery Chronicles* (Durham, NC: Duke University Press, 2019): pp. 14–15.

responses on such an assumption."[108] Many works – popular and scholarly – suggest that there is a connection between how Igbo societies work and how crime takes place. This is usually explained by invoking the historically democratic nature of governance in Igbo villages or Igbos' imbrication in modern commerce.[109] Why a tradition of "acephalous" government or a reputation for commercial savvy might lend itself to crime is never explained.[110] As is often the case for people who constitute a minority in the places where they conduct business, portrayals of Igbos fall into two contradictory stereotypes.[111] The first is that Igbos are rootless cosmopolitans, beholden to no one except themselves and their home villages. The second is that they are part of some vast and powerful cabal, which conspiracy theorists today are most likely to identify as an association of Igbo chiefs called Ohanaeze Ndigbo. Neither description, of course, captures much truth. No one has ever owned 419.

Conclusion

A Nigerian pastor who claimed to have been swindled out of 350,000 US dollars described how deep 419 went in the 2000s: "where do I start to count the census of 419ers, is it from the churches, the politicians, our colonial masters, in the internet cafés, at home, or where? Who am I to judge when almost everyone, even mother nature, plays 419 tricks?"[112] 419 proved adaptable to changes in politics and technology,

[108] Sam Ifeka, *Looking at Ourselves (A Post-Biafra Social Analysis)* (Onitsha, Herald Books, n.d.): p. 7.

[109] Bayart, for example, posited that there was an "affinity" between Igbo traditions of segmentary government and "the market mechanism" – in this case, that of the international drug trade. Bayart, "The 'Social Capital' of the Felonious State," p. 39, as well as pp. 10–11, 19, 29. See also Ellis, *This Present Darkness*, p. 134.

[110] At any rate, while living without kings may be a historically deep tradition, it poorly describes Igbo communities in the twentieth century.

[111] The comparison between Igbos, Jews, and other "Mercurians," as Yuri Slezkine calls those who live and conduct trade in communities where they are minorities, has much popular currency. There are limitations to this historical analogy, but Igbos' experience in Nigeria resonated with, for example, that of Jews in the Russian Empire. Biafra's decision to call the 1966 killings in the north "pogroms" drew attention to that similarity. Yuri Slezkine, *The Jewish Century* (Princeton: Princeton University Press, 2006).

[112] Hugo Africa, *The Man Who Forgave God: Faces of 419 Scam* (Johannesburg: Tsumele Publishing, 2011): p. 78.

and it spiraled into many different forms; but at its heart, it remained what it was during and after the civil war – a tool to survive, and maybe thrive, in conditions of danger and uncertainty. To Nigerians and foreigners alike, 419 defined Nigeria, and it seemed like a permanent, inherent feature of national life. Yet, as the Nigerian adage goes, "no condition is permanent." Just as structural circumstances gave rise to 419, they are bringing it to an end. Crime's stranglehold on Nigerian society is loosening as Nigeria becomes incrementally wealthier, more economically diversified, and less militarized. Nigerians are now more likely to be the victims of international fraud than its perpetrators. As regulatory practices tighten elsewhere, businesses that overlap with fraud – pyramid schemes, stock trading, and gambling outfits among them – are seeking out markets for their "services" in states with fewer resources to protect their citizens.[113] Nigeria is one such state. If it has not already, Nigeria's unwanted distinction as the world's workshop of fraud will soon pass to Russia, Cyprus, or one of a handful of other places vying for it. The scars will take a while to fade.

[113] See, for example, Monica Mark's reportage on the MMM scam in West Africa or the discussion of "Redémar" in nearby Togo in Charles Piot, "Hedging the Future," in Brian Goldstone and Juan Obarrio, eds., *African Futures: Essays on Crisis, Emergence, and Possibility* (Chicago: University of Chicago Press, 2016): p. 108.

Epilogue: War Crimes and Crimes of War

The threads of violence and deceit laced into Nigerian life were not there from the beginning. Some of them were woven in by colonialism and some by events in the more recent past – oil, austerity, militarism, and a rancorous turn to liberal democracy among them. All played their parts in making Nigeria a "counterfeit country," as one polemicist called it.[1] Yet independent Nigeria can only be fully understood in the frame of war, and this is especially true for the history of crime. Crime pervaded Nigerian life during this time, warping Nigeria's internal affairs and its place in the world. It gave the country what Pius Adesanmi called a "stubbornly unrebrandable" bad reputation – one that it still struggles to shake off.[2] As this book has argued, that reputation is the residue of war. The many grim stories related here challenge how we think of war's destructiveness – not in terms of "war crimes" inflicted by states and armies, but in the crimes *of* war that people are driven to when conflict turns life upside-down. This is not an African story; wars always give cover for the violation of norms and laws, even though the damage looks different from one place to another. The cost of war is reckoned not only in body counts and burned buildings, but in its corrosive effects on the beliefs, ambitions, and behaviors of those who survive. The Nigerian Civil War's fragmented legal record is valuable because it shows that corrosion in vivid, unflinching detail.

When people tell stories about crime, they usually do so to indict some social or political dynamic – to show that someone has failed or that something has fallen apart. The argument of this book has been largely in that mold, but it is worth considering what crime produces in addition to what it destroys. What forms of government does it create?

---

[1] Agwagom Vincent Chibueze, *Lawful Nigeria: An Awareness Over-Loading Vibration* (Enugu: Cheston Books, 2011).

[2] Pius Adesanmi, *Naija No Dey Carry Last! Thoughts on a Nation in Progress* (Lagos: Oregami Books, [2015]): p. 163.

What kinds of relationships? How does it reorder the rules of everyday behavior? Of commerce? Crime – real or spectral – creates a grim social world. Fear reigns, self-preservation becomes the guiding principle of life, and crime's suppression causes direct and collateral damage to those who stand in its path. "Cynicism in individual and collective action" sets in, as Célestin Monga writes, and nihilism becomes a shield against the ubiquity of death.[3] Life becomes a war of all against all. Yet outwardly Hobbesian worlds – of which Biafra appears to fit the bill – still have rules, structures of enforcement, and hierarchies of power.[4] Even if they are mimetic, or fragile, these rules *feel* very real indeed to those who live under them. In Biafra, discerning what the rules were, how they were enforced, and how they broke down requires looking through a thick fog of tragedy.

Nigeria has never been a legal void, and the Republic of Biafra was no anarchy, however much it may have looked like one from the outside.[5] If we can find a legal order at work there, what does that imply about law in postcolonial Africa in more ordinary circumstances? Many scholars proceed from the notion that African states have failed, and that, whatever they may be, they do not measure up to the standard of a Weberian nation-state. They posit, implicitly or explicitly, that disorder, patrimonialism, and graft are the fundamental qualities of postcolonial politics. Some construe disorder as a virtue.[6] In

---

[3] Célestin Monga, *Nihilism and Negritude: Ways of Living in Africa* (Cambridge, MA: Harvard University Press, 2016): p. 16.

[4] On the "Hobbesian nightmare" that can transpire, see, in different but complementary registers, Jean Comaroff and John L. Comaroff, *The Truth About Crime: Sovereignty, Knowledge, Social Order* (Chicago: University of Chicago Press, 2016): pp. 207–217; and the memoirist Achike Udenwa, *Nigeria/Biafra Civil War: My Experience* (Ibadan: Spectrum, 2011): p. 184.

[5] As William Reno writes, even the most seemingly nebulous conflicts "do not fit easily into a simple schema of state collapse and ungoverned spaces." William Reno, *Warfare in Independent Africa* (Cambridge: Cambridge University Press, 2011): p. 246. Louisa Lombard makes a similar argument against the notion of state fragility with regard to the Central African Republic. Louisa Lombard, *State of Rebellion: Violence and Intervention in the Central African Republic* (London: Zed Books, 2016): pp. 63–65. See also Judith Scheele *Smugglers and Saints of the Sahara: Regional Connectivity in the Twentieth Century* (Cambridge: Cambridge University Press, 2015); Janet Roitman, *Fiscal Disobedience: An Anthropology of Economic Regulation in Central Africa* (Princeton: Princeton University Press, 2005).

[6] Albeit a mixed one. See Julien Brachet and Judith Scheele, *The Value of Disorder: Autonomy, Prosperity, and Plunder in the Chadian Sahara* (Cambridge: Cambridge University Press, 2019).

the field of law, systemic corruption has led some to conclude that African legal systems are – at best – colonial inheritances with political instrumentality but no freestanding character. The metaphors that describe the archetypal African state include those of shadows, pantomimes, and rhizomatic plants with tangled root systems that burst through the soil in unexpected places. There is some truth to these comparisons; but there is also more logic, and greater intellectual content, to the postcolonial state than they imply. Nothing shows this better than law. Postcolonial Africa is not a "box without a key," as Achille Mbembe has called it – it is a box other keys will not fit. New ones have to be cut for it.[7]

Many former Biafrans wanted a legal reckoning with the war, but the closest they would get was Ali Mazrui's allegorical one in *The Trial of Christopher Okigbo*.[8] They would have no Nuremberg-style day in court, but in 1999 there was a judicial inquiry into the events of military rule, including the war. This was the Human Rights Violations Investigation Commission, popularly called the Oputa Panel after the jurist who convened it.[9] Over several years, the commission heard hundreds of testimonies from war veterans, victims of crime, political dissidents, and the relatives of people who had been killed or disappeared. It made many recommendations, from symbolic apologies to the payment of reparations. None were acted on, and President Olusegun Obasanjo and his successors studiously ignored the panel's report. The case for Igbo injury takes evidence from many places, ranging from the war's death toll to the fact that Nigeria has not had an Igbo head of state since its end.[10] Biafra remains an open wound.

---

[7] Achille Mbembe, *Sortir de la grande nuit: Essai sur l'Afrique décolonisée* (Paris: La Découvert, 2013): p. 173.

[8] Ali A. Mazrui, *The Trial of Christopher Okigbo* (London: Heinemann, 1971).

[9] Chukwudifu Oputa had been a prominent judge in Biafra. The Nigerian government never published the commission's report, but a Nigerian civil society organization in the United States released it unofficially. The inquiry was modeled after the South African Truth and Reconciliation Commission. *Human Rights Violations Investigation Commission Report* (Washington, DC: Nigerian Democratic Movement, 2005).

[10] On these grievances, see Joe Igbokwe, *Igbos Twenty Five Years After Biafra* (Lagos: Advent Communications, 1995); Paul Obi-Ani, *Post-Civil War Political and Economic Reconstruction of Igboland, 1970–1983* (Enugu: Great AP Express, 2009); Otuka Anyasi, *Igbos: What Role in Today's Nigeria* (Lagos: Orient Publishing Company, 1994); Mma Agbagha, *Pressure Group Politics*

More recently, organizations like the Movement for the Actualisation of the Sovereign State of Biafra (MASSOB) and Indigenous People of Biafra (IPOB) have taken one idea of what being Biafran meant – being Igbo – and built a political platform on it.[11] This activism happens in the press, on the street corner, and especially over the Internet.[12] The Biafran cause that attracts young people today is not the same as the one that sparked the civil war, and it is not led by the same people.[13] Even so, law and order remains part of its creed; "Nigeria is a lawless land," reads a poster often seen at pro-Biafra demonstrations.[14] These new separatist movements have been marginal in national politics given Nigeria's other, more potent problems – notably the crisis in the Niger Delta region and the ongoing Boko Haram insurgency in the northeast.[15] Activism has become bolder since the return of democracy, and in the last few years Biafran flags have started to crop up in eastern towns. Young people support Biafra openly, in ways that would have been unthinkable under military rule. On my last flight to Lagos, I sat next to a businessman in his early thirties returning from Thailand, where he had gone to purchase clothing in bulk to sell in Nigeria. We struck up a conversation, and when I asked him where he was from, he replied loudly, "I am from Biafra," causing a small commotion among the Nigerian passengers within earshot, one of whom reached across the aisle to slap him with her

(Never Say Die) (Ibadan: Spectrum Books, 2003); Herbert Ekwe-Ekwe, *Biafra Revisited* (Dakar: African Renaissance, 2007).

[11] Esther Ajiboye and Taiwo Abioye, "When Citizens Talk: Stance and Representation in Online Discourse on Biafra Agitations," *Discourse and Society* vol. 30, no. 2 (2019): pp. 117–134; Johannes Harnischfeger, "Igbo Nationalism and Biafra," *Afrikanistik online*, vol. 2011.

[12] On the importance of the Nairaland internet forum and other sites in the public memory of the war, see Kola Ade Odutola, "The Cyber-Framing of Nigerian Nationhood: Diaspora and the Imagined Nation" (Doctoral dissertation, Rutgers University, 2010): p. 176.

[13] Ike Okonta, "Biafran Ghosts: The MASSOB Ethnic Militia and Nigeria's Democratisation Process," Discussion Paper 73, Nordiska Afrikainstitutet, Uppsala, 2012, p. 19; Uchenna Nwankwo, *Pro-Biafra Movements, Ohanaeze, and the Future of Nigeria* (Lagos: Centrist Books, 2018).

[14] At another rally, the leader of a motorcycle drivers' union warned that past acts of violence against Igbos should not be forgotten: "first fool no bi fool, na second fool be proper foolish." Ernest N. Onuoha, *Biafra: The Victims* (Enugu: Alliance Publications Nigeria Limited, 2012): p. 1.

[15] On the connections between these events, see Edlyne Eze Anugwom, *From Biafra to the Niger Delta Conflict: Memory, Ethnicity, and the State in Nigeria* (Lanham, MD: Lexington Books, 2019).

magazine. It is not clear what will become of this new Biafran movement, but the arrests of several activists and a series of increasingly disruptive demonstrations in the east have put Biafra back in the news. It will probably stay there.

In all this activism, the Republic of Biafra – not the idea but the place that actually existed – sometimes fades into the background. So too do its lessons. The heat of battle makes people think and act differently. In wartime, they reorder their priorities, measure risk in new ways, and accept as normal things that they would usually abhor. When those ways of thinking persist after the last shot is fired, what follows is a "season of anomy," as Wole Soyinka called this period in Nigerian history.[16] Since Biafra, warfare has changed. Wars today end not in victory or defeat, but in some rubble-filled place between them. Some do not end at all. Nigeria has been fighting Boko Haram for a decade, and the United States has been at war for nearly two, but in both places it is remarkably easy to forget that this is the case. Many people live under the flag of war, but we cannot always see it flying above us. The perverse effects of conflict are more obvious looking back at the Biafra War – a war with defined sides, a beginning, and an end – but they are just as present in the more turbid conflicts of our own times.

[16] Wole Soyinka, *Season of Anomy* (New York: The Third Press, 1973).

Archival Collections Consulted

Nigeria:
Nigerian National Archives, Enugu [NNAE]
Nigerian National Archives, Ibadan [NNAI]
Nigerian National Archives, Kaduna [NNAK]
Nigerian National Archives, Calabar [NNAC]
National War Museum, Umuahia [NWM]
Enugu State High Court, Enugu [ESHC]
Arewa House, Ahmadu Bello University, Kaduna [ABUAH]
Lagos State Research and Archives Board [LASRAB]
Biafrana and Achebeana Collections, University of Nigeria-Nsukka
Nigerian Institute of International Affairs, Lagos
Lagos State High Court, Lagos
Imo State High Court, Owerri
Rivers State High Court, Port Harcourt
Nigerian Institute of Advanced Legal Studies, University of Lagos

United Kingdom:
National Archives of the United Kingdom, Kew [NAUK]
Special Collections, School of Oriental and African Studies, London
    [SOAS]
Imperial War Museum, London [IWM]
British Library Newspaper Collection, London
Rhodes House Library, University of Oxford

United States:
Hoover Institution Archive, Palo Alto [HIA]
Special Collections, University of Wisconsin–Madison [SCUW]
Schomburg Center for Research in Black Culture, New York Public
    Library

France:
Centre des archives diplomatiques, Nantes [CADN]

Republic of Ireland:
National Archive of Ireland, Dublin [NAID]

South Africa:
South African National Defence Force Archive, Pretoria [SADF]

Tanzania:
Africana Collections, University of Dar es Salaam

Oral Interviews

Michael Ajogwu, SAN, in his chambers in Independence Layout, Enugu, March 19, 2015.

Kola Babalola, SAN, in his chambers on Harbour Road, Port Harcourt, March 5, 2015.

Comfort Chukwu, Federal Secretariat, Owerri, July 22, 2014.

Chidube Ezebilo, SAN, in his chambers on Oguta Road, Onitsha, March 12, 2015.

Dr. Jacob Ibik, SAN, in his chambers on Owerri Road, Enugu, September 26, 2014.

Chief A. N. Kanu, in his home in Ibeku, Umuahia, March 9, 2015.

Anthony Mogboh, SAN, in his chambers in City Layout, New Haven, Enugu, October 2, 2014.

Emeka Ofodile, SAN, in his chambers on Awka Road, Onitsha, March 16, 2015.

Mary Okehe, State Secretariat Complex, Ikeja, Lagos, July 17, 2013.

Jerome H.C. Okolo, SAN, in his chambers on Zik Avenue, Enugu, September 17, 2014.

A. M. O. Onukaogu, in his chambers in St. Finbarr's St., Umuahia, March 9, 2015.

Mike Onwuzunike, Holy Ghost Cathedral, Enugu, September 14, 2014.

Chief Enechi Onyia, SAN, in his chambers on Zik Avenue, Enugu, September 29, 2014.

Flora Udechukwu, in her home in Old Government Reserve Area, Port Harcourt, February 15, 2015.

Ejike O. Ume, SAN, in his chambers on Enugu Road, Onitsha, March 12, 2015.

Barinua Moses Wifa, SAN, in his chambers on Azikiwe Road, Port Harcourt, March 5, 2015.

Thirteen anonymous interviews

NB: SAN stands for Senior Advocate of Nigeria, an honorific equivalent to Queen's Counsel elsewhere in the Commonwealth.

Index

260

CPSIA information can be obtained
at www.ICGtesting.com
Printed in the USA
LVHW081118270221
680109LV00005B/93